Self-Stabilization

Self-Stabilization

Shlomi Dolev

The MIT Press
Cambridge, Massachusetts
London, England

This book was set in Computer Modern by the author using LATEX.

Library of Congress Cataloging-in-Publication Data

Dolev, Shlomi.
  Self-stabilization / Shlomi Dolev.
    p.   cm.
  Includes bibliographical references and index.
  ISBN 978-0-262-04178-2 (hardcover: alk. paper)—978-0-262-52921-1 (pb. : alk. paper)
  1. Self-stabilization (Computer science).   2. Computer algorithms.   I. Title.
QA76.9.S54D65   2000
005.1'4—dc21   99-38297
                                                                                CIP

The MIT Press is pleased to keep this title available in print by manufacturing single copies, on demand, via digital printing technology.

Contents

Preface

The purpose of this book is to introduce the concept of self-stabilization. Topics were chosen for their lasting impact on the field, the elegance of the results, and their pedagogical usefulness. A rigorous approach to the material is taken, with detailed development of all aspects, including problem specifications, algorithms, and lower-bound description.

The book can be used either as a primary text in an advanced course (for senior undergraduates and graduates) or as a supplementary text in a course on distributed computing or distributed systems. It can also help practitioners and researchers working in the area of distributed systems and communication networks in employing some of the self-stabilization tools. The only background assumed is a level of mathematical sophistication equivalent to that obtained from undergraduate courses in discrete mathematics and algorithms.

The goal of the book is to convey the spirit of self-stabilization; therefore, the main criteria for choosing the subjects and examples were simplicity and generality. I would like to emphasize that the book was not intended to cover all the extensive research activity in the field and that the bibliographic credits are thus not complete.

I would like to thank the people with whom I had the opportunity to collaborate in research and discussion on self-stabilization; first Amos Israeli and Shlomo Moran started exploring this research field with me, and then James Abello, Uri Abraham, Hosame Abu-Amara, Yehuda Afek, Makis Anagnostou, Anish Arora, Hagit Attiya, Baruch Awerbuch, Joffroy Beauquier, Brian A. Coan, Gidi Cohen, Zeev Collin, Ajoy K. Datta, Sylvie Delaet, Mohamed Gouda, Vassos Hadzilacos, Ted Herman, Arkady Kanevsky, Shmuel Katz, Irit Koll, Shay Kutten, Leslie Lamport, Nancy Lynch, Boaz Patt-Shamir, Sergio Rajsbaum, Janos Simon, Marco Schneider, Sebastien Tixeuil, George Varghese, Jennifer L. Welch, Moti Yung, and in fact all the members of the active self-stabilization research community for more than ten exciting years. I would also like to thank the students in my distributed algorithm courses at Ben-Gurion University of the Negev and the students in the international summer schools on distributed computing (organized by Elena Lodi and Nicola Santoro) for helpful suggestions. In addition, Faith Fich, Ted Herman, and Jennifer L. Welch, read an early version of this book and their comments were helpful in improving the presentation. Catherine Logan helped with English editing.

Robert V. Prior and Deborah Cantor-Adams at the MIT Press encouraged me in this long project. Writing this book would not have been possible without the love and support of my wife Gali and my children Noa, Yorai, Hagar, and Eden. This book is also dedicated to my parents, Rachel and Haim.

Self-Stabilization

1 Introduction

The self-stabilization paradigm was introduced by Edsger W. Dijkstra in 1973. A self-stabilizing system is a system that can automatically recover following the occurrence of (transient) faults. The idea is to design systems that can be started in an arbitrary state and still converge to a desired behavior. The occurrence of faults can cause the system to reach an arbitrary state. Self-stabilizing systems that experience faults recover automatically from such faults, since they are designed to start in an arbitrary state.

The craft of designing self-stabilizing distributed algorithms is challenging and exciting, as Edsger W. Dijkstra discovered in designing the first self-stabilizing algorithm. Just before presenting the details of the algorithm, Dijkstra challenges the readers to stop reading and design a self-stabilizing algorithm for mutual exclusion by themselves. It is not only curiosity and intellectual challenge, however, that motivate the extensive study of self-stabilization; the major reason for this wide interest is the applicability of self-stabilizing algorithms to distributed systems.

Existing algorithms such as routing algorithms are designed to stabilize starting from any arbitrary initial state. In a large, distributed, heterogeneous communication network, it is hard to predict in advance the exact combination of failures that will occur or their result. The self-stabilization property handles such a complicated situation by assuming an arbitrary initial state. From any arbitrary initial state, the system should recover and exhibit the desired behavior. For example, it is important that the control system of an autonomous vehicle such as, say, a space shuttle be designed to self-stabilize. The space shuttle may experience a fault — e.g., a power supply problem — and will have to recover automatically. If a space shuttle experiences a fault because of a momentary electrical power problem, it may malfunction for a while, but it will not be lost as long as it uses a self-stabilizing algorithm for its control, since this algorithm will cause the control to recover automatically and continue in its task.

To gain some idea of what a self-stabilizing algorithm is, let us use a pictorial example that we call "the stabilizing orchestra example." On a windy evening, an orchestra is invited to play outdoors. Unfortunately, the conductor is unable to participate. Players listen to the players who are sitting nearby in order to play in harmony. The orchestra is required to play the same piece of music over and over again. Each player has a score to follow in the performance, starting from the beginning of the score again whenever he or she finishes playing the last page.

Since the orchestra is playing outdoors, the wind can, from time to time, turn some of the pages in the score; moreover, the players may not even notice the change. We would like to guarantee that harmony is achieved at some point following the last such undesired page turn. It seems that the demand that harmony be achieved at some point following the last undesired page change is too weak; what happens if the wind continues turning the pages forever, but there are long periods in which no change occurs? Would the players be playing out of synchrony all the time? Fortunately, the players do not know whether a page change is the last page change, so our demand forces them to achieve synchrony during the long periods in which the wind does not turn the pages. Later harmony may be repeatedly lost again due to page changes, and then repeatedly achieved in every long enough period of time.

Imagine that you are the drummer and you find out that each of the violin players sitting near you is playing a different page. What should you do? Since your page may be turned without your noticing, you cannot stick with your current page. So, should you turn to the same page that one of the neighboring violinists is currently playing? Note that it is possible that at the same moment this violin player may change to your page and start playing from the place you are currently playing.

Maybe once asynchrony is detected, a player should start playing from the beginning of the score. In such a case, the drummer and the violin players start simultaneously from the beginning of the score, but a cello player, who is next to the violin player and who playing in synchrony with the violin, may still continue playing, and will restart only after recognizing that the violin player has restarted. Therefore, both the cello and the violin players will restart playing while the drummer continues. This scenario may repeat itself.

Now we are ready to present our first self-stabilizing solution. A self-stabilizing solution would be for every player to join the neighboring player who is playing the earliest page, if this page is earlier than his or her own page. Assuming the scores are long enough, this strategy will reestablish synchrony following the last undesired page change, as shown by the following line of reasoning. Let us assume for now that no player finishes the score and turns to its first page before synchrony is achieved. In such a case, we can find a player who is playing a page with the minimal page number, and this player will cause all the other players to join him: the neighbors of the player who is playing the page with the minimal number will join this player. Once these neighbors play simultaneously, the neighbors of these neighbors will change page and join them, and eventually all players will be playing in harmony.

The case still to be considered is that in which a player goes to the first page of the score before harmony is achieved. This case is discussed in detail in the sequel; at this stage, we give only a sketch of the argument that the reader may choose to skip. It is not possible to argue from some player who is playing the minimal-number page, since some other player starts playing an earlier page later on. However, if the score is long enough, we can argue that all the players will be playing a page in the beginning of the book some time after a player plays the first page. Let us say that the drummer is a player who changed pages to the first page; the neighbors of the drummer will change pages to one of the first pages, as will the neighbors of the neighbors, and so on. Once every player is playing one of the first pages and no player will change pages to the first page for a long enough time, we can therefore use the claims of the first case to convince ourselves that harmony is achieved.

We can conclude that in every long enough period in which the wind does not turn a page, the orchestra resumes playing in synchrony. This is the spirit of self-stabilization — coping with transient faults by designing an algorithm that ensures restablishment of a desired property. In the orchestra case, the transient faults are the wind's page turns and the desired property is the synchronization among the players. After the last transient fault, an arbitrary situation is reached where each player may be playing a different page. From every such arbitrary situation, the orchestra reaches a stage after which it is playing in harmony.

Note that, although the algorithm is guaranteed to achieve synchrony after the last transient fault, the audience may still notice the disturbance that the wind causes (occurrence of the transient faults).

Let us continue with few historical notes. Research on self-stabilizing algorithms started with the pioneering work of Edsger W. Dijkstra in 1973. Dijkstra demonstrated the new self-stabilization concept by presenting self-stabilizing mutual exclusion algorithms. Dijkstra's work was not widely noticed until Leslie Lamport's invited talk at the ACM Symposium on Principles of Distributed Computing in 1983. In his report on Dijkstra's work on self-stabilization, Leslie Lamport stated:

I regard this as Dijkstra's most brilliant work — at least, his most brilliant published paper. It's almost completely unknown. I regard it to be a milestone in work on fault tolerance... I regard self-stabilization to be a very important concept in fault tolerance, and to be a very fertile field for research.

As often happens with Lamport's predictions, self-stabilization research is one of the most active research fields in distributed computing. Innovative theoretical results that can be used in practice have been presented in recent years. Distributed algorithms that were successfully implemented have now been identified as self-stabilizing. Self-stabilization is a concept of interest to both theoreticians and practitioners.

The book starts with the description of basic definitions and techniques to gain basic understanding of what self-stabilization is. Then in chapter 3, using our basic familiarity with self-stabilization, we prove that there are frequent cases in which only self-stabilizing algorithms can automatically resume operation. Chapter 3 concludes with some frequently asked questions.

The remaining chapters are ordered according to their sophistication, starting with basic techniques and continuing with more advanced topics. Chapter 4 is dedicated to the description of the different distributed systems for which self-stabilizing algorithms exist. In fact, it uses the excuse of converting self-stabilizing algorithms (to be executed by different types of distributed systems) to present several fundamental self-stabilizing algorithms. Then in chapter 5 techniques for converting non-stabilizing algorithms to self-stabilizing algorithms are presented. Chapter 6 uses digital clock synchronization task to demonstrate the feasibility of coping with a combination of transient faults and other types of faults. Chapter 7 presents techniques concerned with algorithm behavior during stabilization. In particular, the techniques in chapter 7 ensure fast stabilization when only a few of the processors experience transient faults. The last chapter explores the case of a single machine modeled by a Turing machine.

Notes

The first self-stabilizing algorithms were presented in [Dij73] (See also [Dij74; Dij86]). Three self-stabilizing algorithms for mutual exclusion in a ring are presented in [Dij73]. The invited talk of Leslie Lamport can be found in [Lam83].

2 Definitions, Techniques, and Paradigms

This chapter is devoted to formalizing the distributed system, the basic assumptions, the requirements, and the complexity measures. The formal definitions are then used in the description of basic techniques and paradigms in the design of self-stabilizing algorithms and in proving their correctness.

2.1 Definitions of the Computational Model

The term *distributed system* is used to describe communication networks, multiprocessor computers, and a multitasking single computer. All the above variants of distributed systems have similar fundamental coordination requirements among the communicating entities, whether they are computers, processors, or processes. Thus an abstract model that ignores the specific setting and captures the important characteristics of a distributed system is usually employed.

Each computer runs a program composed of executable statements. Each execution of a statement changes the content of the computer's local memory, including the program counter. In other words, the computer changes state with each statement execution. An abstract way to model a computer that executes a program is to use the state machine model. A distributed system is modeled by a set of n state machines called processors that communicate with each other. We usually denote the ith processor in the system by P_i. Each processor can communicate with other processors, called its neighbors. It is convenient to represent a distributed system by a communication graph in which each processor is represented by a node and every two neighboring processors are connected by a link of the communication graph.

The communication between neighboring processors can be carried out by message passing or shared memory. Communication by writing in, and reading from, the shared memory usually fits systems with processors that are geographically close together, such as multiprocessor computers or processes executed by a multitasking single-processor computer. A message-passing distributed model fits both processors that are located close to each other and wide-area distributed systems, such as communication networks.

In the message-passing model, neighbors communicate by sending and receiving messages. In asynchronous distributed systems, the speed of processors and message transmission can vary. First-in first-out (FIFO) queues are used to model asynchronous delivery of messages. A communication link is either unidirectional or bidirectional. A unidirectional communication link from processor P_i to processor P_j transfers messages from P_i to P_j. The abstraction used for such a unidirectional link is a first-in first-out (FIFO) queue $q_{i,j}$, that contains all messages sent by a processor P_i to its neighbor P_j that have not yet been received. Whenever P_i sends a message m to P_j, the message is enqueued (added to the tail of the queue). P_j may receive the message m that is at the head of the queue; in such a case, the message m is dequeued (removed from the front of the queue). The bidirectional communication link between processors P_i and P_j is modeled by two FIFO queues, one from P_i to P_j and the other from P_j to P_i.

It is very convenient to identify the state of a computer or a distributed system at a given time, so that no additional information about the past of the computation is needed in order to predict the future behavior (state transitions) of the computer or the distributed system. A full description of a message passing distributed system at a particular time consists of the state of every processor and the content of every queue (messages pending in the communication links). The term *system configuration* (or *configuration*) is used for such a description. A configuration is denoted by $c = (s_1, s_2, \cdots, s_n, q_{1,2}, q_{1,3}, \cdots, q_{i,j}, \cdots, q_{n,n-1})$, where s_i, $1 \le i \le n$, is the state of P_i and $q_{i,j}$, $i \ne j$, is the queue of messages sent by P_i to P_j but not yet received.

In the shared memory model, processors communicate by the use of shared communication registers (hereafter *registers*). Processors may write in a set of registers and may read from a possibly different set of registers. The configuration of the system consists of the state of all processors and the contents of the registers. A configuration of a system with n processors and m communication registers is denoted by $c = (s_1, s_2, \cdots, s_n, r_1, r_2, \cdots, r_m)$, where s_i, $1 \le i \le n$, is the state of P_i and for $1 \le j \le m$, r_j is the contents of a communication register.

The future state transitions of a stand-alone computer that executes a (non-interactive) program can be deterministically predicted from its current state. Note that, for a stand-alone computer, the speed of the state transitions may not be fixed (in a multitasking computer environment, the period of time for which each task is executed may change over time); nevertheless, when the tasks are totally independent, we can predict the state of each task following the ith state transition of this task. The situation in distributed systems is different. Nondeterminism due to different speeds of processors and of message delivery can result in totally different state transitions of processors from identical initial states. For example, a processor waiting to receive messages from one of each of its neighbors may act differently if a message from neighbor P_i arrives before a message from P_j, or vice versa. In other words, scheduling of events in a distributed system influences the transitions made by the processors. The situation is even more complicated, since processors execute program statements in parallel at different rates.

The interleaving model is used to reason about the behavior of the distributed system. In this model it is assumed that, at each given time, only a single processor executes a *computation step* (also called an *atomic step*). Each computation step consists of internal computation and a *single* communication operation: a send or receive in message passing systems and a write or read in shared memory systems. Note that a computation step may consist of local computations (e.g., subtraction of the values of two local registers of the processors) in addition to the communication operation. Without loss of generality, the time at which all the local operations between two communication operations of a processor occur is assumed to be immediately before the second communication operation. Thus, it is possible to assume that every state transition of a process is due to communication-step execution (including all local computations that follow the previous step and precede the communication operation of the computation step).

Note that a distributed system allows the processors to execute steps concurrently; however, when processors execute steps concurrently we assume that there is no influence of one step on the other. This is clearly true for send and receive operations that are executed simultaneously, because a message sent cannot be received by a receive operation that is executed at the same time. As for shared memory, it is assumed that the communication register architecture guarantees serialization: the read and write operations can be ordered in a total order such that the result of a read operation from some register is the value that was written last before this read (according to the total order) in that register.

In what follows, we use the term *step* for a computation step and we denote a step (together with the identity of the processor that executes it) by a. Let c_1 and c_2 be two configurations of the system, where c_2 is reached from c_1 by a single step a of a processor; we denote this fact by $c_1 \xrightarrow{a} c_2$. The step a is *applicable* to a configuration c if (and only if) there exists a configuration c' such that $c \xrightarrow{a} c'$. An *execution* $E = (c_1, a_1, c_2, a_2, \cdots)$ (in the interleaving model) is an alternating sequence of configurations and steps such that $c_{i-1} \xrightarrow{a_{i-1}} c_i$ $(i > 1)$; in other words, the configuration c_i $(i > 1)$ is obtained from c_{i-1} by the execution of step a_{i-1}. For instance, if in step a_i the processor P_j writes the value x to a register r_k, then the only components that do not have identical values in c_i and c_{i+1} are the state of P_j and the value of r_k, which were changed according to a_i. A *fair* execution is an execution in which every step that is applicable infinitely often is executed infinitely often. In particular, if (infinitely often) a processor has a step to execute then the processor executes this step (infinitely often).

In a message-passing system, it is possible that a message will be lost during the execution of the algorithm; the reason is unreliable communication media that may lose or corrupt messages in transit. Error-detection codes are used to identify and discard corrupted messages, and these messages can be considered lost messages. To model such systems, we extend the definition of a step to include *environment steps* of type $loss_{i,j}(m)$. The environment step $loss_{i,j}(m)$ is applicable to a configuration c_k in which the queue $q_{i,j}$ contains the message m. The application of $loss_{i,j}(m)$ to c_k results in a configuration c_{k+1} in which m is removed from $q_{i,j}$, and c_k and c_{k+1} are identical in the rest of their components. Unlike steps executed by processors, we do not require that, in every infinite fair execution, the environment steps that are applicable infinitely often will be executed infinitely often. We do require that, in a fair execution in which a message is sent infinitely often, the message must be received infinitely often. To satisfy fairness the receive step must be executed infinitely often, while the loss step should not be executed infinitely often.

Up to this stage, we have presented the class of distributed systems called *asynchronous* distributed systems. The experience of distributed algorithm designers is that algorithms designed for asynchronous systems perform well in communication networks and multiprocessor systems. Yet there is a class of distributed algorithms designed for *synchronous* distributed systems in which a *global clock pulse* (or simply a *pulse*) triggers a simultaneous step of every processor in the system. This class of synchronous algorithms fits multiprocessor systems in which the processors are located close to each other and can therefore be efficiently connected to a common clock pulse. Next we describe the assumptions concerning the steps of the processors in synchronous message-passing and shared-memory systems.

The following actions are performed between each successive pulses of a synchronous message-passing system: the pulse triggers message send operations of every processor to every one of its neighbors, then every message is received by its destination. In the shared memory system, a pulse triggers each processor to read all the registers of its neighbors. Once every processor has finished reading, the processors can write into their registers. Thus, since all the processors execute a step simultaneously, the execution of a synchronous system $E = (c_1, c_2, \cdots)$ is totally defined by c_1, the first configuration in E.

2.2   Self-Stabilization Requirements

A self-stabilizing system can be started in any arbitrary configuration and will eventually exhibit a desired "legal" behavior.

We define the desired legal behavior by a set of legal executions denoted *LE*. A set of legal executions is defined for a particular system and a particular task. Every system execution of a self-stabilizing system should have a suffix that appears in *LE*. For instance, when the task is *mutual exclusion*, the task is defined by the set of legal executions in which, in every configuration, there is at most one processor in the critical section, and in which every processor is in the critical section in an infinite number of configurations of the execution.

A configuration c is *safe* with regard to a task *LE* and an algorithm if every fair execution of the algorithm that starts from c belongs to *LE*.

An algorithm is *self-stabilizing* for a task *LE* if every fair execution of the algorithm reaches a safe configuration with relation to *LE*.

2.3   Complexity Measures

The complexity measures used to evaluate an algorithm include time complexity and space (memory) complexity. At first glance, the attempt to define the time complexity of asynchronous systems may seem to contradict the asynchronous nature of the system. By the definition of asynchronous systems, there is no bound on the rate/speed of step-executions/message-arrivals. However, in order to evaluate and compare different asynchronous algorithms, it is convenient to use the number of *asynchronous rounds* to measure the time complexity of a particular execution. The first *asynchronous round* (or *round*) in an execution E is the shortest prefix E' of E such that each processor executes at least one step in E'. Let E'' be the suffix of E that follows E', $E = E'E''$. The second round of E is the first round of E'', and so on. The number of rounds in the execution of an algorithm is used to measure the time complexity of the algorithm.

Intuitively, the definition of an asynchronous round nullifies the speed differences of the processors by stretching the round to be long enough to

include a step (including a communication operation) of the slowest processor
in this execution segment. Thus, information can be transferred through the
slowest processor even if that processor resides in a node that can separate the
communication graph. Moreover, if the speeds of the processors are identical
and the speeds of message transmission are also identical, every asynchronous
round elapses in the same constant time interval.

A self-stabilizing algorithm never terminates, and processors must repeatedly communicate with their neighbors. In the shared-memory model, processors must repeatedly read the registers of their neighbors and in the message
passing model, processors must continue to send and receive messages forever. The following argument is used to explain why termination cannot be
achieved: assume that every processor P_i has a state s_i in which P_i is terminated. By the self-stabilizing property of the algorithm, the system must reach
a safe configuration from any initial configuration. When the system is started
in a configuration c in which every processor P_i is in state s_i, no processor executes any step, and thus c must be a safe configuration. Therefore the task of
the algorithm is achieved when every processor P_i has only one state, namely
the state s_i. Obviously, such tasks do not require any communication between
the processors and the "algorithm" that is used is not a distributed algorithm.

The non-termination property can be easily identified in the code of a
self-stabilizing algorithm: this code is usually a do forever loop that contains
communication operations with the neighbors. For example, in the shared-
memory case, the code of the algorithm for a processor P_i usually starts
with read operations of the communication registers of P_i and then local
computations that are followed by write operations in the communication
registers of P_i. The number of steps required to execute a single iteration of
such a do forever loop is $O(\Delta)$, where Δ is an upper bound on the degree
(number of neighbors) of P_i. In some of the proofs, it is very convenient to
consider the configuration that follows at least one complete execution of an
iteration of the do forever loop by every processor. Note that a processor can
be started in (a state in which it is in) the middle of executing an iteration of
the do forever loop. However, if x is the number of steps required to complete
an iteration of the do forever loop, then fewer than $2x$ steps are required to
complete an iteration of the loop (from the beginning of the loop to its end)
when P_i is started in an arbitrary state.

For the sake of readability, we extend the definition of an asynchronous
round to an asynchronous *cycle* when convenient. The first *asynchronous cycle*
(or *cycle*) in an execution E is the shortest prefix E' of E such that each

processor executes at least one complete iteration of its do forever loop in E'. Let E'' be the suffix of E that follows E', $E = E'E''$. The second cycle of E is the first cycle of E'', and so on.

Note that if the do forever iteration consists of reading the communication registers of the neighbors, local computations, and writing to the communication registers, then each cycle spans $O(\Delta)$ rounds.

The time complexity of a synchronous algorithm is the number of pulses in the execution (which corresponds to the number of rounds).

The space complexity of an algorithm is the total number of (local and shared) memory bits used to implement the algorithm.

2.4   Randomized Self-Stabilization

So far we have not concerned ourselves with randomized algorithms — i.e., those that use coin-toss or random-function results to determine their actions. An important subject in self-stabilization research is the study of randomized self-stabilizing algorithms. Breaking symmetry is sometimes impossible without using randomization.

In order to define the requirements for randomized self-stabilizing algorithms, we use the following assumptions and definitions. Processor activity is managed by a scheduler. The scheduler is merely an abstraction of the assumption made for the interleaving model, that at most one step is executed in every given time. In any given configuration, the scheduler activates a single processor, which executes a single step. To ensure correctness of the algorithms, we regard the scheduler as an adversary. The scheduler is assumed to have unlimited resources and chooses the next activated processor *on line*, using all the information about the execution so far. A scheduler S is *fair* if, for any configuration c with probability 1, an execution starting from c in which processors are activated by S is fair.

Finally, an algorithm is *randomized self-stabilizing* for a task *LE* if, starting with any system configuration and considering any fair scheduler, the algorithm reaches a safe configuration within an expected number of rounds that is bounded by some constant k (k may depend on n, the number of processors in the system).

Randomized algorithms are often used to break symmetry in a system of totally identical processors in which processors do not have unique identifiers. The terms *uniform* or *anonymous system* are used for such systems.

2.5   Example: Spanning-Tree Construction

To demonstrate the use of our definition and requirements, we present a simple self-stabilizing algorithm for marking a breadth-first search (BFS) spanning tree over the communication graph of the distributed system $G(V, E)$. Each node $v_i \in V$ represents the processor P_i, and each edge $(v_i, v_j) \in E$ indicates that P_i and P_j are neighbors; i.e., they can communicate with each other. For this example we use the shared memory model. A processor P_i communicates with its neighbor P_j by writing in the communication register r_{ij} and reading from r_{ji}. A processor P_i *owns* the register in which P_i writes; i.e., for every neighboring processor P_k, the register r_{ik} is owned by P_i.

The system consists of n processors $P_1, P_2, \cdots, P_n$, where $P_2, \cdots, P_n$ run similar programs while P_1 is a special processor that runs a different program. P_1 is called the *root* processor of the tree. There is a single program that every non-root processor runs. The program has an input parameter that is the number of adjacent links of the processor. Thus, all two (non-root) processors with the same number of neighbors are identical — they run identical programs.

Essentially the algorithm is a distributed BFS algorithm. Each processor is continuously trying to compute its distance from the root and to report this distance to all its neighbors by writing the distance in its registers. At the beginning of an arbitrary execution, the only processor guaranteed to compute the right distance is the root itself. Once this distance is written in all the root's registers, the value stored in these registers will never be changed. Once all processors at distance x from the root have completed computing their distance from the root correctly and have written it in all their registers, their registers remain constant throughout execution, and processors at distance $x + 1$ from the root are ready to compute their own distance from the root, and so forth.

The output tree is encoded by means of the registers as follows: each register r_{ij}, in which P_i writes and from which P_j reads, contains a binary *parent* field denoted by $r_{ij}.parent$. If P_j is the parent of P_i in the BFS tree, then the value of $r_{ij}.parent$ is 1; otherwise the value of $r_{ij}.parent$ is 0. In addition, each register r_{ij} has a *distance* field, denoted by $r_{ij}.dis$, that holds the distance from the root to P_i. The maximal value that can be stored in the *distance* field is N, where N is an upper bound on the number of processors in the system. An attempt to assign a value larger than N to the *distance* field results in the assignment of N.

The code of the algorithm, for the root and for the other processors, appears in figure 2.1. In this code the number of the processor's neighbors is given by

```
01 Root:   do forever
02              for m := 1 to δ do write r_im := ⟨0, 0⟩
03          od
04 Other:  do forever
05              for m := 1 to δ do lr_mi := read (r_mi)
06              FirstFound := false
07              dist := 1 + min {lr_mi.dis | 1 ≤ m ≤ δ}
08              for m := 1 to δ
09              do
10                   if not FirstFound and lr_mi.dis = dist − 1 then
11                        write r_im := ⟨1, dist⟩
12                        FirstFound := true
13                   else
14                        write r_im := ⟨0, dist⟩
15              od
16          od
```

Figure 2.1
The spanning-tree algorithm for P_i

the parameter δ. The program for the root is very simple: it keeps "telling" all its neighbors that it is the root by repeatedly writing the values $\langle 0, 0 \rangle$ in all of its registers. The first 0 tells each neighbor that it is not the parent of the root, the second 0 is the distance from the root to itself. The program for a normal processor consists of a single loop. In this loop, the processor reads all the registers of its neighbors. Processor P_i, which has δ neighbors, keeps δ internal variables corresponding to the δ registers from which P_i reads. The local variable corresponding to register r_{ji}, lr_{ji}, stores the last value of r_{ji} read by P_i. Its two fields are denoted by $lr_{ji}.parent$ and $lr_{ji}.dis$, respectively. Once all these registers are read, P_i computes a value for the variable $dist$ that represents P_i's current idea of its distance from the root. The purpose of the boolean variable *FirstFound* is to make sure that by the end of each pass of the loop each processor has a single parent. The minimum in line 7 is taken over m, $1 \leq m \leq \delta$.

In figure 2.1 we use a program to define implicitly the set of states and the transition function of a processor. The state of a processor consists of the value of the program counter and the values of the internal variables: m, lr_{ji} (for every $1 \leq j \leq \delta$), *FirstFound*, and $dist$. A computation step of the root processor starts with local computations that update the value of m (increment the value of m by one if $m \leq \delta$, or assign $m := 1$ otherwise). The single communication operation that is executed in a computation step of the root is a write operation of $\langle 0, 0 \rangle$ in r_{im} (where the value of m is defined by the preceding local computations). The computation steps end with this write operation. The next computation step starts with the local computation that immediately follows the last write operation, and so on. Similarly, a computation step of the non-root processor terminates in one of the three communication operations (read(r_{mi}), write(r_{im}) := $\langle 1, dis \rangle$ or write(r_{im}) := $\langle 0, dis \rangle$), and the next computation starts immediately following this communication operation. One can argue that, in the context of self-stabilization, the value of the program counter can be arbitrary in the first system configuration and not restricted to the first local computation that follows a communication operation. Thus, it is possible that, in line 10 of the code, a *dist* value that was not computed in line 7 is used. However, following the first computation step every computation step is well structured: it starts immediately following a communication operation and ends with the next communication operation.

The value of each communication register is a combination of a binary value (for the *parent* field) and an integer (no larger than N for the *dis* field). A configuration of the system is a vector of the processor states and a vector of communication register values.

The task *ST* of legitimate sequences is defined as the set of all configuration sequences in which every configuration encodes a *BFS* tree of the communication graph. In fact, a particular *BFS* tree called the *first BFS tree* is encoded. Let $\alpha = (\alpha_1, \alpha_2, ...\alpha_n)$ be the arbitrary ordering of the edges incident to each node $v_i \in V$. The *first BFS tree* of a communication graph G is uniquely defined by the choice of the root v_1 and α. When a node v_i of distance $x + 1$ from v_1 has more than a single neighbor of distance x from v_1, v_i is connected to its first neighbor according to α_i, whose distance from v_1 is x. In the lemma below, we use the definition of the first *BFS* tree to characterize the set of safe configurations for the algorithm.

The lemma below shows that, in every execution, a safe configuration is reached. We use Δ to denote the maximum number of links adjacent to a processor, and use the following definitions of *floating distances* and *smallest floating distance* in our proof.

DEFINITION 2.1:   A floating distance in some configuration c is a value in a register $r_{ij}.dis$ that is smaller than the distance of P_i from the root. The smallest floating distance in some configuration c is the smallest value among the floating distances.

LEMMA 2.1:   For every $k > 0$ and for every configuration that follows $\Delta + 4k\Delta$ rounds, it holds that:

Assertion 1: If there exists a floating distance, then the value of the smallest floating distance is at least k.

Assertion 2: The value in the registers of every processor that is within distance k from the root is equal to its distance from the root.

Proof Note that in every 2Δ successive rounds, each processor reads the registers of all its neighbors and writes to each of its registers. We prove the lemma by induction over k.

Base case: (proof for $k = 1$) Distances stored in the registers and internal variables are non-negative; thus the value of the smallest floating distance is at least 0 in the first configuration. During the first 2Δ rounds, each non-root processor P_i computes the value of the variable *dist* (line 7 of the code in figure 2.1). The result of each such computation must be greater than or equal to 1. Let c_2 be the configuration reached following the first computation of the value of *dist* by each processor. Each non-root processor writes to each of its registers the computed value of *dist* during the 2Δ rounds that follow c_2. Thus, in every configuration that follows the first 4Δ rounds there is no non-root processor with value 0 in its registers. The above proves assertion 1.

 To prove assertion 2, note that the root repeatedly writes the distance 0 to its registers in every Δ rounds. Let c_1 be the configuration reached after these Δ rounds. Each processor reads the registers of the root and *then* writes to its own registers during the 4Δ rounds that follow c_1. In this write operation the processor assigns 1 to its own registers. Any further read of the root registers returns the value 0; therefore, the value of the registers of each neighbor of the root is 1 following the first $\Delta + 4\Delta$ rounds. Thus, assertion 2 holds as well.

Induction step: (assume correctness for $k \geq 0$ and prove for $k + 1$) Let $m \geq k$ be the smallest floating distance in the configuration c_{4k} that follows the first $\Delta + 4k\Delta$ rounds. During the 4Δ rounds that follow c_{4k}, each processor that reads m and chooses m as the smallest value assigns $m + 1$ to its distance and writes this value. Therefore, the smallest floating distance value is $m + 1$ in the configuration $c_{4(k+1)}$. This proves assertion 1.

Since the smallest floating distance is $m \geq k$, it is clear that each processor reads the distance of a neighboring processor of distance k and assigns $k + 1$ to its distance. ■

The next corollary is implied by lemma 2.1. Note that once the value in the registers of every processor is equal to its distance from the root, a processor P_i chooses its parent to be the parent in the first *BFS* tree — P_i chooses the first neighbor according to α_i, with distance smaller than its own.

COROLLARY 2.1:   The algorithm presented above is self-stabilizing for *ST*.

2.6   Example: Mutual Exclusion

Dijkstra, in his pioneering work, presented three elegant, self-stabilizing algorithms for mutual exclusion on a ring. Dijkstra's work is considered to be the first to introduce and demonstrate the self-stabilization concept.

The algorithms presented by Dijkstra are for a system in which processors are activated by a scheduler called *central daemon*, which activates one processor at a time to execute an *aggregate step* consisting of several communication operations. For simplicity we assume that the central daemon is *fair*, activating each processor infinitely often in every infinite execution. The activated processor uses its own state and the states of its neighbors to compute its next state. In other words, the central daemon chooses one processor at a time and lets this processor read the state (that is written in the registers) of its neighbors and change the state (write the new state in the communication registers). Thus, when describing a system configuration there is no need to consider local variables that store the values read from neighbors — the state transition is made according to the values stored in the registers of the neighbors when the (single) processor is scheduled.

The system consists of n processors $P_1, P_2, \cdots, P_n$ that are connected in a ring. Each processor has a *left* and a *right* neighbor. The left neighbor of every processor P_i, $1 < i \leq n$, is P_{i-1} and the left neighbor of P_1 is P_n. Similarly, the right neighbor of every processor P_i, $1 \leq i < n$, is P_{i+1} and the right neighbor of P_n is P_1.

Each processor P_i has a variable x_i that stores an integer value that is no smaller than 0 and no larger than n. The transition functions of the processors $P_2, \cdots, P_n$ are identical, while the transition function of P_1 is distinct. We call

```
1  P₁:          do forever
2                   if x₁ = xₙ then
3                       x₁ := (x₁ + 1) mod (n + 1)
4  Pᵢ (i ≠ 1):  do forever
5                   if xᵢ ≠ xᵢ₋₁ then
6                       xᵢ := xᵢ₋₁
```

Figure 2.2
Dijkstra's algorithm

P_1 the *special processor*. The transition functions (or programs) of P_1 and the other processors P_i $(2 \leq i \leq n)$ appear in figure 2.2.

A configuration of the system is a vector of n integer values, one value for each x variable. A computation step of a processor P_i consists of reading the x variable of the left neighbor and using the value obtained together with the value of x_i to compute a new value for x_i. At any given time, only a single processor is executing a computation step. A processor P_i *can change its state* in a particular configuration c if the next computation step of P_i (when started in c) changes the value of x_i; i.e., $x_i \neq x_{i-1}$ in c, or $x_1 = x_n$ in c.

The task *ME* is defined by the set of all configuration sequences in which exactly one processor can change its state in any configuration and every processor can change its state in infinitely many configurations in every sequence in *ME*. Note that this definition differs from the traditional definition of mutual exclusion that allows processors to be in the reminder section (possibly forever) as long as they do not try to enter the critical section.

A safe configuration for *ME* and Dijkstra's algorithm (figure 2.2) is a configuration in which all the x variables have the same value. This is only one example of a safe configuration, but sufficient for what we need. The next lemma proves that, indeed, every fair execution that starts with such a safe configuration belongs to *ME*.

LEMMA 2.2:   A configuration c in which all the x variables have the same value is a safe configuration for *ME* and Dijkstra's algorithm.

Proof   Clearly the only processor P_i that is able to change the value of x_i in c is P_1. P_1 is activated infinitely often in every fair execution that starts in c. Once P_1 is activated, P_1 assigns x_1 a value that does not exist in any other variable. Let c_1 be the configuration that immediately follows the assignment of this new value in x_1. Clearly, P_1 cannot change the value of x_1 until x_n holds the new value as well. Every other processor P_i cannot change the value of x_i unless $x_{i-1} \neq x_i$. Thus, the only processor P_i that can change the value of x_i is P_2. P_2 is activated infinitely often in every fair execution, and in particular it is activated infinitely often following c_1 of every fair execution. Let c_2 be the configuration reached immediately after P_2 changes the value of x_2. In c_2, it holds that $x_1 = x_2$, $x_2 \neq x_3$, and $x_3 = x_4 = \cdots = x_n$. Thus, the only processor that is able to change a state is P_3. In general, in c_i, $1 \leq i < n$, it holds that $x_1 = x_2 = \cdots = x_i$, $x_i \neq x_{i+1}$, and $x_{i+1} = x_{i+2} = \cdots = x_n$. Thus, the only processor that is able to change the value of its variable is P_{i+1}. Therefore, in c_{n-1}, only P_n is able to change the value of its variable and, once it is activated, a configuration c_n is reached in which the values of all the variables are the same. Note that in every execution that starts in c and ends in c_n exactly one processor is able to change the value of its variable and each processor changes the value of its variable exactly once.

Exactly the same arguments can be applied to c_n; thus it is clear that, in every fair execution, every processor changes the value of its variable infinitely often and, in every execution, there is exactly one processor that can change its state. ∎

To prove that Dijkstra's algorithm is self-stabilizing for *ME*, we need to show that, in every fair execution, a safe configuration relative to *ME* is reached after a finite number of rounds. We first observe that, in any possible configuration, at least one possible value for the x variables does not exist. In fact, the observation that in any configuration at least one value is missing is used in what follows. We call this concept the *missing value* or *missing label concept*.

LEMMA 2.3:   For every possible configuration c, there exists at least one integer $0 \leq j \leq n$ such that for every $1 \leq i \leq n$, $x_i \neq j$ in c.

Proof   There are at most n distinct values in the x variables in c, a distinct value for each processor P_i. There are $n + 1$ possible values that can be stored in each of the x variables. Thus, an integer j must exist that does not appear in any x_i. ∎

The next observation is also simple, claiming that the special processor P_1 changes the value of x_1 infinitely often in every fair execution.

LEMMA 2.4:   For every possible configuration c, in every fair execution that starts in c, the special processor P_1 changes the value of x_1 at least once in every n rounds.

Proof Assume that there exists a configuration c and a fair execution that starts in c and in which P_1 does not change the value of x_1 during the first n rounds. Let c_2 be the configuration that immediately follows the first time P_2 executes a computation step during the first round. Clearly, $x_1 = x_2$ in c_2 and in every configuration that follows c_2 in the next $n - 1$ rounds. Let c_3 be the configuration that immediately follows the first time P_3 executes a computation step during the second round. It holds in c_3 that $x_1 = x_2 = x_3$. The same argument repeats itself until we arrive at the configuration c_n, which is reached in the $(n - 1)$th round and in which $x_1 = x_2 = \cdots = x_n$. In the nth round, P_1 is activated and changes the value of x_1, a contradiction. ∎

We are now ready to prove the main theorem.

THEOREM 2.1:   For every possible configuration c, every fair execution that starts in c reaches a safe configuration with relation to *ME* within $O(n^2)$ rounds.

Proof In accordance with lemma 2.3, for every possible configuration c there exists at least one integer $0 \le j \le n$ such that, for every $1 \le i \le n$, $x_i \ne j$ in c. In accordance with lemma 2.4, for every possible configuration c, in every fair execution that starts in c, the special processor P_1 changes the value of x_1 in every n rounds. Every time P_1 changes the value of x_1, P_1 increments the value of x_1 modulo $n + 1$. Thus, it must hold that every possible value, and in particular the value j, is assigned to x_1 during any fair execution that starts in c. Let c_j be the configuration that immediately follows the first assignment of j in x_1. Every processor P_i $2 \le i \le n$ copies the value of x_{i-1} to x_i. Thus, it holds for $1 \le i \le n$ that $x_i \ne j$ in every configuration that follows c and precedes c_j; it also holds that in c_j, the only x variable that holds the value j is x_1. P_1 does not change the value of x_1 until $x_n = j$. The only possible sequence of changes of the values of the x variables to the value j is: P_2 changes x_2 to the value of x_1 (which is j), then P_3 changes the value of x_3 to j and so on until P_n changes the value of x_n to j. Only at this stage is P_1 able to change value again (following c_j). Let c_n be the configuration reached following the assignment of $x_n := j$. c_n is a safe configuration.

In accordance with lemma 2.4, P_1 must assign j to x_1 in every n^2 rounds. Thus a safe configuration must be reached in $n^2 + n$ rounds. ∎

In fact, Dijkstra's algorithm stabilizes when the number of possible values for the x variable is n. The reason is that, if no possible value is missing in the first configuration, then x_1 has a distinct value; thus, stabilization is guaranteed. Otherwise, at least one possible value is missing in the first configuration and theorem 2.1 holds.

Moreover, a similar argument holds when the number of possible values for the x variables is $n - 1$. In this case, a configuration must be reached in which $x_n = x_1$ (just before the first time P_1 changes the value of x_1). Call this configuration c. If in c every processor P_i, $1 \leq i \leq n - 1$, does not hold a distinct value in x_i, then a missing value j must exist and the stabilization is proved by a proof similar to that of theorem 2.1. Otherwise, each P_i, $1 \leq i \leq n - 1$, holds a distinct value in c. Let j' be the value of x_1 in c and consider the first configuration c' that follows c and in which P_1 is able to change the value of x_1. Consider the following three cases for the first computation step that follows c. Case 1: a processor P_i, $2 \leq i \leq n - 1$, copies the value of x_{i-1} to x_i and, at the same time, eliminates the distinct value stored in x_i from the system. Case 2: P_n copies the distinct value of x_{n-1} to x_n, leaving x_1 with a distinct value. Case 3: P_1 changes the value of x_1 to $k = (j'+1) \bmod (n-1)$; thus, the only x variable that holds j' is x_n. However, P_n must copy the value k within the next n rounds (before P_1 changes the value of x_1 again), eliminating j' from the system.

Will Dijkstra's algorithm stabilize when the number of possible values for the x variables is $n - 2$? Let $c = \{0, 0, 2, 1, 0\}$ be a system configuration. An execution that starts in c and repeatedly activates P_1, P_5, P_4, P_3, P_2, in this order, does not reach a safe configuration:

$$\{0, 0, 2, 1, 0\} \rightarrow \{1, 0, 2, 1, 0\} \rightarrow \{1, 0, 2, 1, 1\} \rightarrow \{1, 0, 2, 2, 1\} \rightarrow$$
$$\{1, 0, 0, 2, 1\} \rightarrow \{1, 1, 0, 2, 1\} \cdots$$

Note that the configuration $\{1, 1, 0, 2, 1\}$ is obtained by incrementing every value in $\{0, 0, 2, 1, 0\}$ by 1, where the increment operation is done modulo $n - 2 = 3$, and therefore the configuration $\{0, 0, 2, 1, 0\}$ is reached again after activating each processor $n - 2 = 3$ times when the processors are repeatedly activated in the order specified above. Thus, there exists an infinite execution in which more than one processor can change a state in every configuration. This execution has no suffix in ME, and therefore the algorithm is not self-stabilizing with relation to ME.

It seems at first glance that the powerful central daemon scheduler guarantees some sort of mutual exclusion by activating one processor at a time. One can ask whether an algorithm in which every processor P_i executes the critical section (whenever the central daemon activates P_i) is a mutual exclusion algorithm.

To answer the above question, let us consider a multitasking single-processor computer in which, at any given time, exactly one process is executed by the single processor. In such settings, one of the processes P_i may enter the critical section (e.g., may start using a resource such as the printer). P_i may be suspended while it is in the critical section by the operating system, due to task switching. We would not want any other process to enter the critical section (and, say, start printing) as long as P_i is in the critical section. Clearly, Dijkstra's algorithm can be used to coordinate the activity of the processes in such a system in the following way: the single process P_i that can change a state is the one that may access the critical section. Only when process P_i is finished with the critical section does it change the value of x_i.

On the negative side, we demonstrate that Dijkstra's algorithm needs more states to work if steps consists of only one communication operation, read or write. (The term *read/write atomicity* describes the operations in such a system.) To do this we introduce an internal variable lx_i for every processor P_i in which is stored the last value read by P_i from the x variable of the left neighbor of P_i. Note that the existence of such a variable is enforced by the new atomicity, since a write operation is not executed in the same atomic step as a read operation and the value written is a function of the last value read. Now a possible configuration is a vector $c = \{(lx_1, x_1), (lx_2, x_2), \cdots, (lx_n, x_n)\}$. A read operation of P_i, $1 < i \le n$, copies the value of x_{i-1} into lx_i; a read operation of P_1 copies the value of x_n into lx_1. A write operation of P_i, $1 < i \le n$, copies the value of lx_i into x_i; a write operation of P_1 assigns $(lx_1 + 1) \bmod K$ to x_1, where, from our previous discussion, $K > (n - 2)$. If we reexamine the operation of every processor in the read/write atomicity model, we discover that the $n-$processor ring in this model is identical to a ring of $2n$ processors in a system with a central daemon. A read operation is essentially a copy of the value of the left neighbor. A write operation by every processor P_i, $i \ne 1$, is also a copy operation from lx_i to x_i. x_1 is the only variable that is incremented modulo K during a write operation. Thus, we can apply our previous proofs and discussion to conclude that K must be greater than $2n - 2$.

In figure 2.3 circles represent processors and rectangles represent communication registers. The left portion of figure 2.3 represents a system for which read/write atomicity is assumed. The arrows in the left portion denote the ability of P_i to write (the value of lx_i, if $i \ne 1$) in x_i and read the value of x_{i-1}

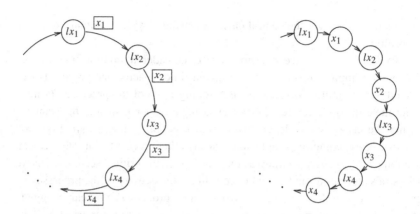

Figure 2.3
Mutual exclusion assuming read/write versus central daemon

(into lx_i). The right portion of figure 2.3 represents a system for which a central daemon is assumed. The arrows in this portion denote the ability of P_i to use the state of its left neighbor together with its own state for its transition function. Note that there is no need to store a value read from a (register of a) processor in a local variable. Whenever the central daemon schedules a processor to execute a step, the state of the left neighbor (the value read from the left neighbor) is used by P_i in the very same (aggregate) step to compute its next state.

2.7 Fair Composition of Self-Stabilizing Algorithms

Several techniques have been proposed for designing, analyzing, and proving the correctness of self-stabilizing algorithms. In this section, we introduce the technique of fair composition of self-stabilizing algorithms. The idea is to compose self-stabilizing algorithms $\mathcal{AL}_1, \mathcal{AL}_2, \cdots, \mathcal{AL}_k$ so that the stabilized behavior (roughly speaking, output) of $\mathcal{AL}_1, \mathcal{AL}_2, \cdots, \mathcal{AL}_i$ is used (as an input) by $\mathcal{AL}_{i+1}$. The algorithms are executed in a fair fashion — each processor executes a step of each algorithm infinitely often. $\mathcal{AL}_{i+1}$ cannot detect whether the algorithms $\mathcal{AL}_1$ to $\mathcal{AL}_i$ have stabilized, but $\mathcal{AL}_{i+1}$ is executed as if these algorithms $\mathcal{AL}_1$ to $\mathcal{AL}_i$ have done so. Thus, when every algorithm up to the ith algorithm has stabilized, $\mathcal{AL}_{i+1}$ is in an arbitrary state from which it starts converging to a legal behavior.

The technique is described for $k = 2$ (i.e., composition of two self-stabilizing algorithms), and the generalization to $k > 2$ is obvious. Two simple algorithms, called a *server* algorithm and a *client* algorithm, are combined to obtain a more complex algorithm. The server algorithm ensures that some properties will hold, and these properties are later used by the client algorithm.

Assume that the server algorithm $\mathcal{AL}_1$ is for a task defined by the set of legal executions $\mathcal{T}_1$, and that the client algorithm $\mathcal{AL}_2$ is for a task defined by the set of legal executions $\mathcal{T}_2$. A processor P_i runs the two algorithms $\mathcal{AL}_1$ and $\mathcal{AL}_2$ in alternation, one step of $\mathcal{AL}_1$ and then a step of $\mathcal{AL}_2$, and so on. Let A_i be the state set of P_i in $\mathcal{AL}_1$ and $S_i = A_i \times B_i$ the state set of P_i in $\mathcal{AL}_2$, where, whenever P_i executes $\mathcal{AL}_2$, it modifies only the B_i components of $A_i \times B_i$ (for simplicity we assume that the communication registers in which a processor writes are parts of the processor state). In other words, whenever P_i executes a step in $\mathcal{AL}_1$, it uses its state in $\mathcal{AL}_1$, ignoring the portion of the state that is modified in the steps of $\mathcal{AL}_2$. Whenever P_i executes a step in $\mathcal{AL}_2$, it uses its state in $\mathcal{AL}_1$ and $\mathcal{AL}_2$ to compute its new B_i portion of its state in $\mathcal{AL}_2$.

The following definitions formalize the concept of an execution of the client algorithm, which assumes self-stabilized execution of the server algorithm. Let $S_i, A_i, B_i, \mathcal{AL}_2$ and $\mathcal{T}_1$ be as above, where $\mathcal{T}_1$ is defined using the A_i portion of the states of every processor P_i. For a configuration c, $c \in S_1 \times ... \times S_n$, define the *A-projection* of c as the configuration $(ap_1, ..., ap_n)$ $\in A_1 \times ... \times A_n$. The *A-projection* of an execution is defined analogously to consist of the *A-projection* of every configuration of the execution.

We say that *algorithm $\mathcal{AL}_2$ is self-stabilizing for task $\mathcal{T}_2$ given task $\mathcal{T}_1$* if any fair execution of $\mathcal{AL}_2$ that has an *A-projection* in $\mathcal{T}_1$ has a suffix in $\mathcal{T}_2$. Finally, an algorithm $\mathcal{AL}$ is a *fair composition* of $\mathcal{AL}_1$ and $\mathcal{AL}_2$ if, in $\mathcal{AL}$, every processor execute steps of $\mathcal{AL}_1$ and $\mathcal{AL}_2$ alternately. In fact it is sufficient that every processor executes steps of $\mathcal{AL}_1$ and $\mathcal{AL}_2$ infinitely often. Note that, for an execution E of $\mathcal{AL}$, the *A-projection* of E is a sub-execution of E corresponding to a fair execution of the server algorithm $\mathcal{AL}_1$.

The following theorem gives sufficient conditions under which the composition of two self-stabilizing algorithms is also self-stabilizing.

THEOREM 2.2:   Assume that $\mathcal{AL}_2$ is self-stabilizing for a task $\mathcal{T}_2$ given task $\mathcal{T}_1$. If $\mathcal{AL}_1$ is self-stabilizing for $\mathcal{T}_1$, then the fair composition of $\mathcal{AL}_1$ and $\mathcal{AL}_2$ is self-stabilizing for $\mathcal{T}_2$.

Proof   Consider any execution E of $\mathcal{AL}$, the fair composition of $\mathcal{AL}_1$ and $\mathcal{AL}_2$. By the self-stabilization of $\mathcal{AL}_1$, E has a suffix E' such that the *A-projection* of E' is in $\mathcal{T}_1$. By the assumption that $\mathcal{AL}_2$ is self-stabilizing given $\mathcal{T}_1$, E' has a suffix in $\mathcal{T}_2$.   ∎

Theorem 2.2 provides a general methodology for constructing self-stabilizing algorithms for complex tasks. Given a task $\mathcal{T}_2$ for which we wish to construct such an algorithm, first define a task $\mathcal{T}_1$ and construct an algorithm $\mathcal{AL}_2$ that is self-stabilizing for $\mathcal{T}_2$ given $\mathcal{T}_1$, and then construct an algorithm $\mathcal{AL}_1$ that is self-stabilizing for $\mathcal{T}_1$. The fair composition of $\mathcal{AL}_1$ and $\mathcal{AL}_2$ is the desired algorithm. Note that this methodology does not require that the algorithm $\mathcal{AL}_1$ reach a "steady state" in which the communication registers (or any other component in the state ap_i of processor P_i) are never changed. Moreover, the fair-composition methodology can be used for message-passing systems. For example, $\mathcal{AL}_1$ can be a self-stabilizing data-link algorithm that uses retransmissions to guarantee that, from some point on, every message sent from one processor to its neighbor reaches its destination. $\mathcal{AL}_2$ can be a self-stabilizing end-to-end algorithm that guarantees that, from some point on, every message sent from one processor in the network to another processor reaches its destination under the assumption that the data-link service is reliable. Clearly $\mathcal{AL}_2$ will not operate correctly until $\mathcal{AL}_1$ is stabilized and operating as it should. Eventually $\mathcal{AL}_1$ reaches a safe configuration with relation to $\mathcal{T}_1$; in this configuration, the B_i components of the state of P_i are arbitrary. Fortunately, $\mathcal{AL}_2$ is self-stabilizing when $\mathcal{AL}_1$ is already stabilized. Therefore a safe configuration for $\mathcal{AL}_2$ with relation to $\mathcal{T}_2$ is reached.

Example: Mutual Exclusion for General Communication Graphs

To demonstrate the power of the fair-composition method, let us compose the spanning-tree construction algorithm of section 2.5 with the mutual exclusion algorithm presented in section 2.6. The combination of these algorithms is a self-stabilizing algorithm for mutual exclusion in systems with general communication graphs. The spanning-tree construction is the server algorithm and the mutual exclusion is the client algorithm.

The mutual exclusion algorithm presented in figure 2.2 is designed for a system in the shape of a ring, assuming that a powerful scheduler schedules the steps of the processors. Note that a slight modification of the algorithm can be applied to systems that support only read/write atomicity as presented in section 2.6. In figure 2.5 we present a version of the mutual exclusion algorithm

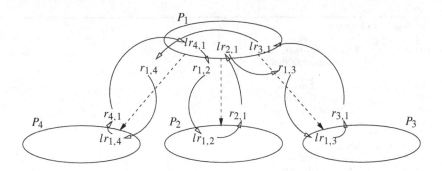

Figure 2.4
Euler tour defines a virtual ring

of figure 2.2 that is designed to stabilize in a system in which a rooted spanning tree exists and in which only read/write atomicity is assumed.

One key observation used to apply the mutual exclusion algorithm to a rooted spanning-tree system is the fact that a Euler tour on a spanning tree defines a (virtual) ring. For example, consider a rooted tree of four processors, where P_1 is the root and P_4, P_2, and P_3 are P_1's children, ordered according to an arbitrary but fixed order chosen by P_1. In this case, the sequence $lx_1, x_1, lx_2, x_2, \cdots$ presented in section 2.6 corresponds to $lr_{4,1}, r_{1,2}, lr_{1,2}, r_{2,1}, lr_{2,1}, r_{1,3}, lr_{1,3}, r_{3,1}, lr_{3,1}, r_{1,4}, lr_{1,4}, r_{4,1}$. Figure 2.4 depicts the virtual ring embedded in the above rooted tree, where P_1 acts as three processors in the ring (one for each attached link). In particular, P_1 acts as the special processor using $lr_{4,1}$ and $r_{1,2}$ — whenever $lr_{4,1}$ equals $r_{1,2}$, P_1 increments the value in $r_{1,2}$ modulo $4n - 5$.

In general, let $\alpha_i = i_1, i_2, \cdots, i_\delta$ be the arbitrary ordering of the tree edges incident to a non-root node $v_i \in V$, where the first edge is the edge leading to the parent of v_i in the tree. For the sake of readability let us use the index j for i_j, resulting in $\alpha_i = 1, 2, \cdots, \delta$. P_i repeatedly executes steps in which P_i reads the register $r_{1,i}$ into $lr_{1,i}$, then writes the value of $lr_{1,i}$ into $r_{i,2}$, and then reads the register $lr_{2,i}$ and writes to $r_{i,3}$, and so on, until it writes the value of $lr_{\delta,i}$ to $r_{i,1}$. The above read/write pattern is repeated. Roughly speaking, P_i plays the role of δ processors in the (virtual) ring. To avoid multiple entries to the critical section, each emulated processor P_i enters the critical section only when the value of $lr_{1,i}$ is not equal to the value of $r_{i,2}$. In contrast, the root processor (i.e., the special processor) enters the critical section whenever the

---

```
01 Root:   do forever
02                lr_{1,i} := read (r_{1,i})
03                if lr_{δ,i} = r_{i,1} then
04                      (* critical section *)
05                      write r_{i,2} := (lr_{1,i} + 1 mod (4n − 5))
06                      for m := 2 to δ do
07                            lr_{m,i} := read (r_{m,i})
08                            write r_{i,m+1} := lr_{m,i}
09                      od
10          od
11 Other:  do forever
12                lr_{1,i} := read (r_{1,i})
13                if lr_{1,i} ≠ r_{i,2} then
14                      (* critical section *)
15                      write r_{i,2} := lr_{1,i}
16                      for m := 2 to δ do
17                            lr_{m,i} := read (r_{m,i})
18                            write r_{i,m+1} := lr_{m,i}
19                      od
20          od
```

Figure 2.5
Mutual exclusion for tree structure: the program for P_i

value of $lr_{δ,i}$ is equal to the value of $r_{i,1}$. The mutual-exclusion algorithm for a spanning-tree system appears in figure 2.5. The indices of $r_{i,m+1}$ are computed modulo $δ$.

The mutual-exclusion algorithm can be applied to a spanning tree of the system using the ring defined by the Euler tour on the tree. However, the mutual exclusion algorithm cannot be applied to a system with a general graph in which a spanning tree is not defined. Fortunately, the value of the parent fields of the server algorithm eventually defines the parent of each processor in the tree, and hence defines the children of each processor as well.

In the composition of the algorithms, each processor alternately executes a step of each of the composed algorithms. Let us consider a particular way to implement such a composition, where an internal binary variable called $turn_i$ is used by each processor P_i to indicate which of the algorithms is to be executed next. P_i maintains a program counter for each of the algorithms. Whenever P_i is scheduled to execute a step and $turn_i = 0$ ($turn_i = 1$, respectively), P_i executes the next step of the spanning-tree construction (the mutual exclusion, respectively) algorithm and assigns $turn_i := 1 - turn_i$. Each processor executes an atomic step infinitely often in every fair execution. This fact, together with the use of the $turn_i$ variable, ensures that every processor executes an atomic step of each of the composed algorithms infinitely often.

The fact that each processor executes the spanning-tree construction infinitely often implies that, at some point of the execution, a fixed spanning tree is defined by the value of the distance fields of the communication registers. When a processor executes the mutual-exclusion algorithm, it uses the value of the parent fields of the tree-construction algorithm for the definition of the tree links that are attached to it. Therefore, when the server algorithm is not yet stabilized the mutual-exclusion algorithm may be executed over a non-tree structure. Hence, it is possible that the execution of the mutual-exclusion algorithm, during the convergence period of the tree-construction algorithm, is not an execution that was considered when the self-stabilizing mutual-exclusion algorithm was designed. Consequently, once the tree is fixed, the self-stabilizing mutual-exclusion algorithm is in an arbitrary state from which it converges to reach a safe configuration.

A different example, demonstrating the applicability of the fair composition technique for the case in which the output of the server is not fixed, is a server algorithm that implements a powerful scheduler — the central daemon. The composition of the previous two algorithms ensures that exactly one processor is executing the critical section and each processor executes the critical section infinitely often. Therefore the composed algorithm can implement a powerful scheduler that chooses one processor at a time to be activated. Again, it is possible that, during the convergence of the server algorithm, several processors are activated simultaneously. However, once the server algorithm stabilizes, only a single processor is activated at a time, ensuring the stabilization of a client algorithm that stabilizes (only) in the presence of such a powerful scheduler (more details are given in section 4.1).

2.8   Recomputation of Floating Output

A large class of distributed algorithms compute a fixed distributed output based on a distributed input. Usually the distributed input of a node is related to its local topology. For example, the input to a processor may be the number of communication links that are attached to the processor, the weight/load of these communication links, or the identifiers of the neighboring processors. The distributed output is a function of the distributed input; the output usually marks links of the communication graph. For example, the output of a processor is the identity of the attached links that participate in a minimum spanning tree of the communication graph.

The recomputation of the floating output is a way to convert a non-stabilizing algorithm $\mathcal{AL}$ that computes a fixed distributed output into a self-stabilizing algorithm. Roughly speaking, the idea is to execute $\mathcal{AL}$ repeatedly. Each time the execution of $\mathcal{AL}$ is over, the output is written in special output variables called *floating output variables*, and then a new execution of $\mathcal{AL}$ starts from the predefined initial state of $\mathcal{AL}$. When the new execution is initialized, every component of the system is assigned a predefined initial state, the only exception being the unchanged value of the floating output variables. The algorithm designer must prove that, from every possible configuration, an execution of $\mathcal{AL}$ will eventually begin from a predefined initial state and that any two executions of $\mathcal{AL}$ that begin from the initial state have identical output. Therefore, the update of the floating output variables, which is executed repeatedly every time an execution of $\mathcal{AL}$ terminates, does not change the output of the system.

Example: Synchronous Consensus

To demonstrate the core idea behind the recomputation of the floating output, we ignore synchronization issues at this stage and assume that the system is a message-passing synchronous system. Consider a distributed system in which every processor P_i has a hardwired binary input I_i and a binary output variable O_i. The *synchronous consensus* task is specified by a set of (synchronous) executions SC in which the output variable of every processor is 1 if and only if there exists an input variable with value 1.

```
01 initialization
02     pulse := 0
03     O_i := I_i
04 while pulse_i ≤ D do
05     upon a pulse
06         pulse_i := pulse_i + 1
07         send (O_i)
08         forall P_j ∈ N(i) do receive (O_j)
09         if O_i = 0 and ∃ P_j ∈ N(i) | O_j = 1 then
10             O_i := 1
```

Figure 2.6
(Non-stabilizing) synchronous consensus algorithm

A non-stabilizing algorithm for the above synchronous consensus task is simple. Starting from an initial state, each processor P_i copies the value of its input I_i to the output O_i. Then each processor repeatedly sends the value of its output to its neighbors. If the value of O_i is 0 and a message with a value 1 reaches P_i, then P_i assigns $O_i = 1$.

A processor P_i with input 1 writes 1 to O_i, sends messages to its neighbors, and receives messages from the neighbors during the first pulse. Thus, during the second pulse, every neighbor P_j of P_i assigns 1 to O_j. In general, following the kth pulse, the output of every processor of distance $k - 1$ from P_i is 1. The *diameter d* of the system is the maximal number of edges (where the maximum is taken over the choice of nodes) in the shortest path that connects a pair of nodes in the communication graph of the system. We can conclude that, following $d + 1$ rounds, the output of every processor is 1 if there exists a processor with input 1. On the other hand, if the input of every processor is 0, then no processor changes its output.

The non-stabilizing algorithm described above does not terminate, since a processor with output 0 cannot be sure whether it is about to receive a message with value 1. However, if every processor knows a bound $D \geq d$ on the diameter of the system, then a processor can count the number of pulses and stop the execution when the counter reaches $D + 1$.

Note that counting pulses by a non-stabilizing algorithm is a simple task. An integer variable, initialized to zero, is incremented by 1 in every pulse. The code for the (non-stabilizing) synchronous consensus algorithm appears in figure 2.6.

Is the above algorithm a self-stabilizing algorithm? The answer is negative. For example, any execution that starts in a system configuration in which the value of at least one output variable is 1, the program counter of every processor is greater than 3, and in which there exists no input variable with the value 1 never reaches a safe configuration. The reason is that no processor assigns 0 to the output variable following the execution of line 3 of the code.

Figure 2.7 presents a self-stabilizing synchronous consensus algorithm. To demonstrate the method of recomputing the floating output, we ignore the fundamental drawback of using unbounded variables in the context of self-stabilization. Every processor has an unbounded integer $pulse_i$. A simple technique ensures that eventually the value of all the *pulse* variables is the same and is incremented by 1 at every pulse. After every pulse, each processor P_i chooses the maximal *pulse* value among the values of $pulse_i$ and the values of the *pulse* variables of its neighbors. The chosen maximal value

---

```
01 upon a pulse
02      if (pulse_i mod (D + 1)) = 0 then
03          begin
04                  O_i := o_i    (* floating output is assigned by the result *)
05                  o_i := I_i    (* initialize a new computation *)
06          end
07      send (⟨o_i, pulse_i⟩)
08      forall P_j ∈ N(i) do receive (⟨o_j, pulse_j⟩)
09      if o_i = 0 and ∃ P_j ∈ N(i) | o_j = 1 then
10          o_i := 1
11      pulse_i := {max(pulse_j, pulse_i) + 1 | P_j ∈ N(i)}
```

Figure 2.7
Self-stabilizing synchronous consensus algorithm

is incremented by 1 and is assigned to $pulse_i$ (we discuss this technique in detail in section 6.1). Let us remark that, starting in a configuration in which a processor P_i holds the maximal $pulse$ value x, among all the $pulse$ variables in the system, it must be the case that after the first pulse, the value of $pulse_i$, and the $pulse$ variables of each of P_i's neighbors is $x + 1$. Thus, after the first d pulses, the value of the $pulse$ variables of all the processors is identical.

The output variable O_i of every processor P_i is used as the floating output, which is eventually fixed and correct. A new variable o_i is used for recomputing the output of the algorithm. Following the first d pulses, the value of the $pulse$ variables of all the processors is identical and the common value is incremented by 1 in each pulse, reaching a pulse number $k(D + 1)$ for some integer k. Once all the processors discover that their pulse number is $k(D+1)$, they start an execution of the non-stabilizing algorithm, using o_i for the output. Then, when the value of the pulse variables is $(k + 1)(D + 1)$, each processor copies the calculated output value o_i into the floating output O_i and starts a new execution of the non-stabilizing algorithm. The floating output is updated again when the value of the pulse variable is $(k + 2)(D + 1)$. Eventually the update of the floating output by the assignment $O_i := o_i$ does not change the value of O_i, since the same (deterministic) calculation is executed between any two complete executions of the non-stabilizing algorithm. Observe that the value of o_i may be changed infinitely often and thus cannot be used as the (fixed) output of the processors that is defined by the set of legal executions SC. Nevertheless, the floating output does stabilize to a fixed and correct output after the processors simultaneously perform a complete execution of the non-stabilizing algorithm.

Let us just note that the floating output method can be used to convert a fixed-output non-stabilizing algorithm into a self-stabilizing algorithm. Let T be the number of pulses required by a synchronous non-stabilizing algorithm to compute the (fixed) output. For every such synchronous algorithm, the conversion method is similar to the conversion used for the synchronous consensus algorithm, with T instead of D.

Asynchronous non-stabilizing algorithms that have a fixed output are also converted to self-stabilizing algorithms by the floating output method. To do this, one needs to use a self-stabilizing synchronizer that simulates a common pulse. Asynchronous algorithms can be executed by synchronous systems by letting processors execute one step in every pulse. Under such a policy, only a single possible execution starts from a predefined initial state and lets each processor execute its next atomic step at every pulse (or simulated pulse, when a synchronizer is used).

An additional conclusion is that the number of pulses in this single execution until a fixed output is reached must be bounded by some integer T; this bound can be used by the floating output method (more details about this technique are given in sections 4.5 and 5.1).

2.9   Proof Techniques

This section describes and demonstrates several basic proof techniques, techniques that we use in subsequent chapters to prove correctness of the self-stabilizing algorithms. Proof techniques demonstrate the difficulties of designing self-stabilizing algorithms and how to cope with them.

Variant Function

The variant function (or potential function) technique is used for proving convergence. The basic idea is to use a function over the configuration set, whose value is bounded, to prove that this function monotonically decreases (or increases) when processors execute a step, and to show that after the function reaches a certain threshold, the system is in a safe configuration.

The above property of the variant function can be used to estimate the maximal number of steps required to reach a safe configuration. In some cases the choice of the variant function is intricate, as the following example indicates.

```
1  do forever
2      if pointer_i = null and (∃ P_j ∈ N(i) | pointer_j = i) then
3          pointer_i := j
4      if pointer_i = null and (∀ P_j ∈ N(i) pointer_j ≠ i) and
5                          (∃ P_j ∈ N(i) | pointer_j = null) then
6          pointer_i := j
7      if pointer_i = j and pointer_j = k and k ≠ i then
8          pointer_i := null
9  od
```

Figure 2.8
Self-stabilizing maximal matching: the program for P_i

Example: Self-Stabilizing Maximal Matching

In the maximal matching algorithm, every processor P_i tries to find a matching neighbor P_j. Assume that each processor P_i has a pointer that either points to one of its neighbors or has a null value. The maximal matching algorithm should reach a configuration c_l in which the existence of a pointer of P_i that points to P_j implies the existence of a pointer of P_j that points to P_i. In addition, assume that in c_l there are no two neighboring processors P_i and P_j, such that both have null pointers. The first condition is the core requirement for matching, while the second requirement guarantees that the solution is maximal.

Our concern in this example is to demonstrate the variant function technique. To simplify the discussion, let us assume the existence of a central daemon that activates one processor at a time; the activated processor reads the state of all its neighbors and changes state accordingly. Only when the activated processor finishes executing the above operations is another processor activated. The algorithm is presented in figure 2.8.

The set of legal executions MM for the maximal matching task includes every execution in which the values of the pointers of all the processors are fixed and form a maximal matching. Given a configuration c_l, we say that a processor P_i is:

• *matched* in c_l, if P_i has a neighbor P_j such that $pointer_i = j$ and $pointer_j = i$.

• *single* in c_l, if $pointer_i = null$ and every neighbor of P_i is matched.

• *waiting* in c_l, if P_i has a neighbor P_j such that $pointer_i = j$ and $pointer_j = null$.

- *free* in c_l, if $pointer_i = null$ and there exists a neighbor P_j, such that P_j is not matched.
- *chaining* in c_l, if there exists a neighbor P_j for which $pointer_i = j$ and $pointer_j = k, k \neq i$.

The correctness proof of the algorithm presented in figure 2.8 uses the variant function $VF(c)$, which returns a vector $(m + s, w, f, c)$, where m, s, w, f, and c are the total number of matched, single, waiting, free, and chaining processors, respectively, in c_l. Values of VF are compared lexicographically: for example, $(5, 3, 4, 7)$ is greater than $(5, 3, 3, 8)$.

Note that every configuration c_l for which $VF(c) = (n, 0, 0, 0)$ is a safe configuration with relation to MM and to our algorithm; also for every safe configuration c_l, $VF(c) = (n, 0, 0, 0)$. Once the system reaches a safe configuration, no processor changes the value of its pointer, while in every non-safe configuration, there exists at least one processor that can change the value of its pointer when it is activated by the central daemon. Next we show that every change of a pointer value increases the value of VF.

An assignment in line 3 of the code reduces the number of free processors and waiting processors by 1 and increments the number of matched processors by 2. An assignment in line 6 of the code reduces the number of free processors by 1 and increments the number of waiting processors by 1. The assignment in line 8 is executed when P_i is chaining. Two cases are considered: first, if no neighboring processor points to P_i. In this case, P_i changes status to free if there exists an unmatched neighbor, or to single if all neighbors are matched. Therefore, the number of chaining processors is reduced by 1 and the number of free or single processors is incremented by 1. In the second case, when at least one neighbor P_k points toward P_i, the status of P_i is changed to free and the status of P_k is changed from chaining to waiting. Hence the number of chaining processors is reduced by 2, while the number of both free and waiting processors is incremented by 1. Thus each of the above assignments increments the value of VF. The system stabilizes once it reaches a configuration in which no increment is possible, which is a safe configuration.

We can conclude that, indeed, every change in a pointer value increments the value of VF. The number of such pointer-value changes is bounded by the number of all possible vector values. The fact that $m + s + w + f + c = n$ implies that the number of possible vector values is $O(n^3)$. A rough analysis uses the following argument. One can choose $n + 1$ possible values for $m + s$ and then $n+1$ values for w and f. The value of n and the first three elements of the vector $(m + s, w, f, c)$ imply the value of c. Therefore the system reaches a safe configuration within $O(n^3)$ pointer-value changes.

Convergence Stairs

It is possible to prove the correctness of a self-stabilizing algorithm by proving that it converges to fulfill $k > 1$ predicates $A_1, A_2, \cdots, A_k$ such that, for every $1 \leq i < k$, A_{i+1} is a *refinement* of A_i. Here a predicate A_{i+1} *refines* the predicate A_i if A_i holds whenever A_{i+1} holds. The term *attractor* is often used for each such A_i predicate. The proof is done in "stairs" by proving that, from some point of the execution, every configuration satisfies A_1 and then proving that an execution in which A_1 holds reaches a configuration after which every configuration satisfies A_2 and, in general, proving that A_{i+1} holds after A_i does. The goal is to prove that the system reaches a configuration in which the last predicate A_k holds, which is a predicate for a safe configuration. The method is demonstrated by a self-stabilizing leader-election algorithm. Leader election is a fundamental task in distributed computing: often a distributed task can be performed by electing a leader and then using a centralized computation by that leader.

Example: Leader Election in a General Communication Network

A self-stabilizing algorithm for this task assumes that every processor has a unique identifier in the range 1 to N, where N is an upper bound on the number of processors in the system. The leader election task is to inform every processor of the identifier of a single processor in the system. This single processor with the elected identifier is the leader. Usually the processor with the minimal (or maximal) identifier is elected to be the leader.

The following simple (non-terminating) algorithm elects a leader in a non-stabilizing manner. Each processor P_i has a candidate for a leader; in the beginning, the candidate is P_i itself. P_i repeatedly communicates the identifier x of its current candidate to its neighbors. Whenever P_i receives an identifier y of a candidate of a neighbor, if $x > y$, P_i changes its candidate to be the processor with identifier y.

The above algorithm is not self-stabilizing, since it is possible that the minimal identifier z — which is a candidate in the first (arbitrary) configuration of the system — is not an identifier of a processor in the system. Nevertheless, eventually every processor declares that z is the identifier of the leader. The term *floating identifier* is used to describe an identifier that appears in the initial

```
01 do forever
02     ⟨candidate, distance⟩ := ⟨ID(i), 0⟩
03     forall Pⱼ ∈ N(i) do
04         begin
05             ⟨leaderᵢ[j], disᵢ[j]⟩ := read(⟨leaderⱼ, disⱼ⟩)
06             if (disᵢ[j] < N) and ((leaderᵢ[j] < candidate) or
07                 ((leaderᵢ[j] = candidate) and (disᵢ[j] < distance))) then
08                 ⟨candidate, distance⟩ := ⟨leaderᵢ[j], disᵢ[j] + 1⟩
09         end
10     write ⟨leaderᵢ, disᵢ⟩ := ⟨candidate, distance⟩
11 od
```

Figure 2.9
Leader election in general graph: the program for P_i

configuration, when no processor in the system with this identifier appears in the system.

We use distance variables and the bound N on the number of processors to eliminate floating identifiers. Each processor P_i has a candidate for a leader $leader_i$ and a value for the distance from this leader dis_i. The program for P_i appears in figure 2.9. A processor P_i repeatedly reads the identifiers chosen by its neighbors for the identifier of the leader. P_i chooses the identifier x that is the smallest among the read values, such that the distance to x is less than N. If y is the minimal distance read from a neighbor together with the identifier x, then P_i assigns $y + 1$ to its distance field.

The proof of correctness uses two convergence stairs. The first convergence stair is a predicate $\mathcal{A}_1$ on system configurations verifying that no floating identifier exists. The second convergence stair is a predicate $\mathcal{A}_2$ for a safe configuration — a predicate that verifies that every processor chooses the minimal identifier of a processor in the system as the identifier of the leader.

The value of a floating identifier can appear in the local arrays of every processor P_i, $l_i[1..\delta]$, in the *candidate* local variable, and in the field $leader_i$ of the communication register. The *distance of a floating identifier* appearing in $l_i[j]$, *candidate*, or $leader_i$ is $d_i[j]$, *distance*, or dis_i, respectively.

To show that the first attractor holds, we argue that, if a floating identifier exists, then during any $O(\Delta)$ rounds, the minimal distance of a floating identifier increases.

LEMMA 2.5: Every fair execution that starts from any arbitrary configuration has a suffix in which no floating identifier exists.

Proof To prove the lemma, we first show that, as long as a floating identifier exists, the minimal distance of a floating identifier increases during any $O(\Delta)$ rounds. Let P_i be a processor that holds in its local variables or in its communication registers a floating identifier with the minimal distance. Once P_i starts executing the do forever loop, it must choose (either its own identifier for $leader_i$ or) a distance that is at least one greater than the distance read from a neighbor (line 8 of the code). Thus, if P_i chooses to assign a floating identifier to $leader_i$, it must choose a distance that is greater by one than the distance it read. Once the minimal distance of a floating identifier reaches N, all processors do not choose a floating identifier. Therefore, all the floating identifiers are eventually eliminated. ∎

The fact that the first predicate $\mathcal{A}_1$ holds from some configuration of the system lets us prove the next theorem using arguments similar to those used for the non-stabilizing algorithm.

THEOREM 2.3:   Every fair execution that starts from any arbitrary configuration reaches a safe configuration.

Scheduler-Luck Game

The analysis of the time complexity (measured in rounds) of distributed randomized algorithms is often a very complicated task. It is especially hard in self-stabilizing algorithms in which no assumptions are made on the initial state of the processors. In this section we describe a useful tool, the *sl-game method*, for proving upper bounds on the time complexity of randomized distributed algorithms, and demonstrate it on self-stabilizing algorithms. The *sl-game* approach tries to avoid considering every possible outcome of the random function used by a randomized algorithm. In fact, it fixes the outcome of the random function, so that the proof arguments are similar to the simpler case of proving correctness of non-randomized algorithms.

Given a randomized algorithm $\mathcal{AL}$, we define a game between two players, *scheduler* and *luck*. The goal of the scheduler is to prevent the algorithm $\mathcal{AL}$ from fulfilling its task; the scheduler can choose the activation interleaving of the processors. The opposing player, luck, may determine the result of the randomized function invoked. The idea is to show that, if luck has a strategy that forces the algorithm to converge to a safe configuration when the game is started in any initial configuration, then the algorithm stabilizes. We show that there is a relationship between the expected time to reach a safe configuration in the game and the expected time to reach a legal behavior when the algorithm is executed.

In each turn of the game, the scheduler chooses the next processor to be activated, which then makes a step. If, during this step, the activated processor uses a random function, then luck may *intervene* — i.e., luck may determine the result (or some subset of the desired results) of the random function. If luck intervenes and fixes the result to be any of g values from the possible h results, then the probability of this intervention is $p = g/h$. Note that luck may choose not to intervene even though the activated processor calls the random function; in this case each possible result has an equal probability of occurrence. Both players are assumed to have unlimited computational resources, and their decisions are based on the history of the game so far. When the step of the activated processor ends, a new turn begins.

If luck intervenes several times, say f times, in order to force the system to reach a safe configuration, and if the probability of the ith intervention is p_i, then the combined probability of these interventions is $cp = \prod_{i=1}^{f} p_i$. Luck has a *(cp,r)-strategy* to win the game if it has a strategy to reach a safe configuration in the game in an expected number of at most r rounds, and with interventions that yield a combined probability of no more than cp. We claim that the existence of a *(cp,r)-strategy* implies that the algorithm reaches a safe configuration within r/cp expected number of rounds.

We give only an informal proof of our claim. When the algorithm is executed it is possible that the results of the random function invocations may differ from the results luck chooses in the *sl-game*. Following such undesired results, the system may reach an arbitrary state. Fortunately, a new *sl-game* can be started from this arbitrary configuration, in which a safe configuration may be reached within r expected rounds and with probability cp. The probability that the second try is successful (in having the results luck chooses) but the first try is not is $(1 - cp) \cdot cp$. In general, the probability that the ith try succeeds is $(1 - cp)^{i-1} \cdot cp$. Thus, the expected number of tries until a safe configuration is reached is $\sum_{i=1}^{\infty} i \cdot (1 - cp)^{i-1} \cdot cp = 1/cp$. Note that the expected number of rounds in each such try is r.

Since the expectation of a sum is the sum of the expectations, the expected number of rounds in an execution until a safe configuration is reached is r/cp. The above discussion is summarized by the following theorem.

THEOREM 2.4: If luck has an *(cp,r)-strategy*, then $\mathcal{AL}$ reaches a safe configuration within, at most, r/cp expected number of rounds.

Example: Self-Stabilizing Leader Election in Complete Graphs

An algorithm that solves the leader election task requires that, when its execution terminates, a single processor be designated as a *leader*, and every processor know whether it is a leader or not. By definition, whenever a leader-election algorithm terminates successfully, the system is in a nonsymmetric configuration. Any leader-election algorithm that has a symmetric initial state requires some means of symmetry-breaking. In *id-based* systems, each processor has a unique identifier called its *id*; thus, the system has no symmetric configuration. In *uniform* (or *anonymous*) systems all processors are identical. Randomization is often used to break symmetry in such systems.

A simple randomized leader election algorithm that stabilizes within an exponential expected number of rounds is presented here. The algorithm works in complete graph systems in which every processor can communicate with every other processor via shared memory. It can be argued that the complete graph topology is too simple. In the id-based model, there exists a trivial self-stabilizing leader-election algorithm for this topology in which each processor repeatedly appoints the processor with maximal *id* as a leader. As often happens, it turns out that the intricacy of the problem depends on the exact system settings. Uniform self-stabilizing algorithms are more subtle than non-stabilizing algorithms, even in such simple topologies.

It is worth mentioning that a simple deterministic (i.e., non-randomized) self-stabilizing algorithm exists for leader election in a complete graph uniform system when the existence of the powerful *central daemon* scheduler is assumed. Say that a group of people is gathered in a circle and that each person can be either sitting or standing. The goal is to reach a situation in which a single person is standing while all others are sitting. A scheduler chooses one person at a time and lets this person look at all the other people and decide to stand up or sit down. A person decides to stand up if no other person is standing; otherwise the person sits down. Clearly there is at least one person standing following the first choice of the central daemon. If more than one person is standing after this first choice — say there are x people standing — then, once $x - 1$ of them are scheduled by the central daemon, a situation in which exactly one person is standing is reached. From this point on, every person except this single person is sitting.

On the other hand, if no central daemon exists, then it is possible to let all the participants find out that no one is standing, decide to stand up (according to their common deterministic algorithm), and then stand up. Once every person

```
1 do forever
2     forall P_j ∈ N(i) do
3         l_i[j] := read(leader_j)
4     if (leader_i = 0 and {∀ j ≠ i | l_i[j] = 0}) or
5         (leader_i = 1 and {∃ j ≠ i | l_i[j] = 1}) then
6             write leader_i := random({0, 1})
7 end
```

Figure 2.10
Leader election in a complete graph: the program for P_i

is standing, it is possible to let each of the participants find out that they should sit and let them sit. This behavior can be repeated forever. Thus, there is no self-stabilizing uniform leader election algorithm without a central daemon.

Our simple randomized self-stabilizing leader-election algorithm does not assume the existence of a central daemon. The settings presented in section 2.1 of this chapter are assumed: each step consists of a single read or a single write operation. Each processor communicates with all other processors using a single-writer multi-reader binary register called the *leader* register, where $leader_i$ denotes the *leader* register of processor P_i. The random function used simulates a coin toss and returns *heads* or *tails* with equal probability. One can assume that heads is mapped to 1 and tails to 0. The algorithm in figure 2.10 is correct in the presence of *coarse atomicity* that assumes a coin toss is an internal operation that is not separable from the next read or write operation. Starting the system with any possible combination of binary values of the *leader* registers, the algorithm eventually fixes all the *leader* registers except one to hold 0. The single processor whose *leader* value is 1 is the elected leader. The algorithm is straightforward: each processor P_i repeatedly reads all *leader* registers; if no single leader exists, P_i decides whether it is a candidate for a leader and, if it is, tosses a coin and assigns its value to its register.

We define the task *LE* to be the set of executions in which there exists a single fixed leader throughout the execution. We define a configuration to be *safe* if it satisfies the following:

- For exactly one processor, say P_i, $leader_i = 1$ and $\forall j \neq i$ $l_i[j] = 0$.
- For every other processor, $P_j \neq P_i$, $leader_j = 0$ and $l_j[i] = 1$.

It is easy to verify that in any (fair) execution E that starts with a safe configuration, as defined above, P_i is a single leader, and thus $E \in LE$.

The stabilization time of the algorithm is exponential, as shown in the next two lemmas.

LEMMA 2.6: The algorithm stabilizes within $2^{O(n)}$ expected number of rounds.

Proof We use theorem 2.4 to show that the expected number of rounds before the algorithm stabilizes is bounded from above by $2n2^n$. To do this, we present an $(1/2^n, 2n)$-strategy for luck to win the *sl-game* defined by the algorithm, the set of all possible configurations, and the set of all safe configurations.

Luck's strategy is as follows: whenever some processor P_i tosses a coin, luck intervenes; if for all $j \neq i$, $leader_j = 0$, then luck fixes the coin toss to be 1; otherwise, it fixes the coin toss to be 0. Since we assume coarse atomicity, the algorithm implies that, at the end of this atomic step, $leader_i$ holds the result of the coin toss. The correctness of this strategy follows from the following observations.

The first observation is that, within less than $2n$ successive rounds, every processor P_i reads all the *leader* registers, and then, if needed, it tosses a coin and writes the outcome in $leader_i$. Therefore, if within the first $2n$ rounds no processor tosses a coin, the system reaches a safe configuration. The reason is that no processor writes in its *leader* register during these $2n$ rounds; therefore every processor reads the fixed value of the *leader* variables during the $2n$ rounds. A processor P_i with $leader_i = 0$ must find another processor P_j with $leader_j = 1$, and a processor with $leader_j = 1$ must find that it is the only processor with $leader_j = 1$.

If there is a processor that does toss a coin, then, in accordance with luck's strategy, it is the case that, after the first coin toss, there is at least one *leader* register whose value is 1. Moreover, once $leader_j = 1$ for some j, there exists a k such that $leader_k = 1$ throughout the rest of the execution. To see this, let S be the set of processors whose *leader* register holds 1 after the first coin toss. If there exists a processor $P_k \in S$ that never tosses a coin again, then $leader_k = 1$ forever. Otherwise, every processor in S tosses a coin; in this case, we take P_k to be the last processor in S that tosses a coin. Luck's strategy guarantees that, during P_k's coin toss, all the remaining *leader* values are 0, and hence luck sets the result of P_k's coin toss to 1. From now on, $leader_k = 1$ and for $j \neq k$, $leader_j = 0$.

Next we compute the combined probability of luck's strategy. Every processor P_i may toss a coin at most once: if the outcome of P_i's first coin toss is set by luck to 0, then, in all successive readings, P_i finds out that $leader_k = 1$ (where P_k is the leader in the safe configuration reached) and hence will not toss a coin again. If the outcome of P_i's first coin toss was set to 1, the *leader* values of all other processors are 0. After this atomic step, P_i finds out that it is the only processor whose *leader* value is 1, and thus it will not toss a coin in this case as well. Therefore, the combined probability of the strategy of luck is at least $1/2^n$.

Thus we conclude that, after a maximum of $2n$ rounds, every processor P_i does not toss a coin anymore; moreover, that during these $2n$ rounds, P_i can toss a coin at most once. Therefore luck wins the game within $2n$ rounds and with $1/2^n$ combined probability. ∎

We have presented a simple proof, using the *sl-game* method, that the algorithm stabilizes within a maximum expected $2n2^n$ rounds. We conclude this section by proving, in the next lemma, that the algorithm does not stabilize under fine atomicity, in which a coin-toss is a separate atomic step. We present a winning strategy for the scheduler, guaranteeing that the obtained schedule is a fair schedule with probability 1.

LEMMA 2.7:   The algorithm is not self-stabilizing under fine atomicity.

Proof The following scheduler strategy ensures that the algorithm never stabilizes under fine atomicity. Start the system in a configuration in which all *leader* registers hold 1. Let one processor notice that it must toss a coin. If the coin toss result is 1, let this processor toss a coin again until the coin toss result is 0. Now, stop the processor before it writes 0 in its *leader* register, and activate another processor in the same way. Once all processors are about to write 0, let them all write. Now, all the *leader* registers hold 0 and the scheduler can force all processors to write 1 in their registers in a similar way, and so on. This strategy thus ensures that the system never stabilizes. ∎

In what follows we give more examples that uses the *sl-game* proof technique to prove the correctness of more complicated randomized self-stabilizing algorithms.

Neighborhood Resemblance

In this section we present a technique used to prove memory lower bounds. In contrast to the scheduler-luck game, which can be used to prove correctness of a self-stabilizing randomized algorithm, the results obtained by the neighborhood-resemblance technique are of the nature of impossibility results — proving that it is impossible to achieve certain tasks with less than a certain amount of memory.

The technique can be applied to a set of self-stabilizing algorithms called *silent self-stabilizing* algorithms. Roughly speaking, a self-stabilizing algorithm is silent if the communication between the processors is fixed from some point of the execution.

We start by defining silent self-stabilizing algorithms for the shared-memory model. A self-stabilizing algorithm is silent if the value stored in every communication register r_i is fixed in every execution that starts in a safe configuration. Note that this definition allows the processors to change state repeatedly. In particular, a processor may repeatedly read and verify that the contents of the registers are not changed due to transient faults. One example of an algorithm in this class is the spanning-tree construction presented in section 2.5. In the message passing case, a self-stabilizing algorithm is silent if, in every execution, each processor P_i repeatedly sends the same message m_{ij} to each neighbor P_j.

The neighborhood-resemblance technique uses a configuration c_0 that is claimed to be a safe configuration and constructs a non-safe configuration c_1 in which every processor has the same neighborhood and therefore cannot distinguish c_0 from c_1.

Example: Spanning-Tree Construction

We are now familiar with the self-stabilizing spanning-tree construction algorithm of section 2.5, which assumes the existence of a special processor, the root, and an arbitrary communication graph. Let us just remind ourselves that, in this rooted spanning-tree algorithm, every processor repeatedly computes its distance from the root and chooses its parent to be a neighbor with the minimal distance from the root. Once the system stabilizes, the contents of the communication registers are fixed. Thus, the spanning-tree algorithm is in fact a silent self-stabilizing algorithm. To implement the distance field, every communication register must be of $\Omega(\log d)$ bits, where d is the diameter of the system. One would like to devise an algorithm that uses fewer resources — an algorithm that uses only a constant number of bits per communication register. This constant number of bits is not a function of the size of the system; in particular, it is not a function of the number of the processors or the diameter of the system. The neighborhood resemblance technique is used to prove that no such silent algorithm exists.

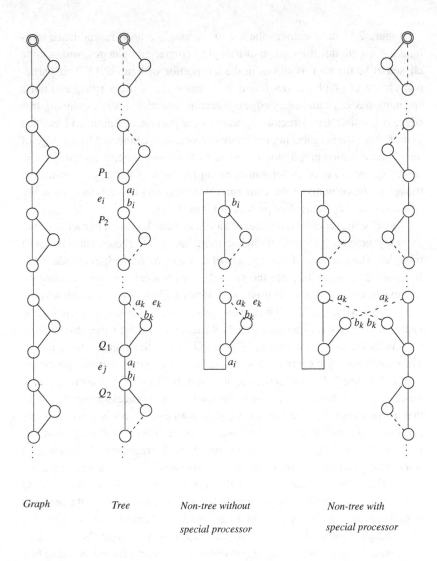

Graph   Tree   Non-tree without   Non-tree with
                             special processor   special processor

Figure 2.11
Construction of a silent non-tree

Figure 2.11 demonstrates the use of the neighborhood resemblance technique. A communication graph of triangles, connected by edges, with a node chosen to be the root, is shown in the left portion of figure 2.11. This particular choice of graph implies that exactly one edge of every triangle is not a spanning-tree edge and every edge connecting two triangles is a spanning-tree edge. A possible tree structure appears in the portion of figure 2.11 entitled *Tree*. Every two neighboring processors (processors connected by an edge of the communication graph) communicate by two communication registers. Examine the contents of the communication registers of the edges connecting triangles (the contents of the communication registers of such an edge e_i are denoted a_i and b_i in the *Tree* portion of figure 2.11).

Let x be the (constant) number of values that can be stored in each register. In every graph of $x^2 + 2$ triangles, there are $x^2 + 1$ edges that connect triangles. The contents of the registers of at least two such edges are identical. In figure 2.11, e_i and e_j are the two edges with identical register contents. The existence of e_i and e_j is used to construct a silent non-tree graph with no special processor. Let P_1, P_2 be the two processors attached to e_i such that the value stored in the register in which P_1 writes is a_i and the value stored in the register in which P_2 writes is b_i. Q_1 and Q_2 are defined analogously for e_j. The neighborhood of every processor in the *Non-tree without special processor* graph in figure 2.11 is identical to the neighborhood of the corresponding processor in the tree. In other words, the state of every processor and the values that the processor can read are the same in both cases. This is clear for every processor different from P_2 and Q_1, since their neighborhood is not changed. It is also clear for P_2, since the value a_i read from the register of P_1 is now read from the register of Q_1. Similarly, the neighborhood of Q_2 is not changed.

At this stage we can conclude that the contents of the registers in the *Non-tree without special processor* graph remains constant, since the registers written and read by every processor have a value identical to their value in a safe configuration for the tree. Can we conclude that every algorithm that uses a constant number of bits per register in order to construct a rooted spanning tree is not stabilizing? The answer is negative, since the *Non-tree without special processor* is not a configuration of a system that fulfills the assumption of the algorithm: that a root processor exists.

To complete the proof and show that no such silent self-stabilizing algorithm for tree construction exists, we need one additional step. Let e_k be an edge of a triangle that is not a tree edge in the *Non-tree without special processor graph*. Let R_1 and R_2 be the two processors attached to e_k. A silent configuration that encodes a non-tree with a special processor is achieved by connecting the *Non-tree without special processor* with the *Tree* in a way that preserves the neighborhood of every processor (see the right portion of figure 2.11). We have reached a silent configuration in which there are processors that are not and never will be connected to the spanning tree of the root.

2.10 Pseudo-Self-Stabilization

To describe the pseudo-self-stabilizing concept, let us start with an example. A computer company found a new technology for personal computers. The cost of a computer produced by this company is much lower than that of other computers. However, the computer has one drawback: it is possible that it will spontaneously turn itself off during operation. The company guarantees that the number of shutdowns is limited to seven, but does not promise if and when they will take place. The customer might choose such a cheap computer because the electricity power supply is not in any case reliable and cannot guarantee continuous operation. Analogously, pseudo self-stabilizing algorithms converge from any initial state to execution, in which they exhibit a legal behavior; but they still may deviate from this legal behavior a finite number of times. A more formal treatment of the pseudo-self-stabilizing concept follows.

We defined a self-stabilizing algorithm as an algorithm for which every fair execution must reach a safe configuration. Since every execution that starts in a safe configuration is a legal execution belonging to LE, it is the case that, once a safe configuration is reached, the system behaves as desired.

The set of legal executions LE defines the desired behavior of the system. In fact, defining the requirements by a set of executions LE is sometimes too restrictive. A task T may be defined in a more abstract way, avoiding the definitions and the description of the implementation details. The variables used by the specific distributed algorithm to achieve the task are not part of this task specification. An *abstract task* is defined by a set of variables and a set of restrictions on their values. For example, let us define the token passing abstract task $\mathcal{AT}$ for a system of two processors: the sender S and the receiver R. S has a boolean variable $token_S$ and R has a boolean variable $token_R$.

Recall that a system execution is a sequence of configurations such that every configuration c_{i+1} is obtained from the immediately preceding configuration c_i by a single atomic step a_i of a processor. The steps of the processors are defined by the distributed algorithm that the system runs. Given an execution of the system $E = (c_1, a_1, c_2, a_2, \cdots)$, one may consider only the values of $token_S$ and $token_R$ in every configuration c_i to check whether the token-passing task is achieved. Let $c_i|tkns$ be the values of the boolean variables $(token_S, token_R)$ in c_i, and let $E|tkns$ be $(c_1|tkns, c_2|tkns, c_3|tkns, \cdots)$. The abstract task $\mathcal{AT}$ can be defined by $E|tkns$ as follows: there is no $c_i|tkns$ for which $token_S = token_R = true$, and there are infinitely many is such that $token_S = true$ in $c_i|tkns$, and infinitely many js such that $token_R = true$ in $c_j|tkns$. In other words, each of the processors holds the token infinitely many times, but the processors never hold tokens simultaneously.

The above specification of the abstract task $\mathcal{AT}$ is a more general specification of the token-passing task than a definition by a legal set of executions LE; the reason is that LE is defined for a specific distributed algorithm. On the other hand, it is impossible to define a safe configuration in terms of $c|tkns$. For instance, we cannot tell whether a configuration in which $token_S = true$ and $token_R = false$ is safe. The reason is that we ignore, say, the state variables of R that specify whether R is about to execute a step in which $token_R$ is assigned to true, while $token_S$ remains unchanged.

An algorithm is *pseudo-self-stabilizing* for an abstract task $\mathcal{AT}$ if every infinite execution of the algorithm has a suffix satisfying the restrictions of $\mathcal{AT}$.

Clearly a self-stabilizing algorithm for a task LE such that every execution in LE fulfills the restrictions of $\mathcal{AT}$ is pseudo-self-stabilizing. However, a pseudo self-stabilizing algorithm may not be self-stabilizing, since it may not reach a configuration such that for *every* execution that starts in it, the restrictions of $\mathcal{AT}$ hold.

Figure 2.12 depicts such a situation: nine configurations and the transitions between them are described. The upper four configurations form a cycle that corresponds to a possible infinite legal execution relative to the abstract task of token-passing. Each of the processors holds a token infinitely often, and at most one processor holds the token at a time. Similarly, the lower cycle of the four configurations in figure 2.12 also corresponds to an infinite legal execution. The configuration in the center of the figure is illegal, since both the processors have a token at the same time. The transition to this configuration may arise from, say, a message loss: only if a message is lost is the transition to the configuration in which both the sender and the receiver hold the token possible. In other words, if no message is lost, the execution depicted by the upper cycle is an infinite legal execution relative to the abstract task $\mathcal{AT}$. Yet the system is not in a safe configuration, and there is no time bound for

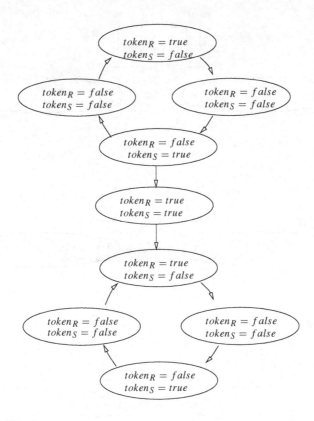

Figure 2.12
Pseudo-self-stabilization

reaching a safe configuration. Only after a message is lost does the system reach the lower cycle of figure 2.12 and, indeed, a safe configuration.

To demonstrate pseudo-self-stabilization, we use the famous alternating-bit algorithm, one of the most basic data-link algorithms used for message transfer over a communication link. The common communication link is unreliable and may lose or corrupt messages. It is assumed that error-detection codes are used to identify and eliminate corrupted messages. We view each such discarded corrupted message as a lost message. The alternating-bit algorithm uses retransmission of messages to cope with message loss. When every corrupted message is identified and the communication links are FIFO (first-in first-out), the alternating-bit algorithm guarantees reliable delivery of (higher-level) messages over such an unreliable communication link. The term *frame* is

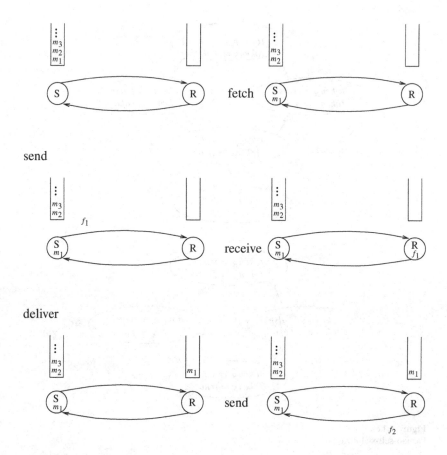

Figure 2.13
Fetch, send, receive, and deliver

used to distinguish the higher-level messages that must be transferred from the messages that are actually sent in order to transfer the higher-level messages; frames are the messages that are actually sent between the sender and the receiver. The algorithm is designed for a system consisting of two processors S and R that are connected by two communication links: one transfers *frames* from S to R, and the other from R to S.

The task of delivering a message from one processor in the network to another remote processor is sophisticated. It is usually partitioned into several layers of algorithms and abstractions: an algorithm of a certain layer uses the services of a lower-level algorithm. The lowest layer is the *physical layer* for which the concern is how the physical device connecting to neighboring processors is used to transmit bits from a processor to its neighbor. Usually the physical layer can ensure transmission of bits with a certain (small) error probability that each bit is corrupted. The next layer is the *data-link layer*, which assumes the existence of a (physical layer) procedure that transmits bits. The task of the data-link layer is to transmit messages from a processor to its neighbor. The data-link layer uses error-detection codes and retransmissions to cope with the probability of bit corruption (introduced by the physical communication device). The *network layer* task is to direct messages sent from one processor to a remote (non-neighboring) processor. Routing algorithms are used to maintain routing databases (routing tables). Whenever a processor must forward an arriving message, it consults the routing database to identify the outgoing link on which the message should be sent; then the data-link procedure of the chosen link is used. Several messages that have to be forwarded may arrive at a processor simultaneously (through its input communication ports). The arriving messages may be stored in input buffers (on a disk) and then *fetched* by the data-link layer algorithm. The data-link algorithm uses *frames* to *send* the fetched message. The data-link algorithm portion that is executed at the receiver receives the sent frames (and sends acknowledgment frames). When the data-link algorithm executed at the receiver side is convinced that the message is received, it *delivers* the message to be handled by the network layer algorithm at the receiver, which in turn consults its routing database.

Figure 2.13 describes the *fetch*, *send*, *receive*, and *deliver* operations. A queue of messages $(m_1, m_2, m_3, \cdots)$ stored in a non-volatile memory are to be transmitted from the sender to the receiver. A fetch operation executed by the sender removes the first message of the queue and stores it in the (volatile) memory of the sender. Then the sender must transfer m_1 to the receiver. In the particular example in figure 2.13, the sender sends m_1 in the frame f_1. This is only one possibility; in fact, other data-link algorithms may send only partial information concerning m_1 in f_1. Note that in addition to the contents of m_1, f_1 may include control information, for example the label of the alternating-bit algorithm. Once the receiver receives f_1, it delivers m_1 to the output queue. Finally, the receiver sends the frame f_2 to the sender in order to notify it sender that a new message can be fetched.

The abstract task of the alternating-bit algorithm can be defined as follows. The sender S has an infinite queue of input messages $(im_1, im_2, \cdots)$ that should be transferred to the receiver in the same order without duplica-

```
Sender:
01      initialization
02      begin
03          i := 1
04          bits := 0
05          send(⟨bits, imi⟩) (* imi is fetched *)
06      end (* end initialization *)
07      upon a timeout
08          send(⟨bits, imi⟩)
09      upon frame arrival
10      begin
11          receive(FrameBit)
12          if FrameBit = bits then (* acknowledge arrives *)
13              begin (* start transmitting a new message *)
14                      bits := (bits + 1) mod 2
15                      i := i + 1
16              end
17          send(⟨bits, imi⟩) (* imi is fetched *)
18      end
Receiver:
19      initialization
20      begin
21          j := 1
22          bitr := 1
23      end (* end initialization *)
24      upon frame arrival
25      begin
26          receive(⟨FrameBit, msg⟩)
27          if FrameBit ≠ bitr then (* a new message arrived *)
28              begin
29                      bitr := FrameBit
30                      j := j + 1
31                      omj := msg (* omj is delivered *)
32              end
33          send(bitr)
34      end
```

Figure 2.14
Alternating-bit algorithm

tions, reordering, or omissions. The receiver has an output queue of messages $(om_1, om_2, \cdots)$. The sequence of messages in the output queue of the receiver should always be a prefix of the sequence of messages in the input queue of the sender. Moreover, to eliminate solutions in which no input message is transfered to the receiver, we require that infinitely often a new message is included in the output queue.

The alternating-bit algorithm in figure 2.14 is not a self-stabilizing algorithm: it is assumed that both the sender and the receiver perform the initialization instructions (lines 1 to 6 and 19 to 23) when the system starts operating. During the initialization the sender fetches the first message im_1 from the buffer of the networks layer, and sends a frame with this message together with label 0 (the value of bit_s) to the receiver. A timeout mechanism copes with frame loss triggering frame retransmission (lines 7 and 8). Once the receiver executes the initialization procedure, it waits for a frame with label 0 (line 27) while acknowledging arriving frames. When a frame with a (new) label different from the current value of bit_r arrives at the receiver, the receiver delivers the message of this frame to the network layer (line 31). The indices i (line 15) and j (line 30) are used only to describe the interface with the network layer. In fact, the input buffer from which im_i is fetched is a queue from which messages are fetched without identifying their index. The first fetch operation (implicitly executed in line 5) fetches the first message in the input queue, the second fetch (implicitly executed in line 17) operation fetches the second message in this queue, and so on. Similarly, the first deliver operation (line 31) delivers the first message to the output queue, the second deliver operation (line 31) delivers the second message, and so on.

Roughly speaking, the abstract task of a self-stabilizing alternating-bit (data-link) algorithm $\mathcal{DL}$ is eventually to guarantee exactly-once message delivery without reordering. More formally, there must exist a suffix of the queue of input messages $I = (im_j, im_{j+1}, \cdots)$ and a k such that the suffix of the output that starts following the first $k - 1$ messages, $O = (om_k, om_{k+1}, \cdots)$, is always a prefix of I. Furthermore, a new message is included in O infinitely often.

Let us consider the sequence of labels stored in bit_s, $q_{s,r}$, bit_r, $q_{r,s}$ in this order. Recall that $q_{s,r}$ and $q_{r,s}$ are the queue of messages in transit on the link from S to R and the link from R to S, respectively. A configuration in which all the labels in the above sequence are 0 is a safe configuration for the alternating-bit algorithm: any execution that starts in such a configuration causes the sender to start sending the next message using the label 1. The sender does not stop sending frames with a certain message im_i and a label 1 until the label used to send the message im_i returns in an acknowledging frame from the receiver to the sender. Note that, since we started in a configuration in which no frame with label 1 exists, the sender receives the label 1 only after the receiver receives a frame with label 1 and the message im_i.

More formally, once the system is in a safe configuration, the value of the labels in the sequence $\mathcal{L} = bit_s, q_{s,r}, bit_r, q_{r,s}$ is in $[0^*1^*, 1^*0^*]$. Roughly speaking, we say that a single *border* between the labels of value 0 and the labels of value 1 slides from the sender to the receiver and back to the sender. For example, let us consider a particular execution that starts in a configuration with the sequence 0^k; for some integer k, the sender receives a frame with sequence number 0 (acknowledgment) and assigns 1 to bit_s. The resulting sequence is $\mathcal{L} = 10^{k-2}$. From this configuration, in our particular choice of execution, the sender sends a frame with label 1. At this stage, the sequence is $\mathcal{L} = 1^20^{k-2}$. Continuing in the same fashion, we reach a configuration in which $\mathcal{L} = 1^i0^{k-i}$ for $2 \leq i \leq k$. In the particular execution we have chosen, neither retransmission due to timeout and nor message loss occurs. Given a configuration with $\mathcal{L} = x^i(1-x)^j$, where x is either 0 or 1, the sequence $\mathcal{L}$ that is the result of retransmission due to a timeout is $\mathcal{L} = x^{i+1}(1-x)^j$. Similarly, the sequence that is the result of losing a frame with, say, label $(1-x)$ is $\mathcal{L} = x^i(1-x)^{j-1}$.

Let us conclude with the following observation: once a safe configuration is reached, there is at most one *border* in $\mathcal{L}$, where a border is two labels x and $x-1$ that appear one immediately after the other in $\mathcal{L}$.

More than a single border can exist in $\mathcal{L}$ in an arbitrary non-safe configuration. For example, there are eight borders in $\mathcal{L} = 110001001101001$. Denote the sequence $\mathcal{L}$ of the configuration c_i by $\mathcal{L}(c_i)$. A *loaded configuration* c_i is a configuration in which the first and last values in $\mathcal{L}(c_i)$ are equal; for example, $\mathcal{L}(c_i) = 00110001001101000$. Consider all the loaded configurations $c_{i_1}, c_{i_2}, \cdots c_{i_k}$, $i_j < i_{j+1}$ in an infinite execution E. Note that, in an infinite execution, there must be an infinite number of loaded configurations, since the sender receives infinitely often an acknowledgment with a label equal to bit_s.

We next show that the number of borders in $c_{i_{j+1}}$ is less than or equal to the number of borders in c_{i_j}. Consider an execution E' that starts in c_{i_j} and ends in $c_{i_{j+1}}$. First let us convince ourselves that any *loss* operation during E' cannot increase the number of borders. This is clear when the lost frame has at least one neighboring frame with the same label value — the loss of a label from a pair 00 or 11 does not change the number of borders. Moreover, the loss of a frame that has no neighboring frame with the same label value reduces the number of borders. The only step that can increment the number of borders is one in which the sender changes the value of bit_s. This change increments the number of borders by 1. Without loss of generality, we assume that $bit_s = 0$ immediately before the sender changes the value of bit_s. The sender receives an acknowledgment with label 0 and changes the value of bit_s to 1. The value of bit_s is 1 until the next loaded configuration is reached; the loaded configuration is reached when the last sequence of frames with label

0 in $\mathcal{L}$ is removed. Therefore, the number of borders is increased by 1 and reduced by 1 because the sender changed the value of bit_s between every two successive loaded configurations. We can conclude that the number of borders in the loaded configurations can only be reduced.

This is the key observation for claiming that the alternating-bit algorithm is pseudo self-stabilizing for $\mathcal{DL}$. From any arbitrary configuration, the number of borders in loaded configurations can be reduced only a finite number of times, but there is no limit on the length of the execution for such a reduction to occur. In fact, it is possible that the number of borders in the loaded configurations will be greater than 0 forever.

Let us describe a specific execution in which the number of borders in the loaded configurations is fixed. Starting in a configuration c, with $\mathcal{L} = 0^*1^*0^*$, the sender receives an acknowledgment with label 0, changes the value of bit_s to 1, and starts sending the message im_j with the label $bit_s = 1$. The resulting value of $\mathcal{L}$ is $10^*1^*0^*$. Next the sender receives all the acknowledgments with label 0 until a configuration in which $\mathcal{L} = 1^*0^*1^*$ is reached. Note that every frame sent following c carries the message im_j. Let us use the notation $\mathcal{L} = (1, im_j)^*0^*1^*$ to denote that the frames with label 1 in the beginning of $\mathcal{L}$ carries the message im_j or an acknowledgment for im_j. Since the number of borders is not reduced, the value of $\mathcal{L}$ in the next loaded configuration is $\mathcal{L} = (0, im_{j+1})^*(1, im_j)^*, 0^*$ and $\mathcal{L} = (1, im_{j+2})^*(0, im_{j+1})^*(1, im_j)^*$ in the following loaded configuration. In such an execution, every input message is output by the receiver exactly once. However, since the number of borders is greater than 0, it is possible that messages will be lost at some point in the execution due to the loss of several frames. For example, if all the frames with label 0 are lost from $\mathcal{L} = (1, im_{k+2})^*(0, im_{k+1})^*(1, im_k)^*$ before they reach the receiver, the messages im_{k+1} and im_{k+2} will be lost, since they have label 1; hence the receiver will not identify these messages as new messages.

To summarize, the alternating-bit algorithm is pseudo self-stabilizing for the data-link task, guaranteeing that the number of messages that are lost during infinite execution is bounded, and the performance between any such two losses is according to the abstract task of the data-link.

Exercises

2.1. A variant of the spanning-tree construction algorithm presented in figure 2.1 is proposed. In this version every processor repeatedly checks whether the value of the *dist* variable of its parent in the tree is smaller than the value of its own *dist* variable. P_i does not execute lines 8 through 16 of the code when the above condition holds. Is the proposed algorithm a self-stabilizing spanning tree construction algorithm? Prove your answer.

2.2. Design a self-stabilizing mutual exclusion algorithm for a system with processors $P_1, P_2, \cdots, P_n$ that are connected in a line. The leftmost processor P_1 is the special processor. Every processor P_i, $2 \leq i \leq n - 1$, communicates with its left neighbor P_{i-1} and its right neighbor P_{i+1}. Similarly, P_1 communicates with P_2 and P_n with P_{n-1}.

2.3. Define a safe configuration for the self-stabilizing synchronous consensus algorithm of figure 2.7.

2.4. Design a self-stabilizing randomized algorithm for leader election in a uniform complete graph system. Use a random function that uniformly chooses a number in the range 0 to 2^n. Use the *sl-game* method to analyze the expected number of rounds required to reach a safe configuration.

2.5. Use the neighborhood-resemblance technique to prove that there is no silent self-stabilizing leader-election algorithm in a ring such that every communication register has a fixed number of bits k.

Notes

Other definitions of the requirements for self-stabilizing algorithms appear in the literature. For instance, an algorithm is self-stabilizing if it fulfills the closure and convergence requirements; see, for example, [AG93]. The closure property is proven for a set of legal configurations, showing that once the system is in one legal configuration it is always in a legal configuration. In a way, the closure requirement is similar to the requirement that, once a safe configuration is reached, the system execution is in the set of legal executions (each configuration in a legal execution is a safe configuration). The purpose of the convergence requirement is to ensure that, from every arbitrary configuration, the system reaches a legal configuration.

The self-stabilizing algorithm for tree construction presented in this chapter is the one in [DIM89; DIM93]. Self-stabilizing algorithms for spanning-tree construction have been extensively studied; see [CYH91; HC92; CD94; AS95; AS97]. A great deal of attention has been paid to reducing the amount of memory required by tree construction algorithms; see, for example, [BJ95; Joh97].

The first self-stabilizing algorithms for mutual exclusion were presented in [Dij73] (see also [Dij74; Dij86]). Three self-stabilizing algorithms for mutual exclusion in a ring are presented in [Dij73]: the first is described in this chapter, and the other two use a smaller number of states (four and three, respectively) per processor. The self-stabilizing mutual exclusion problem has received extensive attention. In [Tch81] Tchuente proves a lower bound for the number of states required for implementing self-stabilizing mutual exclusion algorithms. The missing label concept was formalized in [Var94]. In [FD94] mutual exclusion algorithms that use two states per processor for particular communication graphs, such as rings with additional links from the special processor, are suggested. Other works that consider self-stabilizing mutual exclusion or related tasks, such as $l-exclusion$, are [Lam86; BGW89; Her90; LV92; FDS94; JPT95; ADHK97].

The fair composition technique was introduced in [DIM89; DIM93] and it was further investigated in [GH91; Sto93; Var97]. Recomputation of floating output was used in [AV91] to convert fixed-output algorithms into self-stabilizing algorithms.

Kessels [Kes88] used the variant function to prove the correctness of Dijkstra's self-stabilizing mutual exclusion algorithm [Dij73] that uses only three states. The self-stabilizing maximal matching algorithm appears in [HH92]. Several papers consider the self-stabilizing leader election problem, among them [AG94; AKY90; AKM+93]. Convergence stairs are used in the proofs in [GM91].

The scheduler-luck game technique was suggested in [DIM91; DIM95]. Silent tasks are defined in [DGS96], where the neighborhood-resemblance technique is used to prove lower bounds. The term "non-exploratory self-stabilization" introduced in [PY94] is related to silent self-stabilization, see also [SRR95].

Afek and Bremler presented self-stabilizing leader election and spanning-tree construction algorithms for unidirected networks [AB97].

Pseudo-self-stabilizing algorithms were introduced in [BGM93], and the alternating-bit algorithm appears in [BSW69].

Now that we have some intuition about self-stabilization, it is time for additional motivation. We first examine a basic communication task — that of the data-link layer in the OSI layer model [Tan96]. As we show next, it turns out that there is no reliable data-link algorithm that can withstand processor crashes. We then extend the above result to show that crashes may cause the system to reach an arbitrary state.

3.1 Initialization of a Data-Link Algorithm in the Presence of Faults

The data-link layer is responsible for delivering messages from a *sender* to a *receiver* that are directly connected. Recall that the communication channel connecting the sender and the receiver is not reliable; information sent from the sender to the receiver (and in the opposite direction) can be corrupted or even lost. In order to deliver a message, the sender sends sequences of bits (usually at a constant rate) to the receiver. Each sequence is called a *frame*. The sender stops sending bits for (at least) a short period between two consecutive frame transmissions.

Error-detection codes are used to identify and discard corrupted frames. Frame retransmission is used to cope with the possibility of frame corruption or loss. One retransmission strategy is the alternating-bit algorithm presented in figure 2.14, which can be used to implement a reliable data-link layer. Every message received by the sender from the network layer is repeatedly sent in a frame to the receiver until the receiver acknowledges receipt. The sender is then ready to receive and handle a new message of the network layer.

In more detail: when the system is initialized, there are no frames in transit. Thus, the sender uses the sequence number $bit_s = 1$, while the receiver uses the sequence number $bit_r = 0$. The sender repeatedly sends the frame $\langle m_1, 1 \rangle$ with the first message received from the network layer m_1 and a bit value 1, which is the value of bit_s. The receiver accepts every message from a frame with a bit value different from bit_r. In particular, the receiver accepts m_1 and delivers it to the network layer. At the same time, the receiver changes bit_r to the value of the bit in the frame of the accepted message; i.e., bit_r is assigned the value 1 when m_1 is delivered. In addition, every frame $\langle m, bit \rangle$ that arrives at the receiver is acknowledged by the receiver by the transmission of a frame $\langle bit \rangle$. Therefore, eventually the sender receives a frame $\langle 1 \rangle$ from the receiver that indicates the acceptance of m_1 by the receiver.

The sender changes the value of bit_s to 0 and is ready to send message m_2 by repeatedly transmitting the frame $\langle m_2, 0 \rangle$. Note that when the sender sends the frame $\langle m_2, 0 \rangle$, no frame with sequence number 0 is in the system. Therefore, the sender will receive an acknowledgment $\langle 0 \rangle$ only after bit_r is changed to 0; in other words, only after m_2 is delivered by the receiver to the network layer. Once the sender receives an acknowledgment $\langle 0 \rangle$, no frame with sequence number 1 exists in the system.

Is there a data-link algorithm, such as the alternating-bit algorithm, that can tolerate crashes of the sender and the receiver? To answer this question, we must decide how a crash affects the system. It is usually assumed that a crash causes the sender and receiver to reach an initial state. Therefore, it is obvious that a sender crash occurring immediately after the sender fetches a message m from the network layer, and before any frame is actually sent to the receiver, may result in a message loss, since no information concerning m is available. With this in mind, we want to check whether it can be guaranteed that every message fetched by the sender following the last crash of either the sender or the receiver will arrive at its destination. One way to ensure this is by invoking an initialization procedure; for example, for the alternating-bit algorithm, the initialization procedure initializes bit_s to hold 1 and bit_r to hold 0, and ensures that no frame with label 0 or 1 is in transit. Then the initialization procedure signals the sender to start fetching messages.

Surprisingly, as we now show, no such initialization procedure exists.

Consider an execution in which crashes can also be possible steps; in particular, we denote the sender crash by $Crash_S$ and the receiver crash by $Crash_R$. The effect of a crash step $Crash_X$ is an initialization of the state of the processor X to a special after-crash state. Thus, all the information that X encoded in its state before the crash is totally lost.

We first consider an execution E that starts in a system configuration in which no frames are in transit and in which both S and R are in the special after-crash state. No frame is lost during E and every frame arrives at its destination before the next frame is sent. For example, if the first frame sent following the crash from the sender to the receiver is f_{s1}, then f_{s1} arrives at its destination and the receiver sends f_{r1} as a reaction. This nice "ping-pong" execution is executed until the sender fetches the second message to be sent from the network layer. We denote such an execution by: $E=Crash_S$, $Crash_R, sends(f_{s1}), receive_R(f_{s1}), send_R(f_{r1}), receives(f_{r1}), sends(f_{s2})$, $\cdots, receives(f_{rk})$. We use the term *reference execution* for E. The frame f_{rk} received by the sender during E is the one that convinces the sender in the reference execution to fetch the next message from the network layer.

The idea of the proof, which we call the *pumping technique*, is repeatedly to crash the sender and the receiver and to replay parts of the reference execution in order to construct a new execution E'. During the replay the sender fetches several messages that are identical to m. Note that it is possible for the network layer to use the services of the data-link layer to deliver several identical messages in a row. Figure 3.1 is used below to demonstrate the pumping technique, but first we describe the techniques in words. $Crash_S$ and $Crash_R$ occur at the beginning of our new execution E'; then f_{s1} is sent and arrives at the receiver, and f_{r1} is sent as a reply exactly as in E. Now $Crash_S$ takes place, so we have $Crash_S, Crash_R, send_S(f_{s1}), receive_R(f_{s1}), send_R(f_{r1}), Crash_S$. At the end of the above execution, the sender is in an after-crash state and, according to E, is ready to send f_{s1}. We let the sender send f_{s1} before it receives f_{r1}.

In this configuration, the content of the queue $q_{s,r}$ of frames transmitted over the link from the sender to the receiver is f_{s1}, and the content of the queue $q_{r,s}$ of frames transmitted over the link from the receiver to the sender is f_{r1}. Moreover, the sender is in a state in which f_{s1} was already sent and is now ready to receive f_{r1}.

We let the sender receive the frame f_{r1} that is in $q_{r,s}$ and, since the sender is deterministic, it sends frame f_{s2} as a reaction, exactly as in the reference execution E. Up to this stage, we have constructed the execution $Crash_S, Crash_R, send_S(f_{s1}), receive_R(f_{s1}), send_R(f_{r1}), Crash_S, send_S(f_{s1}), receive_S(f_{r1}), send_S(f_{s2})$. The contents of $q_{s,r}$ in the configuration that is reached at the end of the above execution are f_{s1}, f_{s2}, where f_{s1} is the first frame to reach the receiver. We extend the execution, crashing R and letting it receive f_{s1} and send f_{r1}, receive f_{s2} and send f_{r2}. Now the execution is $Crash_S, Crash_R, send_S(f_{s1}), receive_R(f_{s1}), send_R(f_{r1}), Crash_S, send_S(f_{s1}), receive_S(f_{r1}), send_S(f_{s2}), Crash_R, receive_R(f_{s1}), send_R(f_{r1}), receive_R(f_{s2}), send_R(f_{r2})$. Thus, we reach a configuration in which the contents of $q_{r,s}$ are f_{r1}, f_{r2}.

Let X denote either S or R, where Y denotes S if X denotes R and Y denotes R if X denotes S. In general, we start in a configuration in which all frames sent by X in a prefix of the execution E are in $q_{X,Y}$. We crash Y and let it produce a sequence of frames that it produces in a prefix of E while accepting the frames in $q_{X,Y}$. We then continue crashing X and using the frames in $q_{Y,X}$ in a similar way. With the pumping technique, the length of the prefix of E that is executed by the sender and the receiver grows with the number of crashes.

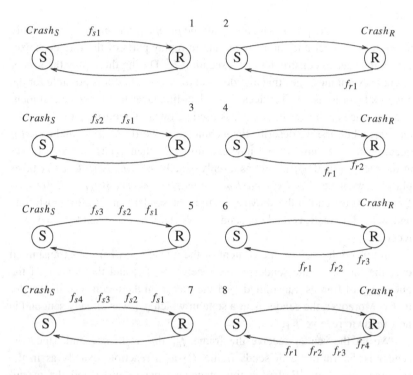

Figure 3.1
Pumping technique

Continuing in the same way, we pump the contents of $q_{r,s}$ until it contains $f_{r1}, f_{r2}, \cdots, f_{rk}$. Then we crash both the sender and the receiver and let the sender receive all the frames in $q_{r,s}$; this, in turn, convinces the sender that the message was sent so that it fetches a new message from the network layer. Now if all frames sent from the sender to the receiver are lost, then no information concerning the first message exists in the system. Therefore, we conclude that the first message that was fetched following the last crash is lost, which proves the impossibility result.

In figure 3.1, we present the eight configurations to describe the pumping technique. Configuration 1 follows a crash of S and the transmission of f_{s1}. Configuration 2 is derived from the first configuration by steps of R in which R receives f_{s1}, sends f_{r1}, and then crashes. Configuration 3 is derived from configuration 2 by steps of S in the following order: a crash of S, a send of f_{s1}, a receive of f_{r1}, and a send of f_{s2}. In general, the even-numbered configurations are reached from the odd-numbered ones by a crash of R, then receipt of the pending frames of the previous odd-numbered configuration, while sending responses. The odd-numbered configurations are reached from the even-numbered ones by a crash of S, then a spontaneous send of frame f_{s1}, followed by receipt of the pending messages of the odd-numbered configuration while sending responses.

We note that the pumping technique can also be used when the first frame sent after the crashes in the reference execution is a frame sent by the receiver, or when several frames are sent by the sender (or the receiver) before an answer is sent by the other side. The details are left as an exercise to the reader.

By similar arguments, it is also possible to show that there is no guarantee that the kth message that is fetched following the last crash will be received. So if no specific guarantee can be given, we may want to require that eventually every message fetched by the sender reaches the receiver — in other words, to require that our data-link algorithm will be self-stabilizing.

3.2   Arbitrary Configuration Because of Crashes

The above technique can be extended to prove that a configuration can be reached in which the states of the processors are any possible state in the execution E described in the previous section, and the messages in the links are any possible sequence of messages sent during E. Before we describe the details, let us note that it is possible that corrupted frames will not be identified as being corrupted and will be accepted by the sender and the receiver, causing an undesired state change and frame transmission.

The error-detection codes augmenting the frames ensure that the probability of such a scenario is small. Nevertheless, even if we assume that no undetected frame corruption is possible, it is still possible that a combination of crashes and frame losses will bring the system to an arbitrary configuration.

Let S (R) be the set of states of the sender (receiver, respectively) during a reference execution E (as defined in the previous section). Let $\mathcal{F}_S$ ($\mathcal{F}_R$) be the set of frames sent by the sender (receiver, respectively) during E. Let C be a set of all configurations for which the state of the receiver is a state in $\mathcal{R}$, the state of the sender is a state in $\mathcal{S}$, and the contents of $q_{r,s}$ and $q_{s,r}$ are any finite possible sequence of frames in $\mathcal{F}_R$ and $\mathcal{F}_S$, respectively.

We will now show that any configuration in C can be reached from the first configuration of E by a sequence of crashes of the sender and the receiver and frame losses. Intuitively, we use the pumping technique to accumulate a longer sequence of frames than was used in proving the impossibility of a crash-resilient data-link algorithm.

Once we have the entire sequence of frames sent from the receiver to the sender during E in $q_{r,s}$, we can start a new replay of E while keeping the frames sent during E in the system. Let us start with the configuration reached by using the pumping technique to accumulate in $q_{r,s}$ all frames sent from the receiver to the sender during E.

We continue from the configuration reached by the pumping technique in which the sequence of frames sent from the receiver to the sender during E are accumulated in $q_{r,s}$. Our first goal is to have two such sequences in a row stored in $q_{r,s}$. To achieve this, we crash the sender, let the sender send the first frame f_{s1} to the receiver, then crash the sender again and let the sender replay E, while accepting the frames stored in $q_{r,s}$. The sequence of frames stored in $q_{s,r}$ will be f_{s1} and then f_{s1} and the rest of the frames the sender sends during E. Now we use the above sequence as an input for the receiver: we crash the receiver, let the receiver accept f_{s1} and send f_{r1}, crash the receiver again, and let it replay E, accepting the frames stored in $q_{s,r}$ while producing f_{r1}, f_{r2}, $\cdots$, f_{rk}.

Our attention returns to the sender: the sender crashes, then sends f_{s1}, receives f_{r1}, and sends f_{s2}. Then we crash the sender again and let it replay E using the rest of the sequence of frames stored in $q_{r,s}$. We obtain a configuration in which the sequence of frames in $q_{s,r}$ is f_{s1}, f_{s2}, f_{s1}, f_{s2}, f_{s3}, $\cdots$ f_{sk}. We continue in the same fashion, reaching a configuration in which f_{s1}, f_{s2}, f_{s3}, $\cdots$, f_{sk}, f_{s1}, f_{s2}, f_{s3}, $\cdots$, f_{sk} appear in $q_{s,r}$. Let us denote f_{s1}, f_{s2}, f_{s3}, $\cdots$, f_{sk} by $\mathcal{F}_{sE}$ and f_{r1}, f_{r2}, f_{r3}, $\cdots$, f_{rk} by $\mathcal{F}_{rE}$. Once we reach a configuration in which $\mathcal{F}_{sE}$ appears twice in a row in $q_{s,r}$, we start accumulating one additional sequence to reach a configuration in which $\mathcal{F}_{sE}$ appears three times in a row in $q_{s,r}$. To do so, we will need to crash the sender (and the receiver) three times: once at the beginning of the replay and once before receiving either of the two $\mathcal{F}_{rE}$ ($\mathcal{F}_{sE}$, respectively), which are already stored in the system.

Let us use the notation $\mathcal{F}_{sE}^2$ to denote the sequence f_{s1}, f_{s2}, $\cdots$, f_{sk}, f_{s1}, f_{s2}, $\cdots$, f_{sk}; in general, the notation $\mathcal{F}_{sE}^i$ denotes a sequence in which $\mathcal{F}_{sE}$ appears i times in a row. For any finite i, this technique can be extended to reach a configuration in which $\mathcal{F}_{sE}^i$ appears in $q_{s,r}$.

Let k_1 (k_2) be the number of frames in $q_{s,r}$ ($q_{r,s}$, respectively) in the arbitrary configuration c_a that we choose from $\mathcal{C}$, and let i be $k_1 + k_2 + 2$. We use the above pumping technique to accumulate $\mathcal{F}_{sE}^i$ in $q_{s,r}$. Then we let the receiver replay E $k_2 + 1$ times using the frames stored in $q_{s,r}$, reaching a configuration in which $q_{s,r}$ contains $\mathcal{F}_{sE}^{k_1+1}$ and $q_{r,s}$ contains $\mathcal{F}_{rE}^{k_2+1}$.

Now we replay E until the desired states of the sender and the receiver are reached. To do this, we let the sender replay using the first copy of $\mathcal{F}_{rE}$ stored in $q_{r,s}$ until the sender reaches the desired state. We lose all frames produced by the sender at this stage and also the leftovers of the copy of $\mathcal{F}_{rE}$ that we used. The same is done for the receiver using the first copy of $\mathcal{F}_{sE}$. At this stage we have the sender and the receiver in the states they have in c_a, and we have to make sure only that the sequences of frames stored in the communication links are identical to the sequence in c_a. Let us consider the frames stored in $q_{s,r}$, since the case of $q_{r,s}$ is analogous. We have k_1 copies of $\mathcal{F}_{sE}$. We can use the first copy to ensure that the first frame f_{s1a} that appears in $q_{s,r}$ of c_a will exist — losing all frames from this copy of $\mathcal{F}_{sE}$ except f_{s1a}. The same can be done for the second frame f_{s2a} that appears in $q_{s,r}$ of c_a, using the the second copy of $\mathcal{F}_{sE}$, and so on.

Figure 3.2 depicts how an additional copy of $\mathcal{F}_{sE}$ is accumulated in $q_{s,r}$. Eight configurations numbered 1 to 8 to are presented. In configuration 1, a single copy of $\mathcal{F}_{rE}$ is in transit from the receiver to the sender. Configuration 2 is derived from configuration 1 by steps of S in which S crashes and then spontaneously sends f_{s1}. Configuration 3 is derived from the second configuration by steps of S in which S crashes and spontaneously sends (an additional) f_{s1}, then S receives f_{r1}, f_{r2} and f_{r3} and sends f_{s2}, and f_{s3} in response (the sender sends a frame upon receiving f_{r3}). Configuration 4 is obtained from the third configuration by a crash of the receiver and then a receive of the first copy of f_{s1} in $q_{s,r}$ and a following send of f_{r1}. Configuration 5 is reached from the fourth configuration by a crash of the receiver, then the acceptance of f_{s1}, f_{s2}, and f_{s3} and send operations of f_{r1}, f_{r2}, and f_{r3} in response.

Crashes are not considered a severe type of fault (e.g., Byzantine faults are more severe, as explained in chapter 6). In this chapter we have proved that it is impossible to achieve a basic task when crashes cause the processors to change state to an after-crash state. One approach to proving correctness of a distributed algorithm is to show that consistency can be preserved by starting in a consistent configuration (a safe configuration) and proving that any step preserves the consistency. The above technique shows that this approach is doomed to failure when crashes are possible, since consistency may not be preserved in the presence of crashes.

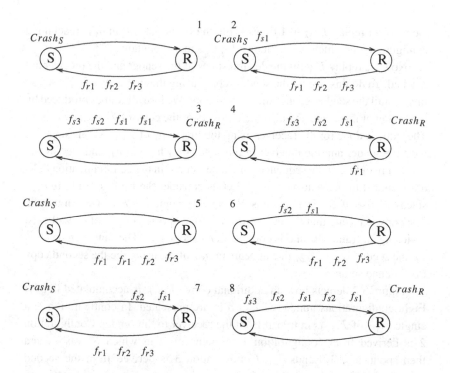

Figure 3.2
Reaching an arbitrary state

Finally, we remark that a crash-resilient data-link algorithm exists when a bound on the number of frames in transit is known. A crash-resilient data-link algorithm also exists when a bound on the transmission time is known. Let us describe a crash resilient data-link algorithm that uses a bound on the number of frames in transit. The algorithm uses an initialization procedure following the crash of the sender or the receiver. This initialization procedure ensures that the alternating-bit protocol presented in figure 2.14 is properly initialized, and that any message that is fetched by the sender following the last crash is delivered.

Let *bound* be the maximal number of frames that can be in transit in the links that connect both the sender to the receiver and the receiver to the sender. Whenever the sender recovers from a crash (starts in an after-crash state) it invokes a clean procedure. The sender repeatedly sends a frame ⟨*clean*, 1⟩

until receiving $\langle ackClean, 1 \rangle$; then the sender repeatedly sends $\langle clean, 2 \rangle$ until receiving $\langle ackClean, 2 \rangle$. This procedure continues until the sender sends $\langle clean, bound + 1 \rangle$ and receives $\langle ackClean, bound + 1 \rangle$.

Once more the missing-label concept presented in section 2.6 is used. In any initial configuration at least one label x in the range 1 to $bound+1$ does not exist. Thus, when the sender receives the first acknowledgment $\langle ackClean, x \rangle$ there is no other label in transit. Moreover, when the sender receives the first acknowledgment $\langle ackClean, y \rangle$, for any $y \geq x$, the only label in transit is y. The sender does not know the value x of the missing label, but nevertheless when the sender receives the first acknowledgment $\langle ackClean, bound + 1 \rangle$ it can be sure that the only label in transit is $bound + 1$. It can therefore initialize the alternating algorithm, in particular assign 0 to bit_s and fetch a new message to send to the receiver. Similarly, whenever the receiver receives a frame $\langle ackClean, bound + 1 \rangle$ it initializes its alternating-bit algorithm, assigning 1 to bit_r. The above initialization procedure ensures that whenever the sender fetches a new message to be sent, all the frames in transit have the same label value.

The actions of the receiver starting from an after-crash state are yet to be defined. As a first try, let us assume that when the first frame $\langle FrameBit, msg \rangle$ arrives at the receiver following a crash, the receiver assigns $bit_r := FrameBit$ and delivers the message msg to the output queue. In such a case it is possible that the receiver delivers an extra copy of msg — one before the crash and one after the crash. This is possible because the sender repeatedly sends the same frame until an acknowledgment arrives, possibly causing the accumulation of several copies of the same frame in the link that transfers messages from the sender to the receiver. Can such duplicate delivery be avoided? In other words, can we guarantee at most one delivery (i.e., no duplication but possibly omission) of messages, and still ensure that every message fetched by the sender following the last crash (of either the sender or the receiver) is delivered — i.e., can we guarantee exactly-once delivery following the last crash? A first try at satisfying this requirement is to change the actions of the receiver following a crash to exclude the output of the message that arrives in the first frame, but still to assign to bit_r the $FrameBit$ of the first arriving frame. In this case it is possible that, following the crash of R, S fetches a message that is not accepted by R — violating the requirement of exactly once delivery following the last crash. bit_r should be somehow initialized to make sure that a message fetched following the crash will be delivered. One solution that satisfies the requirements is to program the sender to send each message in frames with labels 0 until an acknowledgment is received and then to send the same message in frames with label 1 until an acknowledgment is received. The receiver will deliver a message only when the message arrives in a frame with label 1 immediately after it arrived in a frame with label 0. Thus, if the sender fetches a message msg following the crash of R, a frame with $\langle 0, msg \rangle$ must arrive at the receiver before the sender starts sending $\langle 1, msg \rangle$, ensuring that bit_r is set to 0 and then to 1.

3.3 Frequently Asked Questions

To further motivate self-stabilizing algorithms we must answer several important frequently asked questions. One such question is: what is the rationale behind assuming that the states of the processors (the contents of their memory) can be corrupted while the processors' programs cannot be corrupted? After all, the program is usually loaded in exactly the same memory device used to store the content of the program variables. Note that a self-stabilizing algorithm is design to cope with the corruption of variables (including corruption of the value of the program counter) but not with a corruption of the program code. The answer to the above question uses two arguments. The first is that usually the (backup copy of the) program of the processors is stored in a long-term memory device, such as a hard drive, from which it is possible periodically to reload the program statements in order to overcome a possible memory corruption. In addition, in some cases the program is hardwired in a read-only memory device that cannot be corrupted by faults that corrupt the random-access memory contents. The second argument is related to the necessity of having an uncorrupted copy of the program (either in a secondary memory device or in hardware). Let us assume that the program is subject to corruptions as well. In such cases it is impossible to reason about the actions of the processors that have a corrupted code. In fact (as explained in chapter 6), it is possible to cope with only a very limited number of processors that execute corrupted programs.

Another frequently asked question is related to the safety properties of a self-stabilizing algorithm. Usually a distributed algorithm is designed to satisfy safety and liveness properties, where (roughly speaking) safety properties ensures that the system never reaches a bad configuration and the liveness property ensures that the system eventually achieves its goal. The assumption made by the designer of self-stabilizing algorithms is that the algorithm must converge from every possible initial configuration, thus ensuring that, even if a safety requirement is violated, the system execution will reach a suffix in which both the safety and liveness properties hold. At first glance, it seems that the violation of a safety property is a weakness in the self-stabilizing property — what use is an algorithm that does not ensure that a car (controlled by this algorithm) never crashes? This question confuses the severe conditions that a self-stabilizing algorithm assumes with the properties the algorithm achieves. In other words, it is clear that no algorithm can cope with (a set of faults that force it to) any possible initial state and still ensure that certain configurations will never be reached. Thus, if the faults are severe enough to make the algorithm reach an arbitrary configuration, the car may crash no matter what algorithm is chosen. Algorithm designers assume an initial state in which several properties hold and assume that the transitions of the system do not violate these properties; they do not concern themselves with the behavior of the system once these safety properties are violated. A safety property for a car controller might be: never turn into a one-way road when there is no "enter" sign. Thus, if faults cause the car to enter the wrong way on a one-way road, the actions the controller takes are not defined. When no specification exists, the car can continue driving in this road and crash with other cars. On the other hand, a self-stabilizing controller will recover from this non-legal initial configuration (turn the car) and ensure that the safety property (make no further turns in the wrong direction) will hold (as long as no additional unexpected faults occur).

The last question we discuss is related to the fact that processors can never be sure that a safe configuration is reached. What use is an algorithm in which the processors are never sure about the current global state? For instance, when the task is mutual exclusion, processors that enter the critical section cannot be sure that no other processor is in that critical section. This question again confuses the assumptions (transient fault occurrences) with the (self-stabilizing) algorithm that is designed to fit the severe assumptions. A self-stabilizing algorithm can be designed to start in a particular (safe) configuration. As long as the algorithm is started in the above predefined initial configuration and no (transient) fault occurs, each processor's knowledge about the system is accurate. Thus, a self-stabilizing algorithm is at least as good as a non-self-stabilizing algorithm for the same task. In our example, a processor that enters the critical section can be sure that no other processor is in the critical section. Moreover, when a fault does occur, the knowledge of each processor will be eventually accurate. In the terms of our example, a processor knows that *even-*

tually it will enter the critical section by itself (assuming faults do not occur too often).

Exercises

3.1. Use the pumping technique to prove that no crash resilient data-link algorithm $\mathcal{AL}$ exists such that in $\mathcal{AL}$ the sender does not send a frame following a crash.

3.2. Prove that for any given k, there is no data-link algorithm that ensures that the kth message fetched following the last crash (of either the sender or the receiver) is delivered.

3.3. A data-link algorithm guarantees *exactly-once message delivery*, in which exactly one copy of each of the messages fetched by the sender is delivered to the receiver. A more relaxed requirement is *at-least-once message delivery*, where at least one copy of each of the messages fetched by the sender is delivered to the receiver. Does there exist an at-least-once message-delivery data-link algorithm $\mathcal{AL}$ such that $\mathcal{AL}$ guarantees that every message sent following the last crash is delivered at least once? Does your answer depend on whether or not the receiver uses a bounded amount of memory?

3.4. Let $\mathcal{AE}$ be all possible executions of a distributed algorithm executed by a system of two processors S and R. Consider two executions $E_1 \in \mathcal{AE}$ and $E_2 \in \mathcal{AE}$ such that there exist two configurations $c' \in E_1$ and $c'' \in E_2$; here the state x of S in c' does not appear in any configuration in E_2, and the state y of R in c'' does not appear in any configuration of E_1. Prove that crashes can bring the system to a configuration in which S is in state x and R is in state y.

3.5. Let E be an execution of a distributed algorithm for more than two processors. Prove that crashes can bring the system to a configuration in which every processor P_i is an arbitrary state x_i, such that P_i was in the state x_i in some configuration of E. *Hint*: Use the pumping technique on a particular link (or processor), crashing all the processors in the system instead of the single neighbor; accumulate enough copies of the message sent on the link (or all attached links) to make it possible to pump the contents of other links.

Notes

The impossibility results for the existence of a data-link algorithm in the presence of faults appear in [BS88; FLMS93], and the problem was further studied in [ADW95; DW97]. The technique used to bring the system to an arbitrary configuration is based on [JV96].

More motivation for the use of self-stabilizing algorithms can be found in [Lam83; Sch93; FDG94; Tel94; Gou95; Deb95; Bar96].

Several researchers are concerned with demonstrating the applicability of the self-stabilization property to current communication technologies, for instance to high-speed and mobile communication networks; see [DTOF94; DPW95; CGK95; CV96; DW97; CW97].

4 Self-Stabilizing Algorithms for Model Conversions

Previous chapters considered several models of distributed computation. Such models can differ in several aspects. One aspect is whether shared memory or message passing is used for communication; another is whether the existence of a central daemon or a distributed daemon scheduler is assumed, or an interleaving of read/write actions on shared registers (as described in section 2.1). The existence of unique identifiers, a single special processor, or neither of the above (i.e., anonymous processors) can be assumed. In this chapter we design techniques for converting a self-stabilizing algorithm that is designed for one system to work on another system. The designer of an algorithm may then choose the best platform for the algorithm design process and then apply the algorithm to another system with different settings. The framework of algorithm conversion is an opportunity to study self-stabilizing algorithms for fundamental tasks.

4.1 Token-Passing: Converting a Central Daemon to read/write

The literature in self-stabilization is rich in algorithms that assume the existence of powerful schedulers, the *distributed daemon* or the *central daemon*. The distributed daemon activates the processors by repeatedly selecting a set of processors and activating them simultaneously to execute a computation step. Each processor executes the next computation step as defined by its state just prior to this activation. We use read and write operations to describe precisely the meaning of the simultaneous execution of the computation steps. Simultaneous execution starts with all the activated processors reading the states of their neighbors. Once every processor in the set has finished reading, all the processors write a new state (change state). Only then does the scheduler choose a new set of processors to be activated. Note that no non-activated processor changes its state. The central daemon is a special case of the distributed daemon in which the set of activated processors consists of exactly one processor. Note that a synchronous system in which all the processors are activated in every step is also a special case of a system with a distributed daemon.

What are the reasons for using the above special settings in the literature on self-stabilization? One reason is the choices Dijkstra made in the first work in the field. Another is the inherent subtlety of designing self-stabilizing algorithms, which can be started in any possible configuration. The assumption of the existence of a daemon enables the designer to consider only a subset of the possible execution set. In particular, there is no need to use internal variables to store the values read from the communication registers (or to consider the values of these internal variables as subject to corruption by transient faults as well).

The great importance of relaxing the assumption concerning the schedule pattern is obvious. An algorithm designed to work in read/write atomicity can be used in any system in which there exists a central or a distributed daemon, while an algorithm designed for a system with a central or a distributed daemon cannot be used in a system that supports only read/write atomicity. The above facts are our motivation for designing a compiler that receives as an input a self-stabilizing algorithm $\mathcal{AL}$ for some task $\mathcal{T}$ that is designed for systems with the central or distributed daemon, and outputs a version of $\mathcal{AL}$ for task $\mathcal{T}$ for systems that support only read/write atomicity. An algorithm designed to stabilize in the presence of a distributed daemon must stabilize in a system with a central daemon — one possible policy of the distributed daemon is to activate one processor at a time, and an algorithm designed to stabilize under any scheduling policy of the distributed daemon must stabilize when one processor is activated at a time. In this section, we suggest distributively implementing a central daemon by a self-stabilizing mutual exclusion or token-passing algorithm. When a processor enters the critical section in the mutual exclusion algorithm, or when a processor holds the token in the token-passing algorithm, it reads the states of its neighbors and changes state accordingly. Once the processor changes its state, it exits the critical section or passes the token.

The algorithm is designed for a system with an arbitrary communication graph and a single special processor. In what follows, we show how the assumption on the existence of a special processor can be achieved by using a self-stabilizing leader-election algorithm.

We use the algorithm presented in section 2.7, which uses the fair-composition technique to compose the spanning-tree-construction algorithm of section 2.5 with the read/write atomicity version of Dijkstra's mutual exclusion algorithm in section 2.6. Once the spanning-tree construction algorithm stabilizes, a virtual ring forming the Euler tour on the spanning tree is distributively defined. Moreover, the root of the tree acts as the special processor in the ring. Thus, when the mutual exclusion algorithm stabilizes, it is the case that exactly one processor may enter the critical section in every configuration. A processor that enters the critical section of the mutual exclusion algorithm reads the state of its neighbors (or the portion of the state that is communicated to it through the communication registers), changes state and writes its new state to its communication registers, and then exits the critical section. Note that every time a processor enters the critical section it executes a constant number of steps and then exits. Therefore, the convergence of the mutual exclusion algorithm to a safe configuration is still guaranteed.

Our compiler receives as input an algorithm $\mathcal{AL}$ that stabilizes in the presence of a central daemon and composes it with a self-stabilizing mutual exclusion algorithm that schedules the operations of the processors. In an arbitrary initial configuration of the composed algorithm, it is possible that more than a single processor is scheduled to execute a step in $\mathcal{AL}$. Therefore, while the mutual exclusion algorithm stabilizes, it is possible that two neighboring processors will change state simultaneously. Therefore, $\mathcal{AL}$ may not converge to a safe configuration until the mutual exclusion algorithm stabilizes. In fact, however, we are not interested in its exact behavior during this period, since it does not interfere with the activity of the mutual exclusion algorithm. When the mutual exclusion algorithm reaches a safe configuration, the state portion of the processors that is related to $\mathcal{AL}$ is arbitrary. Fortunately, $\mathcal{AL}$ converges to a safe configuration from any arbitrary configuration when it is activated by the central daemon.

4.2 Data-Link Algorithms: Converting Shared Memory to Message Passing

In the study of fault-tolerant message passing systems, it is customarily assumed that messages may be corrupted over links; hence, processors may enter arbitrary states and link contents may be arbitrary. Self-stabilizing algorithms handle these problems as well, since they are designed to recover from inconsistent global states.

Designing a self-stabilizing algorithm for asynchronous message-passing systems can be even more subtle than designing a self-stabilizing algorithm for a system that supports read/write atomicity. The main difficulty is the messages stored in the communication links. A self-stabilizing system must cope with any possible initial state. When modeling asynchronous systems, it is commonly assumed that there is no bound on message delivery time, and the number of messages that can be in (transit and in the buffers of) a link is also unbounded. Thus, there are infinitely many initial configurations from which the system must stabilize. Again, one would like to design a self-stabilizing algorithm for the read/write atomicity model (or even the central daemon model) and then use a compiler that converts this algorithm into a self-stabilizing algorithm in the message-passing model. Our first goal in the design of such a compiler is a self-stabilizing data-link algorithm or token-passing algorithm. A self-stabilizing data-link algorithm will ensure that the unknown contents of the link are controlled, eliminating undesired messages from the link.

Recall that the data-link algorithm is designed for a system of two processors, one of which is the sender and the other the receiver. The task of the data-link algorithm is to use retransmissions in order to deliver messages from the sender to the receiver. The messages that have to be delivered are given to the sender by a higher-level algorithm of the network layer. The messages that are fetched by the sender from the network layer (at the sender side) should be delivered by the receiver to the network layer (at the receiver side) without duplications, omissions, or reordering. A message m that is fetched by the sender from the network layer is sent repeatedly as part of (messages called) *frames* to the receiver until the sender receives an indication that m was delivered by the receiver to the network layer (on the receiver side).

For instance, in the *stop-and-wait* data-link algorithm, each message sent by the sender is acknowledged by the receiver before the next message is sent. This behavior is similar to that of a token-passing algorithm, in which a single token is repeatedly sent from the sender to the receiver and back. First note that a stop-and-wait algorithm implements the token-passing task: each time the sender decides to fetch a new message, a token is present at the sender side; each time the receiver decides to deliver a message, a token is present at the receiver side. On the other hand, a token-passing algorithm implements the data-link task: the token is transferred from the sender to the receiver and back by sending frames between the sender and the receiver. Therefore, roughly speaking, the content of every message that the sender fetches can be attached to every frame sent for transferring the token. A new message is fetched whenever a token arrives at the sender. Once the receiver decides that a token has arrived, it delivers the message that is attached to the last arriving frame. Note that, in both these tasks, it is impossible for the sender and the receiver to hold the token (or fetch and deliver messages) simultaneously. In other words, there is no configuration in which there are two applicable steps a_1 and a_2 such that the sender sends a token (fetches a message) during a_1 and the receiver receives a token (delivers a message, respectively) during a_2.

We abstract the requirements of the data-link algorithm and the token-passing algorithm tasks in a set of executions TP. The task TP of legitimate sequences is defined as the set of all configuration sequences in which no more than one processor holds the token and both the sender and the receiver hold the token in infinitely many configurations in every sequence in TP. In what follows we consider the TP task. Thus, in the next three sections there is no need to use both the terms message and frame — and hence we use only the term message.

Unbounded Solution

The first algorithm we propose uses an unbounded counter to achieve the TP task. A timeout mechanism is assumed to ensure that the system is not started in a *communication-deadlock configuration* in which there is no message in transit in the communication links and neither the sender nor the receiver is about to send a message.

The code for this algorithm appears in figure 4.1. In this algorithm, each message has an integer label called *MsgCounter* and both the sender and the receiver maintain a variable called *counter*. The sender repeatedly sends the value of its counter until it receives a message from the receiver with the same value. Once such a message arrives at the sender, the sender receives the token, increments the value of the counter and sends the new counter value in a message to the receiver. When the new counter is sent, the sender stops holding the token. For every message m received by the receiver, the receiver sends a message m' with a label identical to the label of m. In addition, the receiver stores in its counter variable the last counter value received in a message. Every time a message with a value different from the counter value of the receiver arrives at the receiver, the receiver receives the token, updates its counter value, and sends the message back to the sender. When this message is sent, the receiver stops holding the token.

Recall that a configuration of the system is a tuple $c = (s_s, s_r, q_{s,r}, q_{r,s})$, where s_s (s_r) is the state of the sender (the receiver, respectively) and $q_{s,r}$ ($q_{r,s}$) is the queue of messages sent by the sender to the receiver (by the receiver to the sender, respectively) but not yet received. A computation step a of a processor starts with a single communication operation, message send or message receive, then continues with internal computations, and ends just before the next communication operation. A computation step of the sender can also be started by a *timeout mechanism* instead of message arrival. The timeout mechanism is designed to cope with message loss. A *timeout$_s$* event is an environment step (similar to $loss_{i,j}(m)$) that is executed whenever the system reaches a communication deadlock configuration. For example, a deadlock configura-

---

```
Sender:
01          upon timeout
02              send (counter)
03          upon message arrival
04          begin
05              receive(MsgCounter)
06              if MsgCounter ≥ counter then
                (* token arrives *)
07                  begin (* send new token *)
08                        counter := MsgCounter + 1
09                        send(counter)
10                  end
11                  else send(counter)
12          end
Receiver:
13          upon message arrival
14          begin
15              receive(MsgCounter)
16              if MsgCounter ≠ counter then
                (* token arrives *)
17                        counter := MsgCounter
18                  send(counter)
19          end
```

Figure 4.1
Token-passing with unbounded sequence numbers

tion can be reached due to message loss that eliminates all messages in transit while both the sender and the receiver are waiting to receive a message. An *execution* $E = (c_1, a_1, c_2, a_2, \cdots)$ is an alternating sequence of configurations and steps such that $c_{i-1} \overset{a_{i-1}}{\to} c_i$ $(i > 1)$.

A safe configuration for TP and the algorithm in figure 4.1 is a configuration in which the counter values of all the messages in $q_{s,r}$ and $q_{r,s}$, as well as the values of the counters maintained by the sender and the receiver, have the same value. Interestingly, the correctness proof of the first self-stabilizing datalink algorithm resembles the correctness proof of Dijkstra's mutual-exclusion algorithm presented in section 2.6. According to our definition, the ME task and the TP task are identical. Still in some cases (e.g., section 8.1), we use the TP task to transfer information together with the token. The following lemma proves that, indeed, every fair execution that starts with such a safe configuration belongs to TP.

LEMMA 4.1:   A configuration c in which all the counter variables of the messages and the processors are equal is a safe configuration for TP and the algorithm in figure 4.1.

Proof Following c, the sender must receive a message with a counter value that is equal to its counter variable, because such a message either exists already in one of the queues or is sent due to a timeout. Once the sender receives a message with a counter value that is equal to its counter, the sender has the token. Then the sender increments its counter value and sends a message with the new counter value (releasing the token). Before a message with the new counter value reaches the sender, it must reach the receiver. Therefore, the receiver holds a token before the sender holds the token again. Once the sender receives a message with the value of its counter, a new configuration in which the value of all the counters is identical is reached, and the same arguments can be applied. ■

We are now ready to prove the main theorem.

THEOREM 4.1:   For every possible configuration c, every fair execution that starts in c reaches a safe configuration with relation to TP.

Proof First we claim that, in every fair execution, the value of the sender's counter is incremented infinitely often. Assume, by way of contradiction, that there exists a configuration after which the value of the sender's counter is not changed. Since the execution is fair, every computation step that is applicable infinitely often is executed; in particular, every message that is sent infinitely often is received. The timeout mechanism ensures that at least one message is sent repeatedly by the sender. This message is eventually received by the receiver, which forwards it back to the sender, causing the sender to increment its counter. We conclude that in every fair execution there is no configuration after which the sender does not increment its counter. Let *max* be the maximal value of a counter in a message or in one of the counter variables in the first configuration of the execution c. When the sender assigns the value $max + 1$ to its counter variable, the sender introduces a new counter value not existing in any previous configuration of the execution that starts in c. Thus, when the sender receives a message from the receiver with $MsgCounter = max + 1$, the system is in a safe configuration. ■

A question to ask at this stage is whether an algorithm that uses only bounded memory exists — in particular, whether the unbounded counter and label can be eliminated. We answer this question negatively, proving that the memory of the system must grow at a logarithmic rate, where the memory of the system is the number of bits required to encode the state of the sender, the state of the receiver, and the messages in transit (including the messages in the incoming and outgoing buffers of the links). The lower bound is proved on the *size* of the system configuration, where the size is the number of bits required to encode a configuration.

Lower Bound

Before we present the lower bound, let us discuss issues concerning retransmission and timeouts. One can argue that there is no bound on the size of a configuration when a timeout mechanism is used. The number of messages in $q_{s,r}$ grows each time the timeout mechanism is invoked. Therefore, in an execution in which the sender sends a message at every step due to timeouts, the configuration size grows linearly with the number of steps of the sender. Recall that the timeout mechanism was introduced to cope with situations in which no message is in transit. Therefore, we choose to assume that the time it takes for the timeout mechanism to be triggered is long enough to guarantee that, indeed, no message is in transit in the system.

Can the assumption on the timeout mechanism be used by the algorithm designer? For example, one can propose an algorithm in which the sender waits every so often for a timeout, ignoring any arriving messages. It can be argued that such a technique can be used to eliminate pending messages with undesired labels from the system. However, as we show next, the timeout mechanism should be invoked repeatedly in order to ensure that a safe configuration is reached from every possible system state. This, in turn, implies a long delay in message transmission over the entire execution, not only during convergence. Moreover, it is possible that the timeout mechanism in certain systems does not guarantee that no message is in transit when a timeout is triggered. Therefore, one would prefer an algorithm that stabilizes without using an assumption on the contents of the links when a timeout occurs.

The lower bound presented in this section is proved for an arbitrary *weak-exclusion* task WE. A task is in the weak-exclusion set of tasks if, in every legal execution E, there exists a combination of steps, a step for each processor (the sender and the receiver), such that both steps appear in E but are never applicable simultaneously. In other words, these steps are never executed concurrently. The TP task does not allow two simultaneous steps in which the sender and the receiver receive the token. To simplify the proof of the lower bound, we assume in what follows that every computation step starts with a message receive followed by local computation and ending with a message send. Note that such a scheduling policy results in a possible execution.

For any configuration c and any directed link (x, y) from P_x to P_y (where P_x is the sender and P_y is the receiver or vice versa), let $q_{x,y}(c)$ be the sequence of messages pending on the link from P_x to P_y in c. For any execution E, let $qs_{x,y}(E)$ be the sequence of messages sent by P_x on the link leading to P_y during E. Similarly, let $qr_{x,y}(E)$ be the sequence of messages received by P_y from the link (x, y) during E. We use the notation $p \circ q$ for the concatenation of p and q.

LEMMA 4.2:   For every execution $E = (c_1, a_1, \cdots, a_k, c_{k+1})$ in which no message is lost, it holds that $q_{x,y}(c_1) \circ qs_{x,y}(E) = qr_{x,y}(E) \circ q_{x,y}(c_{k+1})$.

Proof The left-hand side of the equation contains the messages on the link (x, y) in c_1, concatenated with the messages sent during E through (x, y). The right-hand side of the equation contains the messages received during E through (x, y), concatenated with the messages left on (x, y) in c_{k+1}. The proof is completed by a simple induction on k to show that, if no message is lost during E, then both sides of the equation represent the same sequence of messages. ∎

An execution $E = (c_1, a_1, \cdots, c_{\ell-1}, a_{\ell-1})$ whose result configuration c_ℓ is equal to its initial configuration c_1 is called a *circular* execution. Repeating a circular execution E forever yields an infinite execution E^∞. Observe that an execution in which a certain configuration appears more than once has a circular sub-execution $\overline{E} = (c_i, a_i, \cdots, a_{i+\ell-1}, c_{i+\ell}) \equiv (\overline{c}_1, \overline{a}_1, \cdots, \overline{a}_{\ell-1}, \overline{c}_\ell)$, where $c_i = c_{i+\ell} = \overline{c}_1 = \overline{c}_\ell$.

Let $\mathcal{AL}$ be an arbitrary self-stabilizing algorithm for a WE task. To show that, in every execution of $\mathcal{AL}$, all the configurations are distinct, we assume that $\mathcal{AL}$ has a circular sub-execution $\overline{E}$ and reach a contradiction by showing that $\mathcal{AL}$ is not self-stabilizing. Using $\overline{E}$, we now construct an initial configuration c_{init} by changing the list of messages in transit on the system's links. For each link (x, y), the list of messages in transit on (x, y) at c_{init} is obtained by concatenating the list of messages in transit on (x, y) at $\overline{c}_1$ with the list of all messages sent on (x, y) during $\overline{E}$.

Roughly speaking, the effect of this change is to create an additional "padding layer" of messages that helps to decouple each *send* from its counterpart *receive* and achieve additional flexibility in the system, and this which enables us to prove the lower bound. Formally, c_{init} is obtained from $\overline{c}_1$ as follows:

- The state of each processor in c_{init} is equal to its state in $\bar{c}_1$.
- For any link (x, y), $q_{x,y}(c_{init}) = q_{x,y}(c_1) \circ qs_{x,y}(\overline{E})$.

Let $S_x(\overline{E})$ be the sequence of steps executed by P_x during $\overline{E}$. Define $merge(\overline{S})$ to be the set of sequences obtained by all possible merging of the sequences $S_s(\overline{E})$ and $S_r(\overline{E})$, while keeping the internal order in $S_s(\overline{E})$ and $S_r(\overline{E})$. Note that all the sequences in $merge(\overline{S})$ have the same finite length and contain the same steps in different orders.

LEMMA 4.3:   Every $S \in merge(\overline{S})$ is applicable to c_{init}, and the resulting execution is a circular execution of $\mathcal{AL}$.

Proof Let S be an arbitrary sequence in $merge(\overline{S})$ and let P_x be an arbitrary processor of the system. Then we have: (1) The initial state of P_x in c_{init} is equal to its initial state in $\bar{c}_1$. (2) In c_{init}, all messages that P_x receives during $\overline{E}$ are stored in P_x's incoming link in the right order. (3) The steps of P_x appear in S in the same order as they appear in $S_x(\overline{E})$. (1) — (3) imply that the sequence S is applicable to c_{init}, and the application of S to c_{init} yields an execution E_S with result configuration c_{res} whose state vector is equal to the state vector of c_{init} and in which, for every link (x, y), $qs_{x,y}(E_S) = qs_{x,y}(\overline{E})$ and $qr_{x,y}(E_S) = qr_{x,y}(\overline{E})$.

To prove that the execution obtained is circular, it remains to show that the content of every link in the result configuration c_{res} is equal to its content in c_{init}: in other words, that $q_{x,y}(c_{init}) = q_{x,y}(c_{res})$. For every link (x, y), it holds that:

1. $q_{x,y}(c_{init}) \circ qs_{x,y}(\overline{E}) = qr_{x,y}(\overline{E}) \circ q_{x,y}(c_{res})$ (by lemma 4.2 above and the fact that $qs_{x,y}(E_S) = qs_{x,y}(\overline{E})$ and $qr_{x,y}(E_S) = qr_{x,y}(\overline{E})$).

2. $q_{x,y}(\bar{c}_1) \circ qs_{x,y}(\overline{E}) = qr_{x,y}(\overline{E}) \circ q_{x,y}(\bar{c}_1)$ (by lemma 4.2 and the circularity of $\overline{E}$).

Replacing $q_{x,y}(c_{init})$ in equation 1 with its explicit contents yields:

3. $q_{x,y}(\bar{c}_1) \circ qs_{x,y}(\overline{E}) \circ qs_{x,y}(\overline{E}) = qr_{x,y}(\overline{E}) \circ q_{x,y}(c_{res})$.

Using equation 2 to replace $q_{x,y}(\bar{c}_1) \circ qs_{x,y}(\overline{E})$ by $qr_{x,y}(\overline{E}) \circ q_{x,y}(\bar{c}_1)$ in equation 3 gives:

4. $qr_{x,y}(\overline{E}) \circ q_{x,y}(\bar{c}_1) \circ q_{x,y}(\overline{E}) = qr_{x,y}(\overline{E}) \circ q_{x,y}(c_{res})$.

Eliminating $qr_{x,y}(\overline{E})$ from both sides of equation 4 yields the desired result: $q_{x,y}(c_{init}) = q_{x,y}(\overline{c}_1) \circ qs_{x,y}(\overline{E}) = q_{x,y}(c_{res})$, which proves the lemma. $\blacksquare$

Define $blowup(\overline{E})$ as the set of executions whose initial state is c_{init} and whose sequence of steps belongs to $merge(\overline{S})$. Notice that, for every circular execution $\overline{E}$ and every execution $E \in blowup(\overline{E})$, it holds that $S_x(\overline{E}) = S_x(E)$.

LEMMA 4.4: For any set of steps $B = \{a_1, a_2\}$, where $a_1 \in S_s(\overline{E})$ and $a_2 \in S_r(\overline{E})$, there is an execution $E \in blowup(\overline{E})$ that contains a configuration for which the atomic steps in B are concurrently applicable.

Proof Let $S \in merge(\overline{S})$ be the sequence constructed as follows: first take all the steps in $S_s(\overline{E})$ that precede a_1; then take all the steps in $S_r(\overline{E})$ that precede a_2. Applying the sequence constructed so far to c_{init} results in a configuration in which both a_1 and a_2 are applicable. This sequence is completed to a sequence S in $merge(\overline{S})$ by taking the remaining steps in an arbitrary order that keeps the internal order of each $S_x(\overline{E})$. $\blacksquare$

LEMMA 4.5: Let $\mathcal{AL}$ be a self-stabilizing algorithm for an arbitrary weak-exclusion task WE in a system with a timeout mechanism. If $\mathcal{AL}$ has a circular execution $\overline{E}$, then $\mathcal{AL}$ has an infinite fair execution E^∞, none of whose configurations is safe for WE.

Proof Let E be an arbitrary execution in $blowup(\overline{E})$. Define E^∞ as the infinite execution obtained by repeating E forever. We show that no configuration in E^∞ is safe.

Assume by way of contradiction that some configuration c_1 in E^∞ is safe. Now we construct a finite circular execution E' whose sequence of steps S' is obtained by concatenating sequences from $merge(\overline{S})$, that is $S_x(E') = S_x(\overline{E})$. Since $\mathcal{AL}$ is an algorithm for some weak-exclusion task, E' should have some set of steps $B = \{a_1, a_2\}$, where $a_i \in S_i$, that are never applicable to a single configuration c during E'. We reach a contradiction by refuting this statement for E'. To do this we choose some arbitrary enumeration $B = B_1, \cdots, B_e$ of all the sets containing two steps, one of P_s and the other of P_r. Execution E' is constructed by first continuing the computation from c_1 as in E until configuration c_{init} is reached. Then we apply lemma 4.4 to extend E' by

s consecutive executions $E_1, \cdots, E_e$, where E_k, $1 \le k \le e$, contains a configuration in which the steps in B_k are applicable and that ends with c_{init}. The proof follows. ∎

The proof at the lower bound is completed by the following theorem.

THEOREM 4.2:   Let $\mathcal{AL}$ be a self-stabilizing algorithm for an arbitrary weak-exclusion task in a system with a timeout mechanism. For every execution E of $\mathcal{AL}$, all the configurations of E are distinct. Hence, for every $t > 0$, the size of at least one of the first t configurations in E is at least $\lceil \log_2(t) \rceil$.

Proof   Assume by way of contradiction that there exists an execution E of $\mathcal{AL}$ in which not all the configurations are distinct; then E contains a circular sub-execution $\overline{E}$. By lemma 4.5, there exists an infinite execution E' of $\mathcal{AL}$ that is obtained by an infinite repetition of executions from $blowup(\overline{E})$ and that never reaches a safe configuration — a contradiction. ∎

The implication of the above result is that no token-passing or stop-and-wait data-link algorithm exists with bounded memory resources. The memory of at least one of the system components must grow, either the memory of a processor or the number of bits in a message queue. In the next section we propose ways to cope in practice with the implications of the lower bound.

Bounded-Link and Randomized Solutions

It is customarily assumed that a sixty-four-bit counter can implement an unbounded counter for every possible application. The time it takes to reach the largest possible value of this sixty-four-bit counter is enormous. However, in the context of self-stabilizing algorithms, a single transient fault may cause the counter to reach its upper limit instantly.

In light of the lower bound above, it is impossible to devise a self-stabilizing bounded solution for the token-passing task in a completely asynchronous system, where the number of messages in transit is not bounded. In this section we relax the assumptions on asynchronous systems to obtain a bounded self-stabilizing algorithm for the token-passing task TP. For our first algorithm, we assume that a bound on the number of messages in transit is known.

Let *cap* be the bound on the total number of messages in both directions. Interestingly, a bounded version of the algorithm presented in figure 4.1, in

```
Sender:
01      upon timeout
02          send (label)
03      upon message arrival
04      begin
05          receive(MsgLabel)
06          if MsgLabel = label then
                (* token arrives *)
07              begin (* send new token *)
08                  label := ChooseLabel(MsgLabel)
09                  send(label)
10              end
11          else send(label)
12      end
Receiver:
13      upon message arrival
14      begin
15          receive(MsgLabel)
16          if MsgLabel ≠ label then
                (* token arrives *)
17                  label := MsgLabel
18          send(label)
19      end
```

Figure 4.2
Randomized token-passing with bounded sequence numbers

which the counter of the sender is incremented modulo $cap + 1$, is self-stabilizing. Roughly speaking, the reason is that the sender must eventually introduce a counter value not existing in any message in transit.

The second self-stabilizing bounded algorithm that we propose here does not assume any bound on the number of messages in transit. In this algorithm, the sender tosses a coin to decide on the label of messages, and hence the algorithm is randomized. A randomized algorithm requires an additional (hardware) device with random output. Moreover, the stabilization to a safe configuration is with *probability* 1. Thus, there can exist executions E of any finite length such that no safe configuration is reached in E. The code of the algorithm appears in figure 4.2. At least three labels are used, $\{0, 1, 2\}$. The sender repeatedly sends a message with a particular label l until a message with the same label l arrives. Then the sender chooses randomly (by invoking the procedure *ChooseLabel*) the next label $l' \neq l$ from the remaining labels. The program of the receiver is the same as in the unbounded algorithm.

Now we present the main ideas for proving the self-stabilization property of the algorithm in figure 4.2 (similar ideas were presented in section 2.10

for proving that the alternating-bit algorithm is pseudo self-stabilizing). In configuration c, let $\mathcal{L}_{sr}(c) = l_1, l_2, l_3, \cdots, l_k$ be the sequence of the labels of the messages that are pending from the sender to the receiver, and let $\mathcal{L}_{rs}(c) = l_{k+1}, l_{k+2}, l_{k+3}, \cdots, l_{k+q}$ be the sequence of the labels of the messages that are pending from the receiver to the sender. The label l_1 (l_{k+1}) is the label of the last message sent by the sender (receiver, respectively) and the label l_k (l_{k+q}) is the label of the message that is the first to arrive at the receiver (sender, respectively). Let $\mathcal{L}(c) = l_1, l_2, \cdots, l_k, l_{k+1}, l_{k+2}, \cdots, l_{k+q}$ be the concatenation of $\mathcal{L}_{sr}(c)$ with $\mathcal{L}_{rs}(c)$.

A segment of labels $\mathcal{S}(c) = l_j, l_{j+1}, \cdots, l_{j+n}$ in $\mathcal{L}(c)$ is a maximal sequence of labels in $\mathcal{L}(c)$ such that all the labels in $\mathcal{S}(c)$ are identical. Let $SegmentsNumber(\mathcal{L}(c))$ be the number of segments in $\mathcal{L}(c)$.

We use the term *pseudo-stabilized configuration* for every configuration c in which the value of *MsgLabel* of the next (pending) message m_{k+q} to arrive to the sender is equal to the label variable of the sender in c. Note that a pseudo-stabilized configuration c is a safe configuration when $SegmentsNumber(\mathcal{L}(c))=1$. Let c_1 and c_2 be two successive pseudo-stabilized configurations in an arbitrary execution. We claim that $SegmentsNumber(\mathcal{L}(c_1))$ $\geq SegmentsNumber(\mathcal{L}(c_2))$. Moreover, if the number of segments in c_1 is greater than one, then, with probability $1/2$, the number of segments in c_2 is less than the number of segments in c_1.

Starting in c_1, when the sender receives m_{k+q}, the sender chooses a new label — say 2 — that is not equal to the label of m_{k+q}, say $l_{k+q} = 0$. It is easy to see that the segment S to which m_{k+q} belonged is eliminated before the next pseudo-stabilized configuration is reached. At the same time, a new segment with label 2 is introduced as the prefix of $\mathcal{L}$. Moreover, if the label of the segment S' that follows S is 1, S' is eliminated as well. In this latter case the number of segments is reduced. The schedule-luck game technique can be used to prove that the system reaches a safe configuration. Luck always chooses a label that is different from the label of the segment S'. The combined probability of luck's strategy is no more than $2^{-(2 \cdot sn)}$, where $sn = SegmentsNumber(\mathcal{L}(c))$. Luck's strategy ensures that the number of segments is reduced by a factor of two in an execution that starts in c and ends in c', where c' immediately follows a step in which the sender receives an acknowledgment for the first message it sent during the execution. The same holds for the execution that starts in c'. Thus, the number of choices until a safe configuration is reached is $sn + sn/2 + sn/4 + \cdots = 2 \cdot sn$. The number of rounds in the game is $O((k+q) \cdot \log(k+q))$, where $k+q$ is the number of messages in the first configuration c. Thus, a safe configuration is reached within at most $O((k + q) \cdot \log(k + q) \cdot 2^{2 \cdot sn})$ expected number of rounds. We note that the expected number of rounds until a safe configuration is reached can be reduced when the number of labels used is greater than 3.

Self-Stabilizing Simulation of Shared Memory

In this section we present a method for simulating self-stabilizing, shared memory algorithms by self-stabilizing, message passing algorithms. The simulated algorithms are assumed to be in the link-register model in which communication between neighbors P_i and P_j is carried out using a two-way link. The link is implemented by two shared registers that support read and write atomic operations. Processor P_i reads from one register and writes in the other, while these functions are reversed for P_j. In the system that simulates the shared memory, every link is simulated by two directed links: one from P_i to P_j and the other from P_j to P_i. The heart of the simulation is a self-stabilizing implementation of the read and write operations.

The proposed simulation implements these operations by using a self-stabilizing, token-passing algorithm. The token-passing algorithm may be chosen from the algorithms described in the previous section. For any pair of neighbors, we run the algorithm on the two links connecting them. In order to implement our self-stabilizing, token-passing algorithm, we need to define, for each link, which of the processors acts as the sender and which acts as the receiver.

We assume that the processors have distinct identifiers. Every message sent by each of the processors carries the identifier of that processor. Eventually each processor knows the identifier of all its neighbors. In each link, the processor with the larger identifier acts as the sender while the other processor acts as the receiver. Since each pair of neighbors uses a different instance of the algorithm, a separate timeout mechanism is needed for each such pair.

We now describe the simulation of some arbitrary link e connecting P_i and P_j. In the shared memory model, e is implemented by a register r_{ij} into which P_i writes and from which P_j reads, and by a register r_{ji} for which the roles are reversed. In the simulating algorithm, processor P_i (P_j) has a local variable called R_{ij} (R_{ji}) that holds the values of r_{ij} (r_{ji}, respectively). Every token has an additional field called *value*. Every time P_i receives a token from P_j, P_i writes the current value of R_{ij} in the *value* field of that token. A write operation of P_i into r_{ij} is simply implemented by locally writing into R_{ij}. A read operation of P_i from r_{ji} is implemented by the following steps:

1. P_i receives the token from P_j, and then

2. P_i receives the token again from P_j. The value the read operation returns is the *value* attached to the token (when it arrives at this second time).

Note that, during the simulation of a read operation from r_{ji}, P_i does not proceed in its program until the simulated read step is finished. However, P_i continues to send messages (and tokens) to each of its neighbors that serve any read requests.

The correctness of the simulation is proved by showing that every execution E has a suffix in which it is possible to *linearize* all the simulated read and write operations executed in E. Operations in an execution can be linearized if there is a total order of all the simulated operations in which the execution order of the simulated operations of every individual processor is preserved and the result of every read operation from a register r is the last value (according to the total order) written in r, if such a write exists, or a constant value x otherwise. We consider x to be the value of r prior to the first write operation.

Any execution of a simulated read operation by a processor P_i starts in some particular configuration c_r and ends in a later configuration c_{r+k} for some k. P_i does not proceed in executing steps of the simulated program until c_{r+k} is reached; in particular, P_i does not change the value of any $R_{i,l}$ between c_r and c_{r+k}. Therefore, without influencing the operations of the other processors, we can choose any index between r and $r + k$ as the index of the step in which the simulated read operation of P_i occurs. Our simulation method, and in particular the requirement to wait for the second token, guarantees that the result obtained by the simulated read operation is a value of R_{ji} between c_r and c_{r+k}.

The above observations are used to map a time index for each simulated read and write operation. Define the time index of a simulated write operation to r_{ij} to be the index of the step in E in which the corresponding local write operation to R_{ij} is executed. Define the time index of a simulated read operation of P_j from r_{ij} to be the index of the step in E in which P_i sends the value of its local variable R_{ij} attached to the token that later reaches P_j in step (2) of the simulated read.

Once each link holds a single token, all the operations to a register R_{ij} are linearized to be executed in the step with the mapped index, where each read operation from R_{ij} returns the last value written to R_{ij}.

4.3 Self-Stabilizing Ranking: Converting an Id-based System to a Special-processor System

In this section we consider the following conversion: A given self-stabilizing algorithm for a system in which each processor has a unique identifier is converted to work in a system in which all the processors are identical except a single special processor. To do this, we design a self-stabilizing algorithm that assigns unique identifiers to the processors. The *ranking* task is to assign each of the n processors in the system with a unique identifier in the range 1 to n.

The self-stabilizing spanning-tree construction of section 2.5 is composed with a self-stabilizing counting algorithm and a self-stabilizing naming algorithm to form the self-stabilizing ranking algorithm.

The self-stabilizing counting algorithm assumes a rooted spanning tree system in which every processor knows its parent and children in the tree. Each processor P_i has a variable $count_i$ whose value is written by P_i in the communication register that is shared with the parent of P_i in the tree. The self-stabilizing counting algorithm reaches a safe configuration in which the value of $count_i$ is the number of processors in the subtree rooted at P_i including P_i itself. The algorithm appears in figure 4.3. A processor P_i with no children repeatedly assigns 1 to $count_i$. Let the *height* of a processor P_i in a rooted tree be the length of the longest path from P_i to a leaf such that the path does not include the root. Once the value of the *count* variables of all the leaves is 1, we consider processors P_j of height 1. Clearly, when P_j finishes executing a complete iteration of the do forever loop, P_j assigns $count_j$ by the correct number of processors in its subtree. The correctness proof continues by induction on the height of a processor.

The self-stabilizing counting algorithm is an example of the *self-stabilizing convergecast technique*. Intuitively, the *self-stabilizing convergecast* technique is based on the fact that the correct information is repeatedly communicated from the leaves of the tree toward the root.

The naming algorithm uses the value of the *count* fields to assign unique identifiers to the processors. The code for the naming algorithm appears in figure 4.4. The identifier of a processor is stored in the ID_i variable. A processor that executes the do loop of lines 4 through 8 or lines 14 through 18 executes one iteration of the loop for each processor in $children(i)$. The order of the iteration is arbitrary but fixed, say according to the internal labels of the links attached to P_i.

```
01 Root:  do forever
02              sum := 0
03              forall P_j ∈ children(i) do
04                  lr_ji := read (r_ji)
05                  sum := sum + lr_ji.count
06              od
07              count_i := sum + 1
08        od
09 Other: do forever
10              sum := 0
11              forall P_j ∈ children(i) do
12                  lr_ji := read (r_ji)
13                  sum := sum + lr_ji.count
14              od
15              count_i := sum + 1
16              write r_{i, parent}.count := count_i
17        od
```

Figure 4.3
Self-stabilizing counting

```
01 Root:  do forever
02              ID_i := 1
03              sum := 0
04              forall P_j ∈ children(i) do
05                  lr_ji := read (r_ji)
06                  write r_ij.identifier := ID_i + 1 + sum
07                  sum := sum + lr_ji.count
08              od
09        od
10 Other: do forever
11              sum := 0
12              lr_{parent,i} := read (r_{parent,i})
13              ID_i := lr_{parent,i}.identifier
14              forall P_j ∈ children(i) do
15                  lr_ji := read (r_ji)
16                  write r_ij.identifier := ID_i + 1 + sum
17                  sum := sum + lr_ji.count
18              od
19        od
```

Figure 4.4
Self-stabilizing naming

The proof of the stabilization of the naming algorithm (given a safe configuration of the counting algorithm) is by induction on the distance of the processors from the root. The induction starts with the single processor that is

```
01 do forever
02     forall P_j ∈ N(i) do lr_ji := read (r_ji)
03     sum_i := 0
04     forall P_j ∈ N(i) do
05         sum_j := 0
06         forall P_k ∈ N(i) do
07             if P_j ≠ P_k then
08                 sum_j := sum_j + lr_ki .count
09         od
10         count_i[j] := sum_j + 1
11         sum_i := sum_i + sum_j
12         write r_ij .count := count_i[j]
13     od
14     count_i := sum_i + 1
15 od
```

Figure 4.5
Self-stabilizing counting in non-rooted tree

at distance 0 from the root and continues with processors that are at a larger distance. The details are left as an exercise to the reader.

Before continuing to the next conversion method, we present an elegant self-stabilizing counting algorithm for a *non-rooted tree T*. Every processor in such a system knows which of its attached links belong to the tree T. Each processor P_i has a variable $count_i[j]$ for every neighbor P_j. In a safe configuration, the value of every $count_i[j]$ is the number of processors in a subtree of T that is obtained by removing the edge between P_i and P_j. Each such removal of an edge splits the tree into two subtrees; P_i belongs to one such subtree and P_j to the other. The value $count_i[j]$ is related to the number of processors in the subtree to which P_i belongs. The code of the algorithm appears in figure 4.5. Let the *height* of a communication register r_{ij} be the depth of the tree rooted at P_i upon removing the edge between P_i and P_j, where the depth of a rooted tree is the maximal number of edges from the root to a leaf. The correctness proof is by induction on the height of the registers. In the first cycle of every fair execution, the $r_{ij}.count$ field of every register of height 0 (a register of a leaf) is assigned the value 1 by P_i. Clearly, every further assignment of the leaf processor P_i in $r_{ij}.count$ does not change the value of $r_{ij}.count$. Now observe that the value of every register of height 2 is computed using only values of registers of height 1. In general, the value of every register of height h is computed using the values of registers of smaller height. The height of the registers is bounded by the diameter of the system d; hence, it holds that a safe configuration is reached within $O(d)$ cycles. The counting algorithm can be used to elect a leader (or two leaders if symmetry cannot be broken) in the tree and assign unique identifiers to the processors (assuming that the symmetry in the two leaders case can be broken).

4.4   Update: Converting a Special Processor to an Id-based Dynamic System

In this section we present a self-stabilizing algorithm for the update task. The task of the most basic form of the update algorithm is to inform each processor of the identifiers of the processors that are in its *connected component*. Processors that can communicate directly or indirectly are in the same connected component. Therefore, every processor knows the maximal identifier in the system and a single leader is in fact elected. The self-stabilizing algorithm for the leader-election task given in section 2.9 can be used to convert self-stabilizing algorithms that are designed for systems with a unique leader to id-based systems.

The leader-election algorithm presented in section 2.9 stabilizes in $O(N)$ cycles, where N is an upper bound on the number of processors in the entire system. This is a drawback in dynamic systems where link and processor failures can partition the system into several connected components, each with a small number of processors. A question to ask at this stage is whether there is a leader-election algorithm that stabilizes within $O(d)$ cycles, where d is the actual diameter of the connected component. The self-stabilizing update algorithm that is presented here gives a positive answer to the above question.

Before describing the update algorithm, let us gain some intuition about the importance of a special processor in many self-stabilizing systems. Dijkstra presented the first self-stabilizing mutual-exclusion algorithm for a ring of processors in which all processors are identical except a single special processor. Dijkstra proved that, without this special processor, it is impossible to achieve mutual exclusion in a self-stabilizing manner. In distributed systems, it is difficult to guarantee that a special processor will always exist. Moreover, the assumption that such a special processor exists contradicts the distributive nature of the system. Active paths of research were triggered by this impossibility result. Self-stabilizing randomized leader election algorithms can be used to ensure that a single special processor, namely the elected leader, acts as the special processor. Other self-stabilizing distributed algorithms, such as the update algorithm presented in this section, assume that each processor has a unique identifier. Unique identifiers exist in several distributed systems, for instance in the widespread Ethernet local communication network.

Dijkstra's proof is for a composite (non-prime) number of processors connected in a ring and activated by the central daemon. Recall that the central daemon activates a single processor at a time and that the activated processor then reads the state of its neighbors and changes its state accordingly. A processor P_i can execute the critical section in a configuration c if, and only if, P_i changes its state when it is the first processor to be activated by the central daemon following c. Therefore, every fair execution of a self-stabilizing mutual-exclusion algorithm must have a suffix in which exactly one processor may change a state in every configuration.

To demonstrate the technique for proving the impossibility result, we consider a special case in which the system is an oriented ring of four processors. Let P_1, P_2, P_3, P_4 be the processors in the ring, where P_i is connected to P_{i+1} for every $1 \leq i \leq 3$ and P_4 is connected to P_1. The ring is oriented so that P_1 is the left neighbor of P_2, P_2 is the left neighbor of P_3, P_3 is the left neighbor of P_4, and P_4 is the left neighbor of P_1. A processor P_j is the right neighbor of a processor P_i if P_j is connected to P_i and P_j is not the left neighbor of P_i.

The proof considers executions that start in a symmetric configuration c in which P_1 and P_3 are in the same state s_0 and P_2 and P_4 are in the same state s_0'. We show that there is an execution in which symmetry (between P_1 and P_3, and between P_2 and P_4) is never broken. The specific execution in which symmetry is preserved is the execution in which the processors repeatedly execute steps in the following order: P_1, P_3, P_2, P_4. Since there is no special processor, all the processors have the same transition function, denoted $f(s_l, s, s_r)$. The transition function $f(s_l, s, s_r)$ of a processor P_i is a function of s_l, the state of the processor to the left of P_i, s, the state of P_i, and s_r, the state of the processor to the right of P_i.

In our execution, P_1 is the first activated processor following c, changing state according to f and the state $s_l = s_0'$ of P_4, state $s = s_0$ of P_1, and state $s_r = s_0'$ of P_2. Denote the new state of P_1 by $s_1 = f(s_0', s_0, s_0')$. The second activated processor is P_3, which changes state according to the states $s_l = s_0'$ of P_2, $s = s_0$ of P_3 and $s_r = s_0'$ of P_4; therefore, P_3 changes its state to $s_1 = f(s_0', s_0, s_0')$. Similarly, P_2 is activated next and changes state to $s_1' = f(s_1, s_0', s_1)$, and so does P_4. Thus, in the configuration c_4 that follows the first activation of all the processors, P_1 and P_3 are in state s_1, while P_2 and P_4 are in state s_1'.

The proof is almost completed since, in the above execution, whenever P_1 may change a state from s_m to s_{m+1}, P_3 may also change its state from s_m to s_{m+1}. Analogously, the above holds for P_2 and P_4. Thus, in every configuration in which P_1 has permission to execute the critical section, P_3 has permission as well; and in every configuration in which P_2 may execute the critical section, P_4 may execute the critical section as well.

Note that when no central daemon exists, the impossibility result for the existence of a self-stabilizing mutual exclusion algorithm in a system of identical processors holds also for a ring of a prime number of processors. When we start in a configuration c_0 in which all the processors are in the same state — say s_0 — and the contents of the communication registers are identical, symmetry can be preserved forever. An execution that preserves symmetry is one in which every processor reads the communication registers of its neighbors before any processor writes a new value to its communication registers. Such a schedule guarantees that configurations in which all the states of the processors and the contents of registers are identical are reached infinitely often. Moreover, in the particular execution that we chose, each processor reads and writes the same values from/to the communication registers. Therefore, if a processor P_i enters the critical section following a particular read or write operation, so does every processor that executes the same operation just before or just after P_i. Thus, there is no suffix of the execution in which, in every configuration, only one processor is in the critical section.

It is good practice to design an algorithm that is as general as possible; such an algorithm will fit a large class of systems. The impossibility results above motivate the restriction we make when designing the update algorithm: that each processor has a unique identifier.

In a distributed system, processors and communication links can fail and recover repeatedly. At any given time, a processor is connected directly or indirectly to a set of processors. Processors that can communicate directly or indirectly are in the same *connected component*. The update algorithm gathers information in a processor P_i from all the processors in P_i's connected component.

We define the task *UP* to be the set of executions in which every processor has a set of identifiers consisting of an identifier for every processor in its connected component. Our update algorithm constructs n directed *BFS* trees. For every processor P_i, the algorithm constructs a directed *BFS* tree rooted at P_i. Roughly speaking, each *BFS* tree is a copy of the algorithm in section 2.5.

The update algorithm constructs the *first BFS tree* that is rooted at each processor: a graph may have more than a single *BFS* tree rooted at the same node. We define the *first BFS tree* of G relative to P_i to be a *BFS* tree rooted at P_i. When a node P_j of distance $k + 1$ from P_i has more than one neighbor at distance k from P_i, P_j is connected to the neighbor with the maximal identifier among all its neighbors whose distance from P_i is k (other conventions such as the *last BFS tree* could be used as well, as long as the *BFS* tree is fixed).

Denote the upper bound on the number of processors in the system by N. During the execution of the algorithm, each processor P_i maintains a set $Processors_i$ of no more than N tuples $\langle id, dis \rangle$. Each tuple in $Processors_i$ represents a processor in the system, where id is the identifier of the processor and dis is the distance (i.e., the number of edges) from P_i to the processor with the identifier id. The value of the id and the dis fields is in the range 0 to N. P_i communicates with any of its neighbors $P_j \in N(i)$ by writing (or sending) the value of $Processors_i$ and reading (or receiving, if message passing is used for communication) the value of $Processors_j$. In what follows, we describe the case when the processors communicate using shared memory. However, the same algorithm can be applied to message passing when each message arriving from P_i to P_j is written in an input buffer r_{ij} of P_j.

Let $n \leq N$ be the number of the processors in the system. After the system stabilizes, it holds that $Processors_i$ contains n tuples — a tuple $\langle j, x \rangle$ for every processor P_j in the system — such that P_j is at distance x from P_i.

A processor P_i repeatedly reads the set $Processor_j$ of every neighbor P_j and assigns $Processors_i$ by a set of tuples according to the sets P_i reads. The tuples P_i reads from its δ neighbors are stored in an internal set, $ReadSet_i$, of no more than δN $\langle id, dis \rangle$ tuples.

The code of the algorithm appears in figure 4.6. P_i repeatedly executes lines 2 through 10 of the code. P_i initializes $ReadSet_i$ in line 2, and then P_i accumulates the tuples in the sets of its neighbors into $ReadSet_i$ (lines 3 and 4). Note that the current contents of $Processors_i$ are not used for computing the new contents of $Processors_i$. The distance of P_i to a processor $P_j \neq P_i$ is the distance of a processor P_k to P_j, where P_k is next to P_i, plus one; obviously, the distance of P_i from itself is 0. In line 5, P_i removes every tuple with an identifier field that is equal to the identifier of P_i, and then P_i increments by 1 the distance of every remaining tuple (line 6). The semantics of the operators $\backslash\backslash$ and $++$ are implied in a straightforward manner by the above description. Next, P_i adds the tuple $\langle i, 0 \rangle$ to $ReadSet_i$. In computing the distance from P_i to P_j, P_i believes a neighbor P_k that is closest to P_j. In lines 8 and 9, for every

```
01 do forever
02      ReadSet_i := ∅
03      forall P_j ∈ N(i) do
04          ReadSet_i := ReadSet_i ∪ read(Processors_j)
05      ReadSet_i := ReadSet_i \\ ⟨i, *⟩
06      ReadSet_i := ReadSet_i + +⟨*, 1⟩
07      ReadSet_i := ReadSet_i ∪ {⟨i, 0⟩}
08      forall P_j ∈ processors(ReadSet_i) do
09          ReadSet_i := ReadSet_i \\ NotMinDist(P_j, ReadSet_i)
10      write Processors_i := ConPrefix(ReadSet_i)
11 od
```

Figure 4.6
Update algorithm for processor P_i

processor P_j, P_i removes each tuple with the identifier of P_j except for the tuple with the smallest distance among these tuples.

An important issue in the design of the self-stabilizing update algorithm is how the algorithm rapidly eliminates floating tuples; a *floating tuple* is a tuple with an identifier of a processor that does not exist in the system. The operation *ConPrefix(ReadSet_i)* is the core technique used to eliminate floating tuples. Let y be the minimal missing distance value in $ReadSet_i$. $ConPrefix(ReadSet_i)$ eliminates every tuple with a distance greater than y in $ReadSet_i$. Intuitively, *ConPrefix* eliminates tuples of processors that cannot be reached via a closer processor. Note that, in line 10, P_i assigns to $Processors_i$, which may contain no more than N tuples, a subset of $ReadSet_i$, which may contain δN tuples. When the number of tuples assigned to $Processors_i$ in line 10 is greater than N, P_i chooses N tuples with the smallest distances among the tuples in $ReadSet_i$.

To prove the correctness of the algorithm, we define a *safe configuration*. A configuration is *safe* if, for every processor P_i, it holds that:

• *Processors_i* includes n tuples, a tuple $⟨j, y⟩$ for every processor P_j in the system, where y is the distance of P_j from P_i, and

• the tuples that are included in $ReadSet_i$ will cause P_i to rewrite exactly the same contents to $Processors_i$.

According to our definition, in a safe configuration, every processor P_i knows the set of processors in the system and the distance from each such processor. In addition, each tuple read by P_i does not conflict with the knowledge of P_i. Therefore, in an execution that starts with a safe configuration, the value of $Processors_i$ is the same in every configuration.

Recall that, in every asynchronous cycle of an execution E, each processor executes at least one complete iteration of its do forever loop.

LEMMA 4.6:   In every arbitrary execution following the kth cycle, it holds for all processors P_i and P_j that are at distance $l < min(k, d + 1)$ that (1) a tuple $\langle j, l \rangle$ appears in $Processors_i$, and (2) if a tuple $\langle x, y \rangle$, such that $y \leq l$ appears in $Processors_i$, then there exists a processor P_x at distance y from P_i.

Proof The proof is by induction on k, the number of cycles in the execution.

Base case: (Proof for $k = 1$) During the first cycle, each processor executes line 7 of the code, adding the tuple $\langle i, 0 \rangle$ to $ReadSet_i$. By the increment operation of line 6 of the code, the distance of every tuple that is different from $\langle i, 0 \rangle$ in $ReadSet_i$ is greater than 0; therefore the tuple $\langle i, 0 \rangle$ is not eliminated in lines 8, 9 and 10. Thus, in the last write of P_i to $Processors_i$ during the first cycle, the tuple $\langle i, 0 \rangle$ is written in $Processors_i$. Moreover, each further write operation follows the execution of lines 5 through 9 and therefore results in writing the tuple $\langle i, 0 \rangle$ to $Processors_i$. The above completes the proof of assertion (1) of the lemma. To prove assertion (2), we note that the distance field of every tuple is positive. Therefore, once the increment of line 6 is executed, no tuple of distance 0, except for $\langle i, 0 \rangle$, is written in $Processors_i$.

Induction Step: We assume that, following the first k cycles of the execution, assertions (1) and (2) hold for $l < min(k, d + 1)$. We prove that, after one additional cycle, assertions (1) and (2) hold for $l < min(k + 1, d + 1)$.

By the induction assumption, following the first k cycles of the execution, each tuple of distance $l < min(k, d + 1)$ that should appear in $Processors_i$ does indeed appear there. Moreover, no tuple with distance $l < min(k, d + 1)$ that should not appear in $Processors_i$ appears in $Processors_i$. In other words, the $Processors$ variables are correct up to distance $l - 1$.

In the $k + 1$ cycle, every processor reads the tuples of its neighbors — in particular, it reads all the correct tuples with distances up to $l - 1$. Therefore, every tuple of distance l that is computed during the $k + 1$ cycle is a correct tuple — indeed, a processor at distance l with the identifier of the tuple exists. Moreover, since every tuple of distance $l - 1$ appears following k cycles, no tuple of distance l is missing following the $k + 1$ cycle. ■

LEMMA 4.7:   In every arbitrary execution following $d + 2$ cycles, it holds for every tuple $\langle x, y \rangle$ in every $Processors_i$ variable that a processor x exists in the system.

Proof In accordance with lemma 4.6, it holds that, following $d + 1$ cycles, every tuple with distance d or less is not a floating tuple; therefore, if a floating tuple $\langle x, y \rangle$ (with a nonexistent identifier x) appears in a *Processors* variable, then $y > d$. During the cycle that follows the first $d + 1$ cycle, every processor that reads the tuple $\langle x, y \rangle$ increments y (line 6 of the code) to be greater than $d + 1$. The proof is complete, since no tuple of distance $d + 1$ exists, and therefore the operation in line 10 of the code removes every floating tuple.   ∎

COROLLARY 4.1:   In any execution, any configuration that follows the first $d + 3$ cycles is a safe configuration.

Proof In accordance with lemma 4.6, it holds that, in every configuration that follows the first $d + 1$ cycles, every tuple with distance d or less is not a floating tuple; and for every two processors P_i and P_j at distance $l \leq d$, a tuple $\langle j, l \rangle$ appears in $Processors_i$. In accordance with lemma 4.7, in every configuration that follows the first $d + 2$ cycles, no tuple of greater distance exists in the *Processors* variables. Therefore, during the $d + 3$ cycle, a safe configuration is reached immediately after every processor reads the tuples of its neighbors.   ∎

Self-Stabilizing Convergecast for Topology Update

We now show how the convergecast technique is composed with our update algorithm to yield a topology-update algorithm that stabilizes within $O(d)$ cycles. In the topology-update algorithm, the information that is convergecast is the local topology, i.e., the identity of the neighbors of each descendant. The local topology information may be collected through every tree or only through the tree of the processor with the maximal identifier, which we call the leader.

The convergecast mechanism assumes that every processor knows its parent and children in T, the *BFS* tree of the leader. Note that this assumption is valid after $O(d)$ cycles. The convergecast uses for every processor P_i a variable up_i in which P_i writes to its parent in T. When P_i is a leaf in T, P_i writes its own local topology in up_i. Otherwise P_i concatenates the values of the up_i variables of all its children in T and its own local topology, and writes the result in up_i. The stabilization of the convergecast mechanism is based on the correct information in the leaves and the direction in which information is collected, namely from the leaves toward the root of the tree.

Let the *height* of a processor P_i in a rooted tree be the length of the longest path from P_i to a leaf such that the path does not include the root. Obviously, following one cycle, the value of up_i of every leaf processor is fixed and consists of its local topology. Therefore, following the second cycle of the execution, every processor whose children are leaves has fixed and correct topology information about its subtree. Similarly, following h cycles, every processor of height $h - 1$ or less has the correct topology on its subtree.

Self-Stabilizing Broadcast for Topology Update

When the information concerning the topology is collected only on the tree of the leader, the convergecast results in correct data for the single leader. But, the rest of the processors do not know the topology. In order to inform every processor of the collected topology, we use a self-stabilizing *broadcast* mechanism. The broadcast uses for every processor P_i a variable $down_i$ in which P_i writes to its children. If P_i is the leader, then P_i repeatedly writes the value of up_i in $down_i$. Otherwise, P_i assigns the value of the $down$ variable of its parent to $down_i$. The stabilization of the broadcast mechanism is based on the fact that the (fixed) information that is broadcast is copied in a fixed direction from a parent to its children. Therefore, following the first cycle, after the root has the right information to broadcast, all of the root children have the correct information. Similarly, following the ith cycle, every processor within distance i from the root has the right information.

Adaptive Self-Stabilizing Algorithms

The update algorithm is one of the best examples of a *memory-adaptive*, *time-adaptive*, and *communication-adaptive* self-stabilizing algorithm. In dynamic systems, the parameters of the system, such as the diameter, the number of processors, and the number of bits required to store the largest identifier in the system, are not fixed. For example, a link failure can partition the system into two independent connected components. Each connected component should stabilize independently and achieve its task. A self-stabilizing algorithm is *time-adaptive* if the number of cycles necessary to converge to a safe configuration is proportional to the actual parameters of the system, such as the *actual* diameter or *actual* number of processors in the system. Hence, the self-stabilizing leader election algorithm of section 2.9, which stabilizes in $O(N)$ cycles, is not time-adaptive, while the self-stabilizing update algorithm is time-adaptive.

A self-stabilizing algorithm is *memory-adaptive* if the amount of memory used in the system after a safe configuration is reached is proportional to the *actual* parameters of the system, such as the *actual* diameter or the *actual* number of processors. In contrast, a self-stabilizing algorithm is not memory-adaptive if the amount of memory used by the algorithm is proportional to an upper bound on the parameters of the system.

Recall that a silent self-stabilizing algorithm (see section 2.9) is one for which the communication between processors is fixed. A silent self-stabilizing algorithm designed for shared memory systems guarantees that, once a safe configuration is reached, the contents of the registers are fixed. A silent self-stabilizing algorithm designed for message passing systems guarantees that the only communication between any two neighboring processors that communicate between themselves is a single message that is sent repeatedly. A silent self-stabilizing algorithm is *communication-adaptive* if the number of bits that are (repeatedly) communicated between neighbors is proportional to the *actual* parameters of the system.

The self-stabilizing update algorithm stabilizes within $O(d)$ cycles and therefore is time-adaptive. The update algorithm repeatedly writes and reads $O(n)$ tuples in the communication registers, and is therefore memory-adaptive and communication-adaptive.

4.5   Stabilizing Synchronizers: Converting Synchronous to Asynchronous Algorithms

Designing algorithms for asynchronous systems can be a sophisticated task. Every configuration can be extended to a set of executions that differ in the order in which applicable steps are scheduled. In contrast, when the system is synchronous, all the processors in the system change state simultaneously. Thus, a configuration uniquely defines the execution that follows it. The tasks of the *synchronizer* is to emulate distributively a synchronous execution in an asynchronous system. The output of the synchronizer can be used by a synchronous algorithm to invoke steps. Roughly speaking, the synchronizer outputs a signal to every processor to execute a step.

Before presenting self-stabilizing synchronizers, let us note that, in some cases, there are drawbacks to using synchronizers. The restriction of the execution of steps to be scheduled slows down the fastest processors to executing steps at the speed of the slowest processor. Intuitively, in a non-restricted asynchronous execution, the fast processors may make progress, thus helping the slow processors to execute the system's task.

Next we describe two self-stabilizing synchronizers, the α and β synchronizer. To demonstrate once again that the communication model does not influence the algorithmic concept of the solutions, we present the α synchronizer for a message passing system and the β synchronizer for the shared-communication-registers model.

In designing the α synchronizer, we use a self-stabilizing data-link algorithm like that presented in section 4.2. Once stabilized, it is guaranteed that every message sent by a processor is received. An acknowledgment mechanism is assumed such that a processor P_i, when it has sent a message m to P_j, receives an acknowledgment from P_j before sending a new message m'. The acknowledgment itself may carry information concerning the state of P_j between the time P_i starts sending the message and the arrival of the acknowledgment. In other words, every time a processor P_j sends an acknowledgment, the acknowledgment is augmented with the current value of variables of P_j.

Every processor P_i has an integer *phase$_i$* variable. The task of the α synchronizer is defined by a set of execution $\mathcal{AS}$ such that, in every execution in $\mathcal{AS}$, the values of the *phase* variables of each two neighboring processors differ by no more than 1, and the value of each *phase* variable is incremented infinitely often, where every increment is an increment by 1.

For ease of presentation, let us first assume that every processor has an unbounded *phase* variable.

Self-Stabilizing Unbounded α Synchronizer

The code for the unbounded version of the α synchronizer appears in figure 4.7. The send and receive operations in the code use a stabilized data-link algorithm on each link. Therefore, when a send operation to a neighbor P_j terminates, P_j indeed receives a message with *phase$_i$* and P_i receives the value of *phase$_j$* with the acknowledgment. The DLsend operation starts a send operation of the data-link algorithm on each link attached to P_i. The DLsend operation involves retransmission of frames with appropriate labels until an acknowledgment with the proper label is received. An acknowledgment received from a processor P_j includes the value of *phase$_j$*. While P_i is waiting for acknowledgment from all its neighbors (lines 3 to 10 of the code), P_i may receive messages with an acknowledgment and *phase* value (line 5 of the code) or messages with only

```
01 do forever
02     forall P_j ∈ N(i) do received_j := false
03     do
04         DLsend(phase_i) (* start send to all neighbors *)
05         upon DLreceive(ack_j ,phase_j)
06             received_j := true
07             phase_ji := phase_j
08         upon DLreceive(phase_j)
09             phase_ji := phase_j
10     until ∀ P_j ∈ N(i) received_j =true (* all send terminated *)
11     if ∀ P_j ∈ N(i) phase_i ≤ phase_ji then
12         phase_i := phase_i + 1
13 od
```

Figure 4.7
Self-stabilizing α synchronizer (unbounded version)

a *phase* value (line 8 of the code). In the latter case, the message received is originated by P_j in line 4 of P_j's code; P_i answers these messages by sending $(phase_i, ack)$ to P_j.

Can we convince ourselves that every execution reaches a safe configuration with relation to $\mathcal{AS}$? Starting in any configuration, we see that, by the self-stabilization property of the data-link algorithm, eventually a configuration c_a is reached in which the data-link algorithm executed on each link is stabilized. In addition, we choose c_a to be a configuration such that following c_a, for every processor P_i, every value that is received by P_i from a neighboring processor P_j and is not yet acknowledged is indeed currently sent by P_i.

Our first observation is that, from some configuration on, for all neighboring processors P_i and P_j, the values of $phase_i$ and $phase_j$ differ by no more than one. Then we show that the value of every phase variable is incremented infinitely often.

LEMMA 4.8:   In every fair execution, for every processor P_i and every neighbor P_j, it eventually holds in every configuration c that the value of $phase_i$ in c is at most the value of $phase_j$ in c plus one.

Proof Assume that the value of $phase_i$ is greater by two or more than the value of $phase_j$ in infinitely many configurations. Since the value of $phase_j$ cannot be decremented, one of the two following cases must hold:

Case 1: P_i increments the value of *phase*$_i$ infinitely often, and the value of *phase*$_i$ is greater by more than one than the value of *phase*$_j$ in infinitely many configurations; or

Case 2: from some configuration of the execution, P_i does not increment the value of *phase*$_i$ and P_j does not increment the value of *phase*$_j$ as well.

The self-stabilizing data-link algorithm, and the fact that the value of every phase variable is not decremented, ensures that eventually, whenever P_i increments the value of *phase*$_i$ by one (executing lines 11 and 12 of the code), it holds for every neighbor P_j that *phase*$_i$ $\leq$ *phase*$_j$. Therefore, case 1 above is impossible. Now consider case 2. If P_i does not increment the value of *phase*$_i$ from some configuration on (if the condition in line 11 does not hold forever), it must hold that a neighboring processor P_x exists with a smaller phase value. Moreover, from some configuration of the execution, P_x does not increment *phase*$_x$. The same argument holds for P_x and a neighboring processor P_y with *phase*$_y$ < *phase*$_x$. The contradiction is completed by using the above argument repeatedly until a processor P_z is reached such that P_z has no neighbor with a smaller *phase* variable. ∎

COROLLARY 4.2:   In every fair execution there exists a configuration after which the difference in the *phase* value of every two neighboring processors is no greater than one.

Proof In accordance with lemma 4.8, it eventually holds for every processor P_i that the value of *phase*$_i$ is not greater than *phase*$_j$ of every neighboring processor P_j. Lemma 4.8 holds for P_j as well. Therefore, there exists a configuration in which the maximal difference between *phase*$_i$ and *phase*$_j$ is one. ∎

To prove that the algorithm stabilizes, we need to show that the phase variable of every processor is incremented infinitely often. Clearly, by the conclusion of corollary 4.2, it is sufficient to show that at least one phase variable is incremented infinitely often.

LEMMA 4.9:   In every fair execution, a *phase* variable is incremented infinitely often.

Proof Assume that there exists a configuration c after which no processor increments its phase variable. Let P_i be a processor with the minimal phase variable in c. By the fairness of the execution, P_i must execute lines 2 through 12 of the code infinitely often, receiving the constant value of the phase variables of its neighbors and then incrementing the value of its phase variable by one (in line 12 of the code). ∎

Self-Stabilizing Bounded α Synchronizer

The bounded version of the α synchronizer increments the value of the phase variables modulo M, where M is any constant greater than n. When the system stabilizes, a processor P_i with phase value $M - 1$ increments its phase variable by 1 modulo M, assigning 0 to *phase*$_i$.

The code of the algorithm appears in figure 4.8. The DLsend and DLreceive operations are used just as the unbounded solution, as discussed above.

The technique for achieving a bounded α synchronizer is to assign all the phase variables to zero upon detecting that two phase variables of neighboring processors differ by more than one (where 0 and $M - 1$ are considered to differ by one). Essentially this is a *reset* technique that initializes the value of the phase variables. The reset technique ensures that processors resume operation from a configuration in which the value of all the phase variables is zero.

To implement such a reset, every processor P_i has a *reset*$_i$ variable. Whenever *reset*$_i$ is assigned to zero, it causes the neighboring processors to have a value not greater than 1 in their *reset* variables. The neighbors, in turn, ensure that their neighbors have a value not greater than 2 in their *reset* variables. In general, a processor P_j at distance l from P_i assigns the value l in *reset*$_j$ (if *reset*$_j > l$) because of the zero assignment in *reset*$_i$.

Informally, a reset wave propagates in the system, causing the processors to reduce the value of their *reset* variables. An important observation is that, while the reset wave propagates, no processor that has already reduced the *reset* variable can increment it beyond $2N$, where N is a bound on the number of processors.

To demonstrate the above property, consider a system in the form of a chain P_1, P_2, P_3, P_4, where $N \geq 4$ and P_i communicates with P_{i+1}, $1 \leq i \leq 3$. Further assume that P_1 assigns *reset*$_1 := 0$ (in line 26 of the code). P_1 sends the value of *reset*$_1$ to P_2 (in line 6) and continues only after receiving acknowledgment from P_1 (at this stage the data-link algorithm is stabilized). Thus, P_2 must receive (line 10 of the code) a message with *reset*$_1 = 0$ and execute the *UpdatePhase()* procedure. When *reset*$_2$ is greater than 0, P_2

```
01 do forever
02    forall P_j ∈ N(i) do received_j := false
03    PhaseUpdated := false
04    ResetUpdated := false
05    do
06       DLsend(phase_i, reset_i) (* start send to all neighbors *)
07       upon DLreceive(ack_j ,phase_j , reset_j )
08          received_j := true
09          UpdatePhase()
10       upon DLreceive(phase_j , reset_j )
11          UpdatePhase()
12    until ∀ P_j ∈ N(i) received_j =true (* all send terminated *)
13    if ResetUpdated = false then
14       if ∀ P_j ∈ N(i) reset_i ≤ reset_ji then reset_i := min(2N, reset_i + 1)
15       if  PhaseUpdated = false and
16          ∀ P_j ∈ N(i) phase_i ∈ {phase_ji,(phase_ji − 1) mod M} then
17          phase_i := (phase_i + 1) mod M
18 od

19 UpdatePhase()
20    phase_ji := phase_j
21    reset_ji := reset_j
22    if reset_i > reset_ji then
23       reset_i := min(2N, reset_ji + 1)
24       ResetUpdated := true
25    if phase_ji ∉ {(phase_i − 1) mod M, phase_i, (phase_i + 1) mod M} then
26       reset_i := 0
27       ResetUpdated := true
28    if reset_i ≠ 2N then
29       phase_i := 0
30       PhaseUpdated := true
```

Figure 4.8
Self-stabilizing α synchronizer (bounded version)

assigns $reset_2 := 1$ (line 23). Then, P_2 sends the value of $reset_2$ to P_3 (and P_1), ensuring that the clock value of P_3 is not greater than 2. At this stage the value of $reset_4$ is not yet influenced by the assignment of 0 in $reset_1$. Nevertheless, P_1 can assign $reset_1$ to 1 in line 14 of the code and then assign $reset_1$ to 2 (again in line 14 of the code; recall that the value of $reset_2$ is 1 at this stage). Now P_2 can assign $reset_2$ to 3 since both its neighbors have the value 2 in their reset variables. Thus, P_1 can increment its reset variable value to hold 4. In the configuration reached, $reset_1 = 4, reset_2 = 3, reset_3 = 2$ and the value of $reset_4$ is not yet determined by the send operation of $reset_3 = 2$ that P_3 has not yet finished. Clearly, P_2 must increment the value of $reset_3$ before P_1 can further increment the value of $reset_1$. The complete and detailed proof that no processor can increment the value of its *reset* variable beyond $2N$ when the propagation of the reset is not yet terminated follows from the above discussion.

A self-stabilizing data-link service is assumed where every message is sent repeatedly until it is received and acknowledged by the neighboring processors. A configuration c is a *safe data-link configuration* if the data-link algorithm executed on every link is in a safe configuration. In the sequel, we consider only execution that starts from safe data-link configurations.

LEMMA 4.10:   Every fair execution in which no processor P_i assigns 0 in *reset$_i$* has a suffix in which the value of the reset variable of every processor is $2N$ in each of its configurations.

Proof Let x be the minimal value of a *reset* variable in the first configuration of the execution. The minimal value of a *reset* variable in each of the following configurations is at least x. Moreover, following the first execution of lines 2 through 4 of the code, no processor P_i with *reset$_i$* $= x$ assigns *ResetUpdate* := true. Therefore, if $x < 2N$, then every processor with *reset$_i$* $= x$ increments the value of *reset$_i$* by 1. Hence, a configuration c in which the minimal value of a *reset* variable is $x + 1$ is reached. The same arguments can be applied to c, resulting in a configuration in which the minimal value of a *reset* variable is $x + 2$, and so on. ∎

LEMMA 4.11:   Every fair execution in which no processor P_i assigns 0 to *reset$_i$* reaches a safe configuration.

Proof Assume that there are two neighboring processors P_i and P_j such that *phase$_j$* $\neq$ (*phase$_i$* $- 1$) mod M, *phase$_j$* $\neq$ *phase$_i$*, and *phase$_j$* $\neq$ (*phase$_i$* $+ 1$) mod M in infinitely many configurations.

When the values of *phase$_j$* and *phase$_i$* are not changed during execution, then P_i assigns *reset$_i$* := *true* after the first time P_i receives the value of *phase$_j$* and executes the *UpdatePhase()* procedure. Otherwise, either P_i or P_j infinitely often assigns its phase variable to a *wrong value*: a value that is not one greater than, one less than, or equal to the value of the phase variable of the neighboring processor (where greater and less are evaluated modulo M).

By lemma 4.10, it holds that every fair execution in which no processor P_i assigns 0 to *reset$_i$* has a suffix in which *reset$_i$* $= 2N$ in each of its configurations. Thus, there exists a suffix of the execution E' in which:

(1) the value of $phase_i$ is not assigned to 0 in line 29 of the code, and

(2) in every configuration of E', the values of both the *ResetUpdated* and the *PhaseUpdated* variables are false.

Consider a suffix E'' of E' that follows the first time each processor executes the data-link send operation on every link and receives an acknowledgment from each of its neighbors. Without loss of generality, let P_i be the processor that assigns infinitely often a *wrong value* in $phase_i$ during E''. Clearly, by the condition of line 16 of the code, it must hold that P_j has changed the value of $phase_j$ between the last receive operation of $phase_j$ and the assignment of the *wrong value* by P_i. According to the definition of E'', the only possible change in the value of $phase_j$ is an increment by 1 modulo M (note that an additional increment by P_j requires an additional receive of the current value of $phase_i$). Thus the value of $phase_{ji}$ can either be equal to the value of $phase_j$ or one less (modulo M); in both cases, P_i does not assign a *wrong value* to $phase_i$. ∎

LEMMA 4.12: Every fair execution in which a processor P_i assigns 0 to $reset_i$ reaches a safe configuration.

Outline of proof: Consider an execution that starts with the assignment of 0 in $reset_i$, and consider the set of processors in every configuration that received a message with a *causal relationship* to the above assignment: every message sent by P_i following the assignment of 0 in $reset_i$ has a causal relationship to the assignment. In addition, every message sent by a processor that has already received a message that is causally related to P_i's assignment is also causally related to this assignment.

Following the assignment of 0 to $reset_i$, the value of *ResetUpdated* is assigned *true*, and therefore the value of $reset_i$ is not changed until the value of $reset_i$, namely 0, is acknowledged by every neighbor P_j of P_i. P_j acknowledges P_i only after verifying that $reset_j \leq 1$.

When P_j receives a $reset_i$ value that is less than $reset_j$, P_j assigns *ResetUpdated* := *true* (in line 24 of the code). Therefore, P_j does not increment the value of $reset_j$ before a send of $reset_j$ operation to every neighbor of P_j is completed.

The other possibility is that P_j receives a $reset_i$ value x that is equal to or greater than the value y of $reset_j$. In such a case (by lines 22 through 24 of the code), before the value of $reset_j$ is incremented to $x + 2$, P_j sends a value not greater than $x + 1$ to every neighbor P_k, causing $reset_k$ to have a value not greater than $x + 2$.

Thus, we conclude that, when the first causally related (to the assigment $reset_i := 0$) message arrives at a processor P_l, the $reset_l$ variable of P_l is assigned to a value not greater than $N - 1$, the maximal length of a path from P_i to P_l.

The next argument of the proof is the following easily verified property: any processor P_k that has already received a message causally related to P_i's assigment cannot increment the value of its $reset$ variable beyond $2N - 1$ while there exists a processor P_m that has not yet received a causally related message.

Therefore, a configuration is reached in which the value of all the reset variables is less than $2N$ and the value of all the phase variables is zero. No processor assigns $reset$ to zero thereafter. ■

Note that the bounded α synchronizer does not assume the existence of a unique identifier for the processors. Therefore, the α synchronizer can be used in uniform systems (as suggested in section 5.1).

To complete this section, we need to describe explicitly how to execute synchronous algorithms on an asynchronous system using the α synchronizer. A step of a processor in a synchronous algorithm starts by sending messages to all the neighbors; then it receives a message from every neighbor and finally last changes state accordingly. Note that a processor that executes a step of a synchronous algorithm does not necessarily communicate with all its neighbors in every pulse. Such a policy can reduce the amount of communication bandwidth used, i.e., fewer bits are transmitted through the communication chanals. Moreover, information can be "transmitted" from one neighbor to the other without sending messages: e.g., a processor can conclude that no leader exists if no messages are received in a period of at least k successive pulses, knowing that a leader must send a message every k pulses.

In the execution of the α synchronizer, however, every processor repeatedly sends messages to every of its neighbors just to implement a pulse signal at every processor. Thus, reducing the number of messages used by the synchronous algorithm is not an issue. To simplify our discussion, we assume that a null message, instead of no message, is sent by the synchronous algorithm.

The heart of the conversion is the simulation of the synchronous steps. To simplify our discussion further, let us modify the synchronous algorithm $\mathcal{AL}$ so that it sends its entire state to its neighbors. Note that the state of a processor P_i defines the messages P_i sent in $\mathcal{AL}$.

The synchronizer guarantees that eventually the values of the phase variables differ by at most one. A processor with phase number t must receive the states of its neighbors that are related to phase number t in order to compute its next state. To ensure that processors will be able to change states, every processor attaches its current state s_t and the previous state s_{t-1} to every message it sends in the execution of the α synchronizer.

Finally, just before a processor P_i increments its phase value by 1, it also computes a new state according to the states received from its neighbors and its current state. P_i uses s_{t-1} as the state of a neighbor with a phase value greater than its own, and uses s_t otherwise. Note that the greater-than relationship is well defined for $M \geq 3$.

Self-Stabilizing β Synchronizer

Another classical way to implement a synchronizer uses a rooted spanning tree of the communication graph. Recall that a rooted spanning-tree structure can be marked on an arbitrary connected communication network (of processors with unique identifiers) by the leader-election algorithm presented in section 2.9. Therefore, a self-stabilizing (synchronization) algorithm that assumes the existence of a rooted spanning tree can be composed with the leader election algorithm of section 2.9. The fair composition of these algorithms (using the technique presented in section 2.7) yields a self-stabilizing synchronizer for systems with an arbitrary communication graph.

The root repeatedly *colors* the tree. Each processor P_i has a $color_i$ internal variable that can contain a value in the range 0 to $5n - 2$ (in section 8.1, we show that a constant number of colors is, in fact, sufficient). Whenever the root P_r discovers that the subtrees rooted at its children are colored by its current color, it chooses a new color and communicates the new color to each of its children P_i by writing in $r_{ri}.color$. A processor P_i communicates its color to every one of its children P_j by writing in $r_{ij}.color$. Let P_{parent} be the parent of P_i in the tree; P_i repeatedly reads the value of $r_{parent,i}.color$ and assigns it to $color_i$. In other words, the color of a parent propagates to the processors in its subtree. In addition, P_i writes $r_{i,parent}.color := color_i$ whenever P_i discovers that the subtrees rooted at its children are colored by the color of its parent.

```
01 Root:  do forever
02              forall P_j ∈ children(i) do lr_ji :=  read (r_ji)
03              if ∀ P_j ∈ children(i)  (lr_ji.color = color_i) then
04                  color_i := (color_i + 1) mod (5n - 3)
05              forall P_j ∈ children(i) do write r_ij.color := color_i
06          od
07 Other: do forever
08              forall P_j ∈ {children(i) ∪ parent} do lr_ji :=  read (r_ji)
09              if color_i ≠ lr_parent,i.color then
10                  color_i := lr_parent,i.color
11              else if ∀P_j ∈ children(i) (lr_ji.color = color_i) then
12                  write r_i,parent.color := color_i
13              forall P_j ∈ children(i) do write r_ij.color := color_i
14          od
```

Figure 4.9
Self-stabilizing β synchronizer

The code of the algorithm appears in figure 4.9. The first observation we make is that the root changes its color infinitely often.

LEMMA 4.13:   In every fair execution, the root changes color at least once in every $2d + 1$ successive cycles.

Proof   Assume that, from some configuration of the execution, the root P_r does not change its color variable for $2d + 1$ cycles. Therefore, every processor P_j that is a child of P_r must copy the color of P_r during the first cycle of the execution.

Similarly, every child of P_j copies the color of P_j (which is equal to the color of P_r) during the second cycle of the execution.

Continuing in the same manner, we can conclude that, following d cycles, the color of every processor is equal to the color of P_r.

Thus, during the $d + 1$st cycle, each leaf P_l in the tree reports to its parent P_k that it has finished coloring its (empty) subtree with the color of the root. During the $d + 2$nd cycle, each processor P_k, all of whose children are leaves, reports that its subtree is colored with the color of the root.

Repeating the same arguments, we can conclude that each of the children of the root reports that its subtree is colored with the color of the root within the first $2d$ cycles. ∎

The next lemma uses the missing-label concept.

LEMMA 4.14: A configuration in which the color of all the processors is equal is reached within $O(dn)$ cycles.

Proof There are n internal color variables in the system, $2n - 2$ color fields in the communication registers, and $2n - 2$ internal variables that store a color value. Thus, the total number of distinct colors in any given configuration is no more than $5n - 4$. Therefore, at least one color value is missing in any configuration.

In accordance with lemma 4.13, the root changes its color at least once in every $2d + 1$ successive cycles. The root changes colors by incrementing its color by 1, modulo $5n - 3$. Hence, in every $(2d + 1)(5n - 3)$ successive cycles, the root must assign its color to a color value that does not exist in the system.

It is easy to check that, once the root assigns a nonexistent color value x, every processor P_i reports that its subtree is colored with x only when indeed every $color_j$, $r_{jk}.color$, and $lr_{jk}.color$ in its subtree is colored by x. Therefore, the entire tree is colored by x when the children of the root report to the root that their subtree is colored by x. ∎

To complete the description of the β synchronizer, we need to define how a synchronous step is executed. A synchronous step consists of reading the communication registers of the neighbors. Once every processor has finished reading, processors change state and write new values in their communication registers according to the value they read.

Note that the communication register fields used for executing the synchronous algorithm are different from the color fields used by the synchronizer.

To implement such a synchronous step, we let each processor read the communication registers of its neighbors when a new color propagates from the root to the leaves, and let each processor change the contents of the communication registers according to the synchronous step when the completion of subtree coloring is reported.

In more detail: just before each time a processor P_i changes its color, it reads the communication registers of its neighbors, as in the synchronous step. Just before each time a non-root processor P_i writes a color to its parent in the tree (reports the termination of the coloring process in its subtree), P_i writes new values to its communication registers, as in the second part of the synchronous step.

Similarly, the root processor writes new values to its communication registers when all its children have reported completion of coloring.

4.6 Self-Stabilizing Naming in Uniform Systems: Converting Id-based to Uniform Dynamic Systems

The self-stabilizing update algorithm presented in section 4.4 is designed to stabilize in an *id-based* system, in which every processor has a unique identifier. Assigning unique identifiers to processors in dynamic systems requires continuous bookkeeping to ensure that every processor joining the system has a nonexistent identifier, i.e., an identifier unique in the system. For instance, a manufacturer of Ethernet cards receives a range of identifiers to be used for the Ethernet cards it produces. A single authority is responsible for the identifier range distribution, and the manufacturer is responsible for using every identifier no more than once. In practice, the required global coordination and distribution of responsibility can lead (although in rare cases) to the assignment of a single identifier to more than one processor.

The above discussion motivates the following question: Can the tasks achieved in id-based systems also be achieved in a uniform (or anonymous) dynamic system? We already know that breaking symmetry is impossible when the processors are identical. For example, leader election in an id-based synchronous system of two processors is a trivial task. Yet no deterministic distributed algorithm exists for such a uniform system: the states of both processors are identical in every configuration of a synchronous execution that starts in a configuration in which both processors are in identical states. Fortunately, randomization can be used to break symmetry.

In this section, we present a randomized self-stabilizing leader-election and naming algorithm for dynamic systems. The algorithm stabilizes within an expected $O(d)$ cycles, where d is the actual diameter of the system. The design of the naming algorithm and its proof of correctness use several basic techniques. In particular, the core ideas of the update algorithm and the β synchronizer are an integral part of the final algorithm. The *sl-game* is used to prove the correctness of the algorithm. The way in which basic tools are integrated gives us an opportunity to demonstrate the design process of a complex, self-stabilizing, distributed algorithm. Thus, we choose to describe this algorithm differently by discussing the design decisions and process within the detailed description of the algorithm.

In a uniform system, the processors $P_1, P_2, \cdots, P_n$ are anonymous. The subscripts $1, 2, \cdots, n$ are used for ease of notation only. For simplicity of presentation, we assume that every processor P_i has a single communication register r_i in which P_i writes to its neighbors. Similarly to the self-stabilizing up-

date algorithm of section 4.4, the naming algorithm constructs a *BFS* spanning
tree rooted at each processor P_i in the system.

Informally, each tree is marked by a randomly chosen identifier. When several processors have an identical chosen identifier x, the algorithm constructs
a spanning forest of trees. Each tree of this forest is rooted at a processor with
identifier x. In order to detect the existence of other processors with the same
identifier, each processor repeatedly colors its tree with randomly chosen colors. Let T_1 and T_2 be two trees marked by the identifier x such that there exist
two neighboring processors P_i in T_1 and P_j in T_2. The repeated coloring technique ensures that P_i and P_j identify the existence of more than one processor
with identifier x. P_i notifies the root of its tree upon such an indication. A root
processor P_k that receives notification of the existence of another tree, rooted at
a processor with the same identifier, chooses a new identifier. A new spanning
tree is constructed with the new identifier. The tree is constructed during the
processes of propagating the new identifier and sending feedback to the root
on the termination of the tree construction. The root receives a list of identifiers together with the notification of the completion of the tree construction.
The root broadcasts all the identifiers that appear more than once in the list of
identifiers it received. A processor that recognizes its identifier in the list of
conflicting identifiers randomly chooses a new identifier.

A more detailed description follows. We first describe the data structure
and then the several techniques that are composed to form the final algorithm.

Denote the upper bound on the number of processors in the system by
N. Each processor P_i maintains a set *Processors$_i$* of at most N items, an
item for each (possible) processor in the system. In addition, P_i maintains
an array *Queue$_i$* of N^2 items. Every item in *Processors$_i$* and *Queue$_i$* is a
tuple $\langle tid, dis, f, color, ackclr, ot, ack, list, del \rangle$ of fields, where tid is an
identifier of a root of a tree and the range of tid is 0 to N^{10}. The rest of the
fields in the tuple are related to the tree rooted at a processor with an identifier
tid: the dis field is the distance of P_i from the root of this tree, the range of
dis being 0 to N, and f is a pointer to the parent of P_i in the tree, the range
of f being 0 to Δ, where Δ is an upper bound on the degree of a node in the
communication graph.

The *color* field is used to identify other trees with the same tid, and the
range we chose for the color is 0 to N^{10} (a much smaller range can also be used;
the range chosen does not increase the space complexity of the algorithm).
$ackclr$, ot and ack are boolean variables: $ackclr$ is used by P_i to acknowledge
to its parent that the color of the parent has been propagated to every processor

in the subtree rooted at P_i. The ot field is used to notify the parent of the existence of another tree with the same tid; ack is used to notify the parent of P_i of the termination of the propagation of its new identifier. Each of the *list* and *del* fields may contain up to N identifiers. The *list* field is used by P_i to report to its parent the identifier of the processors in its subtree, and the *del* field is used by P_i to notify its children in the tree of conflicting identifiers.

Next we present details of each technique separately and then of how they are integrated. First we describe the update technique, which is based on the update algorithm in section 4.4.

The Update Technique   Every processor P_i has a variable ID_i with its current chosen identifier. To compute the values of $Processors_i$ and $Queue_i$, P_i uses two internal variables $Processors_{ji}$ and $Queue_{ji}$ for each neighbor P_j. The program of P_i consists of reading the value of the $Processors_j$ and $Queue_j$ variables of every neighbor P_j, and writing new values for $Processors_i$ and $Queue_i$ accordingly. P_i repeatedly reads the value of $Processors_j$ into $Processors_{ji}$ and the value of $Queue_j$ into $Queue_{ji}$.

The algorithm uses the tid and dis fields similarly to the update algorithm. Let $ReadSet_i$ be the union of the tuples in the $Processors_{ji}$ variables read by P_i.

The value of the f field of every tuple in $Processors_{ji}$ (read from $Processors_j$) is set to j before it is included in $ReadSet_i$. The value of the dis field of every tuple in $ReadSet_i$ is incremented by 1, unless this value is N. P_i adds a tuple with $tid = ID_i$ and $dis = 0$ to the $ReadSet_i$ obtained.

For every $id = x$ that appears in a tuple in $ReadSet_i$, P_i removes every tuple with $id = x$ except for a single tuple t. The value of the dis field of t is the minimal dis value y among the tuples with $id = x$ in $ReadSet_i$. Moreover, if there is more than one tuple t with $id = x$ and $dis = y$ in $ReadSet_i$, P_i checks whether there exists a tuple t such that a tuple t' exists in $Processors_i$ or $Queue_i$ for which $id = x$ and the values of f in t and t' are equal. In such a case, t is chosen; otherwise, an arbitrary tuple with $id = x$ and $dis = y$ is chosen.

P_i sorts the remaining tuples in $ReadSet_i$ by the value of their dis field, where the first tuple is the tuple with $tid = ID_i$ and $dis = 0$. When there are more than N tuples left in $ReadSet_i$, P_i assigns the first N tuples to $Processors_i$ and the rest are enqueued in $Queue_i$.

Like the update algorithm in section 4.4, the above technique ensures that, when every processor has a unique identifier, a *BFS* tree rooted in each processor is constructed within $O(d)$ cycles. However, the value of ID_i chosen by a processor P_i is not necessarily different from the value of ID_j chosen by P_j. If more than one processor has the same $id = u$ value, then a spanning forest is constructed, with a tree rooted at each such processor. To overcome such a situation, a coloring technique based on the β synchronizer presented in section 4.5, is used.

The Coloring Technique In order to ensure that no two processors have the same chosen identifier, each processor repeatedly colors its tree with a randomly chosen color. The following description of the coloring technique is for a particular tree T with $tid = x$. Whenever a processor P_i reads that, for every processor P_j of P_i's children, $P_i.color = P_j.color$ and $P_j.ackclr = true$, P_i randomly chooses a new color (from the range 0 to N^{10}) and assigns it to $P_i.color$. Each non-root processor P_j in T repeatedly copies the color of its parent P_k in T by assigning the value P_j read from $P_k.color$ to $P_j.color$. If this assignment changes the value of $P_j.color$, P_j simultaneously assigns $P_j.ackclr := false$. In addition, whenever P_j reads that $P_k.color = P_j.color$ and for every processor P_l of P_j's children $P_j.color = P_l.color$ and $P_l.ackclr = true$, P_j assigns $P_j.ackclr := true$.

Since colors are chosen from a large range, it holds with very high probability that when a processor P_i chooses a new color this color does not appear in the tree. Therefore, P_i discovers that $P_j.color = P_i.color$ and $P_j.ackclr = true$ for any of its children P_j when indeed the subtree rooted at P_j is colored by $P_i.color$.

Whenever a processor P_j changes the value of $P_j.color$ from color y to color z, P_j checks whether it read a tuple from a neighboring processor with $tid = x$ and color different from y and z. In such a case, P_j concludes that more than a single root of a tree with $tid = x$ exists, and sets the value of ot field to true.

To gain some more understanding for the additional building blocks used by the naming algorithm, we present arguments based on the scheduler-luck technique described in section 2.9.

The Scheduler-Luck Game Luck's strategy in the scheduler-luck game is to intervene whenever a processor chooses a new identifier, and to choose an identifier that does not exist in the system. With this strategy, we can show that every processor selects a new identifier no more than once, and that the system reaches a safe configuration in an expected $O(d)$ cycles. Certainly, it is possible that during an execution of the algorithm the result of the random function will not be identical to luck's choice in the game — it may choose an identifier that already appears in the system configuration. In such a case, an arbitrary configuration is reached from which there is high probability that a new sequence of choosing n distinct identifiers is started.

Note that it is most important that, under luck's strategy, each processor selects an identifier no more than once. Otherwise, if a processor can repeatedly choose a new identifier, the probability of choosing an existent identifier will not be negligible. Thus, as long as each identifier selection selects a nonexistent identifier, the design of our algorithm does not allow more than one new selection of an identifier by each processor.

Let us examine whether any additional mechanisms are needed to prevent repeated identifier selection by a processor. A processor is triggered to choose a new identifier after reading an indication $ot_j = true$ from one of its children P_j. When a processor P_i chooses a new identifier, a tuple with $tid = ID_i$ and $dis = 0$ is repeatedly written in $Processors_i$. Each neighboring processor P_j reads the tuple with $tid = ID_i$ and $dis = 0$ from $Processors_i$ and includes a tuple with $tid = ID_i$ and $dis = 1$ in $Processors_j$. These actions start the construction of the spanning tree rooted in P_i that is identified by $tid = ID_i$. Still, tuples with the previous identifier of P_i may be present in $Processors$ variables. Thus, since the number of tuples in each $Processors$ variable is bounded, it is unclear whether every processor can include the new tuple in its $Processors$ variable. Roughly speaking, a processor that chooses a new identifier leaves floating tuples with small distances in the system. These tuples compete with entries of the $Processors$ variables. Thus, it is possible that part of the tree will be disconnected, not participating in the coloring process, and thus cause a false other-trees indication. To overcome such a scenario each processor maintains a queue.

The Queue When each processor chooses an identifier no more than once, the number of distinct identifiers present in the $Processors$ variables during the entire execution is no greater than $N + N^2$. Therefore, it is possible to use a queue of N^2 entries to ensure that, once a tuple with a specific identifier is included in $Processors_i$, a tuple with this identifier exists in either $Processors_i$ or $Queue_i$.

Whenever P_i computes a new value for $Processors_i$, it deletes every tuple t in $Queue_i$ such that there exists a tuple t' in $Processors_i$ and the tid fields in both t and t' are identical. In addition, P_i guarantees that there are no two tuples with an identical tid value in $Queue_i$. If two or more tuples with $tid = x$ exist in $Queue_i$, then P_i deletes all the tuples with $tid = x$ except the one with the smallest index in $Queue_i$. Let k be the index of a tuple t in $Queue_i$ that P_i deletes. P_i deletes t by assigning $Queue_i[l] := Queue_i[l + 1]$ for every $k \leq l < N^2$, starting by assigning a value to $Queue_i[k]$ and continuing with increasing values of l until $Queue_i[N^2 - 1]$ is assigned by $Queue_i[N^2]$. P_i then assigns $Queue_i[N^2].tid := 0$, indicating that there is no tuple in the N^2 index of $Queue_i$. Finally, P_i enqueues each tuple t that exists in the current $Processors_i$ but not in the computed new value of $Processors_i$. P_i enqueues a tuple t by assigning $Queue_i[l + 1] := Queue_i[l]$ for every $N^2 > l \geq 1$, starting by assigning a value in $Queue_i[N^2]$ and continuing with decreasing values of l until assigning $Queue_i[2] := Queue_i[1]$. P_i then assigns $Queue_i[1] := t$, and finally writes the computed values of both $Processors_i$ and $Queue_i$ in its communication register.

At this stage, we introduce several techniques ensuring that, once a new chosen identifier is included in $Processors_i$, it exists in either $Processors_i$ or $Queue_i$ (recall that, according to luck's strategy, each processor chooses no more than one identifier). The propagation of a chosen identifier is based on a fundamental technique called propagation of information with feedback.

Propagation of Information with Feedback The task of the algorithm for propagation of information with feedback is to send information stored in a particular processor P_i to all the processors in the system and to notify P_i of the completion of this information propagation. In our case, the information is the new identifier chosen by P_i, assuming that this identifier does not exist in the system. During feedback, the processors collect a list of the values in the ID variables of the processors. Our goal is to give P_i the above list $O(d)$ cycles after P_i chooses a new identifier x. Moreover, we would like to ensure that, once P_i receives feedback on the completion of the propagation, the parent-child relation (in the tree rooted at P_i) is unchanged. This last requirement ensures that no false indication of the existence of other trees with identifier x will be received.

A straightforward argument shows that the propagation phase takes $O(d)$ cycles: the update technique ensures that a new tid value read by a processor P_j is included in either $Processors_j$ or $Queue_j$. Recall that a cycle may include steps of many processors, while a certain processor executes only a single step. Thus, for instance, when the communication graph is a ring, it is possible that all the processors to the left of P_i will receive a tuple with $tid = x$

before the neighbor to the right of P_i receives such a tuple. Our technique of propagation of information with feedback, which we describe below, ensures that, when the feedback arrives at P_i, a fixed *BFS* tree identified by $tid = x$ is encoded in every system configuration.

The processor P_i that initiates the propagation repeatedly writes a tuple with $tid = x$ and $dis = 0$ in $Processors_i$. In more detail, P_i writes the tuple $\langle x, 0, 0, 1, false, false, \emptyset, \emptyset \rangle$ in $Processors_i$ (recall that the fields of a tuple are $\langle tid, dis, f, color, ackclr, ot, ack, list, del \rangle$). P_i repeatedly reads the shared registers of its neighbors. When P_i discovers that, for every neighbor P_j, there is a tuple in $Processors_i$ with $tid = x, dis = 1$ and $ack = true$, P_i concludes that feedback arrived.

Each processor P_j participates in the propagation of information with feedback from every other processor, including P_i. When a processor P_j includes for the first time a tuple t_j with $tid = x$ in $Processors_j$ as a consequence of reading a tuple t_k with $tid = x$ from a neighbor P_k, P_j copies the value of the fields $\langle color, ackclr, ot, ack, list, del \rangle$ of t_k to the corresponding fields of t_j. P_j then modifies the value of the fields f, dis, ack, and $list$ of t_j as follows. P_j repeatedly reads the communication registers of its neighbors and uses the value read to determine the value of the above fields. Let $\mathcal{X}$ be the set of P_j's neighbors such that for every $P_k \in \mathcal{X}$, P_j reads a tuple t_k for which the value of the tid field is x. From this point on, we consider only tuples with $tid = x$. We use the notation t_j for the tuple with $tid = x$ in $Processors_j$ or $Queue_j$, and we refer to a specific field z in t_j by the notation $t_j.z$. Let $\mathcal{X}' \subset \mathcal{X}$ be the maximal set of processors such that $\forall P_l \in \mathcal{X}'$ and $\forall P_m \in \mathcal{X}$, the value y of the distance field of the tuple t_l is not greater than the value of the distance field of t_m. P_j assigns $y + 1$ to $t_j.dis$. If the value of the f field of t_j is a label of a link connecting to a neighbor $P_k \in \mathcal{X}'$, then P_j does not change the value of the f field. Otherwise, (1) P_j assigns to the f field of t_j the label of a link that connects P_j with a neighbor $P_k \in \mathcal{X}'$, and (2) P_j assigns *false* to the ack field of t_j, and $\emptyset$ to the $list$ field.

P_j assigns *true* to the ack field of t_j when the following hold: (1) every neighbor has a tuple with $tid = x$ and the distance field of every such tuple is no more than one smaller or one greater than the value of the dis field of t_j, and (2) for every neighbor P_k of P_j such that $t_k.f$ is the label of P_k to the link that connects P_j and P_k (in other words, P_j is the parent of P_k in the tree), it holds that $t_k.dis = t_j.dis + 1$ and $t_k.ack = true$. Whenever P_j assigns $t_j.ack := true$, P_j simultaneously computes a new value for $t_j.list$. If P_j has no children, then P_j assigns its identifier ID_i to $t_j.list$; otherwise,

P_j concatenates the value of the *list* fields of all its children and the value of ID_i and assigns the concatenated list to $t_j.list$.

We now make several observations about the proposed propagation-with-feedback technique. The first is that no processor P_j can assign a distance in $t_j.dis$ that is less than the distance from P_i to P_j. Thus, after P_j assigns the correct minimal distance to P_i in $t_j.dis$, the values of $t_j.dis$ and $t_j.f$ are unchanged.

An induction argument on the distance from P_i proves that P_i terminates the propagation when every processor P_j has a tuple t_j such that the value of $t_j.dis$ is the distance of P_j from P_i and $t_j.ack = true$.

The base case, which is proven for each neighbor of P_i, is clear. Let us assume correctness of the above assertion for processors at distance l and prove it for processors at distance $l + 1$. Let P_j be a processor at distance l from P_i and let P_k be a processor at distance $l+1$ from P_i. Before the last assignment of $t_j.ack := true$, P_j reads that the value of $t_k.dis$ is the minimal distance of P_k to P_i and $t_k.ack = true$. Thus, following this configuration, P_k cannot change the value of $t_k.dis$, and hence cannot change the value of $t_k.f$ and $t_k.ack$.

Furthermore, when P_i concludes termination, $t_i.list$ consists of $n - 1$ identifiers, an identifier id_j for each processor P_j in the system such that there exists a configuration during the execution of the algorithm for propagation of information with feedback in which the value of ID_j is id_j. Therefore, assuming that every new identifier is a nonexistent identifier, P_i reveals all the conflicting identifiers in the system. The conflicting identifiers appear more than once in $t_i.list$. Now we are ready to examine the resulting algorithm.

Integrated Algorithm The design of the algorithm has two goals: to ensure that (1) when an identifier x is used by two or more processors as their identifier, at least one processor chooses a new identifier in expected $O(d)$ cycles; and (2) following the first choose operation (if such an operation is executed), every processor that does not have a distinct identifier chooses one in $O(d)$ cycles.

The first goal is achieved by the use of the multiple *BFS* trees and the global synchronization algorithms, while the second is achieved by the propagation of information with feedback. The elimination of the conflicting identifiers uses the *del* fields. Each processor copies the *del* field of its parent. Thus, the value of *del* computed by the root is broadcast over the tree to the entire system. When a processor P_j finds the value of ID_j in the *del* field of a tuple, P_j chooses a new identifier.

Let us establish several steps toward proving the correctness of the algorithm.

LEMMA 4.15:   In any given configuration, the number of distinct identifiers is less than N^8.

Proof Each tuple may contain no more than $2N + 1$ distinct identifiers (in *tid*, *list* and *del*). The sum of the numbers of tuples in both $Processors_i$ and $Queue_i$ is no more than $N + N^2$. In addition to $Processors_i$ and $Queue_i$, P_i maintains $Processors_{ji}$ and $Queue_{ji}$, internal variables for each neighbor P_j.

Thus, the total number of distinct identifiers encoded in the state of a processor is no greater than $(2N + 1)(N + N^2)(1 + N - 1)$, and no more than $N(2N + 1)(N + N^2)N < N^8$ (for $N \geq 2$) in the entire system.   ■

LEMMA 4.16:   The probability that every identifier-choose operation in a sequence of N identifier-choose operations results in a nonexistent identifier is greater than $1/2$.

Proof The probability that a single identifier choose operation results in a nonexistent identifier is at least $(1 - N^8/N^{10}) = (1 - 1/N^2)$, yielding $(1 - 1/N^2)^N > 1/2$ for a sequence of N choose operations ($N \geq 2$).   ■

We can conclude that:

THEOREM 4.3:   A safe configuration is reached in an expected $O(d)$ cycles.

Outline of proof: The combined probability of the scheduler-luck game is greater than $1/2$, and the expected number of cycles of the execution of the game is $O(d)$.   ■

Exercises

4.1. Complete the details of the stabilization proof of the algorithm in figure 4.4. Are the numbers assigned to the processors related to a *DFS* tour on the tree?

4.2. Why is the second part of the definition of a safe configuration for the update algorithm in figure 4.6 necessary?

4.3. Does the impossibility result for breaking symmetry from section 4.4 work in the case of a distributed daemon?

4.4. Design a self-stabilizing β synchronizer that uses a number of colors proportional to the depth of the tree.

4.5. Does the self-stabilizing update algorithm of section 4.4 stabilize with relation to the update task (UP) when it is executed in a unidirected strongly connected system? Prove your answer. Recall that, in unidirected systems, the fact that P_i can read a register of P_j does not imply that P_j can read a register of P_i. Each of these communicating neighbors is connected by an arrow from P_j to P_i in the communication graph. A communication graph is strongly connected if there exists a directed path from every processor to every other processor.

Notes

The self-stabilizing mutual exclusion algorithm presented in section 4.1 assumes read/write atomicity, like the algorithm presented in [DIM93]. We note that the algorithm presented in [DIM93] uses less memory and stabilizes faster.

The method for simulating self-stabilizing shared memory algorithms by self-stabilizing message passing algorithms presented in section 4.2 was introduced in [DIM97a].

One of the earliest reported studies on self-stabilizing message passing systems was made by Gouda and Multari [GM91], who developed a self-stabilizing sliding window algorithm and two-way handshake that used unbounded counters. They proved that any self-stabilizing message passing algorithm must use timeouts and have an infinite number of safe states. Afek and Brown [AB93] presented a self-stabilizing version of the well-known alternating-bit algorithm (see [BSW69]) that used either randomization or an aperiodic sequence (an infinite sequence is aperiodic if it has no suffix that is a repetition of a finite sequence). In [DIM97a], it was proven that the size of the configuration of every self-stabilizing token-passing algorithm must grow at a logarithmic rate, and three token-passing algorithms that match the lower bound were presented.

The problem of self-stabilizing ranking in a rooted tree studied in section 4.3 was considered in [DIM97b].

The impossibility result for achieving mutual exclusion in a ring of a composite number of processors appeared in [Dij73]. This impossibility result motivated a study by Burns and Pachel [BP89] in which they presented a self-stabilizing mutual exclusion algorithm for a ring of a prime number of identical processors. The algorithm presented in [BP89] assumed the existence of a powerful central daemon. The update algorithm is due to [Dol93; DH95]. A different self-stabilizing topology update algorithm was presented in [SG89].

Synchronizers were introduced in [Awe85]. Awerbuch suggested the α, β and γ (non-stabilizing) synchronizers, where the γ synchronizer combines the α and β synchronizers in a clustered system. One of the first self-stabilizing β synchronizers was presented in [Kru79]. The coloring technique presented in [DIM91] is essentially a self-stabilizing β synchronizer. The unbounded α synchronizer in this chapter is a version of the one proposed in [CFG92]; a similar technique was proposed in [AKM$^+$93].

Algorithms for self-stabilizing leader election in anonymous systems appeared in [AKY90; DIM91; AV91; AEY91; AEYH92; AK93]. These algorithms make different assumptions concerning the amount of memory available to the processors. Some of these studies assumed that the number of bits used by the processor to store identifiers was not bounded [DIM91; AEY91; AEYH92; AK93], while others assumed that a bound on the number of processors is known [Dol94]. The expected time complexity of these algorithms is a function of the number of the processors n, the diameter d, or a function on a bound on these values, namely N and D. The naming algorithm presented in this chapter appeared in [Dol94; Dol98], and uses an improved version of the basic algorithms for propagation of information with feedback presented in [Seg83]. A detailed description of the propagation of information and feedback procedure can be found in [DIM97b].

5 Stabilizers

In this chapter we introduce methods for converting non-stabilizing algorithms to self-stabilizing algorithms. We start with a method used for converting fixed-input fixed-output algorithms to self-stabilizing algorithms.

5.1 Resynchronous Stabilizer

We use the term *resynchronous stabilizer* for the transformer that converts any non-stabilizing synchronous or asynchronous algorithm $\mathcal{AL}$ with distributed input and fixed output to its stabilizing version $\mathcal{SA}$, where $\mathcal{SA}$ stabilizes in both synchronous and asynchronous systems. An example of such an algorithm $\mathcal{AL}$ is a spanning-tree construction in which each processor knows its neighborhood (distributed input) and the output is a (fixed) spanning tree of the system. Note that a mutual exclusion algorithm is not a fixed-output algorithm and therefore is not a possible input for the resynchronous stabilizer.

Let the *synchronous execution time* of an algorithm $\mathcal{AL}$ be the number of steps a processor executes until the (synchronous or asynchronous) algorithm produces the desired output, when the algorithm is executed in a synchronous system. Note that any fixed-output asynchronous algorithm works in synchronous systems as well. Clearly, there exists an asynchronous schedule that is equivalent to the synchronous schedule. For example, if in the synchronous system every (simultaneous) step starts by reading the communication registers of the neighboring processors followed by a simultaneous write to the communication registers (where the communication registers are assumed to be atomic), then, in the equivalent asynchronous schedule, the processors are scheduled to execute the read operations (one after the other in our interleaving model) and only then to perform the write operations (again, one after the other).

For a given algorithm $\mathcal{AL}$ with synchronous execution time t, the stabilizer maintains an array of $t + 1$ states at each processor (a state for each time unit). The kth entry in the array of a processor P_i should reflect the state of P_i following the $k - 1$th step of $\mathcal{AL}$. In particular, the first entry of the array is the initial state of P_i as defined by $\mathcal{AL}$. In each computation step, every processor P_i receives the arrays of every neighbor P_j. P_i uses the arrays received and the program of P_i in $\mathcal{AL}$ to recompute every entry of its array except the first. P_i assigns the initial state of P_i in $\mathcal{AL}$ to the first entry of the array, and then P_i uses the first entries of the received array together with the first entry of its own array to compute the second state of P_i in $\mathcal{AL}$. P_i stores this second state in the second entry of its array and then continues computing the next $t - 1$ entries of its array one by one. P_i uses the kth entry of every received array together with its own (just computed) kth entry to compute the $k + 1$th entry.

The correctness of the above algorithm is proved by induction on the steps of the execution, the assumption being that, after the kth cycle, all the entries of index $l \le k$ in the arrays are the states of P_i in the simulated $l - 1$ step of $\mathcal{AL}$ (the state in which P_i would be if $\mathcal{AL}$ were executed in a synchronous system).

One can argue that storing the entire computation sequence in the memory of the processors is too expensive. A possible extension of the resynchronous technique is to use the self-stabilizing synchronizer of section 4.5. The phase value of a self-stabilizing synchronizer can be used by the processors to initialize the execution whenever a certain value, e.g., zero, is assigned to the phase variable. Then two states are used in a fashion similar to the one described in section 4.5. Finally, whenever the execution terminates the value of a floating output variable is updated (see section 2.8). This technique dramatically reduces the amount of memory and communication used by the stabilizer.

The α synchronizer does not assume distinct identifiers and can be executed by a uniform system. Is there a stabilizer that uses the technique described above to convert a randomized algorithm to a self-stabilizing algorithm? There are two problems to solve in designing of a such stabilizer. The first is that usually no bound on the execution of the randomized algorithm can be given, even if the algorithm is executed in a synchronous system. The reason is that a randomized algorithm can be designed to terminate in an expected number of rounds, permitting (with low probability) executions with number of rounds greater than any given integer k. The second subtle point is the fact that the floating output may not be fixed. Different executions are possible, each with different return values for the random function. Thus, the result of two executions may differ, and the floating output of the processors may be changed infinitely often. For example, a randomized leader-election algorithm may elect a different leader in each of its executions.

To overcome the above difficulties, the floating output is examined whenever zero is assigned to the phase variable. For example, in the leader-election task, the examination procedure starts when the value of the phase variable of a processor is zero and continues until the phase value is D (recall that D is the bound on the diameter of the system and is known to every processor). Each processor P_i has a floating boolean output variable $leader_i$. In the beginning of the floating output examination, each processor P_i with $leader_i = true$

randomly chooses an identifier id_i from a large enough range, e.g., $1 \cdots N^{10}$. Then during the next D phases, P_i broadcasts the value of id_i. Every processor P_j has a variable $MaxId_j$ in which it stores the maximal identifier it has received so far. In the beginning of the floating output examination, each processor P_j with $leader_j = false$ assigns $MaxId_j := 0$, and each processor P_i with $leader_i = true$ assigns $MaxId_i := id_i$. When a processor P_j receives a message with $id_i > MaxId_j$ during the floating output examination, P_j assigns $MaxId_j := id_i$, $leader_j := false$, and sends the arrival message to all its neighbors. Thus, if the value of $MaxId_j$ following the first D phases is zero, then P_j may conclude that no leader exists and assign $leader_j := true$. On the other hand, if several processors are leaders in the first configuration, then with high probability there exists a single processor with the maximal identifier, and this processor is elected as the leader. The elected leader remains fixed throughout the execution. Notice that if two or more processors have the same identifier then each of these processor will randomly choose a new identifier at the beginning of the next floating output examination.

Can the above scheme for leader election be generalized for use in any randomized algorithm that assumes anonymous system and has a fixed output? A scheme that collects and examines the outputs of all the processors using the leader election, ranking, and update algorithms is a positive answer to this question. The details are left to the reader.

5.2   Monitoring and Resetting

We now describe the main ideas of a general stabilizer for a fixed-output and a non-fixed-output algorithm $\mathcal{AL}$. Two mechanisms are used: one to monitor the consistency of the system and the other to repair the system configuration when inconsistency is detected. The combination is not trivial. The consistency-checking mechanism should let the correction process complete its task successfully without repeatedly triggering new correction processes because consistency is not yet achieved. A consistency-checking process that triggers a global reset in an incautious way may repeatedly invoke resets and thus not allow the reset mechanism to execute a complete and successful reset. A successful reset should bring the system to a consistent (safe) configuration in which no reset activity takes place.

The general stabilizer repeatedly invokes a self-stabilizing *distributed snapshot* algorithm and examines the snapshots obtained. For simplicity, let us assume that the leader (elected by a self-stabilizing leader-election algorithm) is the only processor that repeatedly invokes a distributed snapshot algorithm. Furthermore, assume that the leader initiates the variables of the distributed snapshot algorithm by invoking a self-stabilizing *distributed reset* algorithm (like the one described in this chapter) between every two invocations of the snapshot algorithm. Thus, we need only describe a distributed snapshot algorithm that is initiated by a single processor starting in a predefined initial state. Roughly speaking, the distributed snapshot algorithm collects a (possible) configuration of the system without stopping its activity. Each processor records its state and the contents of the communication links attached to it. Then the records can be collected and examined. The description assumes the message passing model. A self-stabilizing data-link algorithm is executed over each communication link. The snapshot algorithm records (in local variables) the (current) state of each processor and the messages that are in transit in each communication link. Then the records are collected at the leader and examined.

• The leader records its current state in a local variable and repeatedly sends a (message with a) marker to each of its neighbors.

• Each processor P_i that receives a marker for the first time records its current state in a local variable and repeatedly sends a marker (with each message sent) to each of its neighbors.

• After P_i has recorded its state (due to the arrival of the first marker from a neighbor P_j), P_i starts recording the arriving messages from every neighbor P_k, $k \neq j$, in a local variable lq_{ki}. P_i stops recording the arrival messages when a marker arrives from P_k.

• P_i can send its records to the leader after receiving markers from each of its neighbors.

It is assumed that there is a predicate that identifies whether a configuration is a safe configuration or not. A global reset is invoked upon collecting a snapshot that describes an unsafe configuration; the global reset ensures that the system is started in a pre-defined safe configuration. Note that, once the system is in a safe configuration, it remains in a safe configuration unless another transient fault occurs.

For a subset of non-stabilizing algorithms, it is possible to replace the global snapshot with a local snapshot and to replace the global reset with a reset of subsystems. For example, in the spanning tree-construction algorithm presented in section 2.5, each processor checks whether x, its current distance from the root, is greater by one than y, the minimal distance of a neighbor from the root. This local consistency-check process guarantees that, if no processor detects inconsistency, the system encodes a rooted spanning tree. The next subsection develops the consistency-check idea by presenting a set of processes called transient fault detectors.

Transient Fault Detectors

In this section, we discuss a hierarchy of *transient fault detectors* that includes global and local monitoring as its two extremes. The idea is to augment each processor with information about the system up to a certain distance from the processor. The processors check that their information about the system is consistent and that the overall information maintained describes a safe configuration.

First note that a processor cannot "know" whether the system is in a safe configuration or not. Assume, for a moment, that there is a boolean variable $safe_i$ for every processor P_i such that $safe_i$ should be true when the system is in a safe configuration and false otherwise. Since a self-stabilizing system can be started in an arbitrary configuration, the value of every $safe_i$ variable cab be *true* while the system is not in a consistent state. In other words, it is impossible for a processor to know whether the system is in a safe configuration, as its safe variable indicates, or whether a transient fault has just corrupted the consistency of the system. In light of the above observation, a mechanism called *transient fault detector* is proposed. The transient fault detector guarantees that a fault is detected by *at least one processor* when the system is not in a safe configuration. In other words, the transient fault detector does not guarantee that every processor detects that the system is in an inconsistent configuration; it ensures only that at least one processor detects inconsistency.

The transient fault detector itself is an algorithm using variables that are subject to transient faults as well. It is possible that, due to such a corruption, the transient fault detectors indicate inconsistency even though the system is in a safe configuration of the original algorithm examined. Obviously, to make the transient fault detector useful, no failure should be detected when both the system and the fault detector are in a safe configuration. On the other hand, a failure must be detected when the algorithm is not in a safe configuration.

Let us first describe failure detectors for silent abstract tasks. An *abstract task* is defined as a set of executions in which only the values of a subset of the state variables, called the *output variables*, are shown in each configuration. A task is a *silent task* if the output of the system that implements the task is fixed.

Note that the output is fixed for a particular system but can be changed if the system undergoes topological changes such as processor or communication-link failures or additions. For example, the rooted spanning-tree abstract task that we now define is a silent task.

DEFINITION 5.1:   The *rooted tree abstract task* is defined as follows: each processor P_i maintains two (output) boolean variables $P_i[j]$ and $C_i[j]$ for each neighbor P_j. The value of $P_i[j]$ or $C_i[j]$ is true if P_i considers P_j to be its parent or one of its children, respectively, in the tree. There exists a single processor P_r that has a hardwired false value in every $P_r[j]$.

To detect a fault in an algorithm that implements a silent task, every processor must communicate with its neighbors. Starting in any arbitrary configuration, after the first time every two neighbors communicate, a fault is detected if the system configuration is not consistent. To implement a failure detector, each processor P_i maintains a variable $\mathcal{V}_i^d$ with the view of P_i on the topology of the system and the output of every processor up to distance d from P_i. We say that the *radius* of $\mathcal{V}_i^d$ is d.

It turns out that a failure detector exists that can detect inconsistency of every silent task within the time it takes for every two neighboring processors to send and receive a message from each other. The distance d used for the view $\mathcal{V}_i^d$, in this particular failure detector, is the diameter of the system, so that every processor has the entire output of the system in its view.

The program that implements the failure detector at a processor P_i repeatedly communicates $\mathcal{V}_i^d$ to each of its neighbors P_j. Whenever P_i receives a view $\mathcal{V}_j^d$ from a neighbor P_j, P_i verifies that $\mathcal{V}_i^d$ is equal to $\mathcal{V}_j^d$ and the value of the output variables of P_i appear in $\mathcal{V}_i^d$ (and hence in $\mathcal{V}_j^d$). In addition, P_i checks whether $\mathcal{V}_i^d$ satisfies the requirement of the task. P_i detects inconsistency whenever the views $\mathcal{V}_i^d$ and $\mathcal{V}_j^d$ do not agree, the value of the output variables of P_i do not appear correctly in $\mathcal{V}_i^d$, or the view $\mathcal{V}_i^d$ does not satisfy the requirement of the task.

In the case of the rooted tree abstract task, the view of each processor includes all the (output) boolean variables $P_i[j]$ and $C_i[j]$. Clearly, if no processor detects a failure after communicating with its neighbors, then, by transitivity of the equality relation, it must hold that all the views of the processors are identical and that they encode a spanning tree of the system rooted at P_r.

The implementation of a transient failure detector by augmenting each processor with a view of the entire system is a memory consuming solution. One can ask whether it is possible to reduce the radius of the views used to implement a failure detector. The answer is positive: there exist tasks for which a view of radius one is sufficient. The coloring task is one example. The task is to color the processors, so that no two neighboring processors have the same color.

DEFINITION 5.2: The *coloring abstract task* is defined as follows: each processor P_i maintains an output variable C_i to which it assigns a value. For every two neighboring processors P_i and P_j, the value of C_i and C_j should be different.

A failure detector for the coloring task employs a view of diameter one. To detect a failure each processor P_i communicates to each of its neighbors P_j the portion (state of processors and value of variables) of P_i's view that also appear in P_j's view.

Every processor P_i has a view V_i^1 that includes its own color and the color of all of its neighbors. P_i repeatedly communicates to each neighbor P_j the portion of its view V_i^1 that is shared with the view V_j^1. Thus, every processor communicates its color to its neighbors. A fault is detected whenever a processor detects that a neighbor's color is equal to its own. On the other hand, a failure detector that uses views of radius 0 cannot detect inconsistency in the coloring task. A view of radius 0 includes only the color of the processor; therefore there is no shared portion in neighboring views, and no communication is performed by the failure detector. These means that a failure is not detected when the system is in an inconsistent state in which two neighbors have the same color.

The radius of the view required for implementing a transient failure detector gives some indication of whether the task requires global coordination or only local coordination. The coloring task is defined by a state relationship of neighboring processors and is therefore local in nature. Hence it is not surprising that a view of diameter one is sufficient for the coloring task. There are tasks, however, that are defined by a global relationship on the states of the processors and for which a failure detector with radius one is still sufficient, for instance the *topology update task*.

DEFINITION 5.3: The *topology update abstract task* is defined as follows: each processor P_i maintains an output variable $\mathcal{T}_i$ containing the representation of the communication graph.

Interestingly, although the task specification requires each processor to have global knowledge, the transient fault detector for the topology update abstract task uses a view of diameter one. The view $\mathcal{V}_i^1$ of the processor P_i includes the output variable $\mathcal{T}_i$ and the output variable $\mathcal{T}_j$ of every neighbor P_j of P_i. Note that every output variable $\mathcal{T}_i$ contains the representation of the entire communication graph. P_i repeatedly sends the shared portion of $\mathcal{V}_i$ and $\mathcal{V}_j$ to P_j. In particular, P_i sends $\mathcal{T}_i$ to P_j; therefore, if two processors P_i and P_j have different values in $\mathcal{T}$, this fact is detected after the first communication between neighbors. Thus, if no fault is detected all the processors have the same view. It is assumed that every processor P_i knows its local topology and P_i checks whether its local topology appears in $\mathcal{T}_i$. If no processor detects a fault, then the view held by the processors is correct.

We note that there are tasks, such as the rooted tree construction abstract task (see definition 5.1), that require a radius of view that is smaller than d and greater than 1.

There are several possible ways to assign a value to the view variables. One possible way is related to a reset procedure described below. The reset procedure may be invoked by the transient failure detector to initialize the state of every processor in the system. An update procedure may follow the execution of the reset procedure, collecting information from the view variables up to the desired radius. Once the reset and the update finish their tasks, the failure detector starts operating, using the data accumulated in the view variables.

Up to this point, we have presented failure detectors that detect inconsistency for silent tasks. The tasks of distributed systems are often non-silent and even involve user interaction. Is there a transient fault detector for such tasks? It turns out that it is possible to monitor the consistency of each distributed algorithm. In other words, the failure detector presented next receives as an input a non-stabilizing algorithm $\mathcal{AL}$ for a task in order to implement a failure detector for it. Again, starting in any arbitrary configuration, after the first time each pair of neighbors communicates, a fault is detected if the system configuration is not consistent.

Note that, unlike silent tasks, for which the views of the processors are not changed, here the views must be constantly updated. Moreover, we require that a non-consistent configuration be identified after every two neighboring processors exchange messages once. If a message transmission takes one time unit, then after one time unit a fault should be detected. At first glance this seems impossible, since the number of time units required to gather the information about the current configuration is proportional to the diameter of the system. However, a special data structure called a *pyramid* can be used in order to achieve fault detection within a single time unit.

Our description is for synchronous systems; however, we can augment the processors with a synchronizer to apply the scheme to asynchronous systems. A *pyramid* $\Delta_i = \mathcal{V}_i[0], \mathcal{V}_i[1], \mathcal{V}_i[2], \cdots, \mathcal{V}_i[d]$ of views is maintained by every processor P_i, where $\mathcal{V}_i[l]$ is a view of all the processors that are within a distance of no more than l from P_i, l time units ago. In particular, $\mathcal{V}_i[d]$ is a view of the entire system d time units ago. Neighboring processors exchange their pyramids and check whether they agree on the shared portions of their pyramids. If indeed the shared portions are equal then all the $\mathcal{V}[d]$ views are equal. In addition, every processor checks whether $\mathcal{V}_i[d]$ is a *consistent configuration* for the input algorithm $\mathcal{AL}$ and the task of the algorithm. A *consistent configuration* for a non-stabilizing algorithm $\mathcal{AL}$ is any configuration that is reachable from the initial state of $\mathcal{AL}$. Thus, if no fault is detected after every two neighboring processors exchange messages, it holds that all the processors have the same $\mathcal{V}[d]$ and this view is a view of a consistent configuration.

It is still not clear, however, whether or not the *current* configuration is a consistent configuration. The next test ensures that the current consistent is indeed consistent. Every processor P_i checks that its state in the view $\mathcal{V}_i[l]$, $0 \leq l \leq d - 1$, is obtained by executing algorithm $\mathcal{AL}$ using the state of P_i and the state of P_i's neighbors in $\mathcal{V}_i[l + 1]$. This last test ensures that the current configuration is indeed a consistent configuration. Thus by starting in a consistent configuration and continuing according to the steps of the algorithm, a consistent configuration is reached.

To complete the description of the failure detector, we need to describe how the pyramids are updated in every time unit. A processor P_i receives the pyramid $\Delta_j = \mathcal{V}_j[0], \mathcal{V}_j[1], \mathcal{V}_j[2], \cdots, \mathcal{V}_j[d]$ of every neighbor in every time unit. P_i uses the received values of $\mathcal{V}_j[d - 1]$ to construct the value of the new $\mathcal{V}_j[d]$. The construction is straightforward since $\mathcal{V}_j[d - 1]$ of all the neighbors of P_i contains information about every processor at distance d from P_i, $d - 1$ time units before the current time unit. Analogously, P_i uses the received values of $\mathcal{V}_j[k - 1]$, $1 \leq k \leq d$, together with the value of $\mathcal{V}_i[k - 1]$ to compute the new value of $\mathcal{V}_i[k]$.

Self-Stabilizing Reset

A common technique for converting a distributed algorithm $\mathcal{AL}$ to a self-stabilizing algorithm for a certain abstract task $\mathcal{T}$ is to compose a failure detector, a self-stabilizing reset, and the algorithm $\mathcal{AL}$. The composition of a failure detector $\mathcal{D}$, self-stabilizing reset $\mathcal{R}$, and algorithm $\mathcal{AL}$ yields a self-stabilizing algorithm $\mathcal{DRA}$ for the abstract task $\mathcal{T}$. A processor executes steps of each of the composed algorithms infinitely often.

The task of the self-stabilizing reset is to initialize the system, upon request, to a predefined initial safe configuration c of $\mathcal{DRA}$ with relation to the abstract task $\mathcal{T}$. Thus, roughly speaking, once such a safe initial configuration c is reached, the activity of the failure detector and the reset algorithm does not interfere with the execution of $\mathcal{AL}$.

Every processor may invoke a reset at any of its execution steps. To make the description simple, let us assume that every processor has a boolean *invoke* variable. A processor invokes a reset by assigning *true* to its invoke variable. The cause for invoking a reset may be *external* or *internal*. External causes are outside events that influence the system, such as a topology change or a user request. Internal causes, however, are part of the distributed algorithm activity; for example, a distributed inconsistency-detecting mechanism like the one described above.

The reset procedure can be repeatedly invoked externally, and in such a case the system may never reach a safe configuration with relation to $\mathcal{T}$. Therefore, the behavior of the reset task is defined for executions with no external cause for invoking a reset, or equivalently, after the last such external reset is invoked, or between every two consecutive invocations far enough apart. In every fair execution that starts in an arbitrary state of $\mathcal{DRA}$, a safe configuration with relation to the abstract task $\mathcal{T}$ must be reached.

Let us present a self-stabilizing reset algorithm that is implemented by the use of a fair composition (see section 2.7) of a self-stabilizing leader-election and a spanning tree-construction algorithm with a version of the β synchronizer. The choice of the particular reset algorithm demonstrates, once again, how the basic self-stabilizing algorithm can be composed to result in a self-stabilizing algorithm for a new (and a more complicated) task.

Observe that the self-stabilizing leader-election algorithm presented in section 2.9 constructs a spanning tree rooted at the elected leader. Similarly, the self-stabilizing update algorithm presented in section 4.4 constructs a spanning tree rooted at every processor. Each of the above algorithms can be used as the server algorithm in the fair composition. Hence, in what follows we design a reset algorithm for a system in which a rooted spanning tree exists.

The client self-stabilizing algorithm that is served by the leader election and spanning tree construction algorithm is a variant of the self-stabilizing β synchronizer presented in section 4.5. Recall that the β synchronizer repeatedly colors the tree in such a way that eventually, whenever the root chooses a new color, all the processors in the tree have the same color.

```
01 Root:  do forever
02              forall P_j ∈ N(i) do lr_{ji} :=  read (r_{ji})
03              if (∀ P_j ∈ children(i)  (lr_{ji}.color = color_i)) then
04                    color_i := (color_i + 1) mod (5n − 3)
05                    if (∀ P_j ∈ children(i)  (lr_{ji}.ResetRequest = false)) and
06                        invoke_i = false then
07                        reset_i := false
08                    else
09                        reset_i := true
10                        invoke_i := false
11                        InitializeState(DA)
12              forall P_j ∈ children(i) do
13                    write r_{ij}.⟨color, reset⟩ := ⟨color_i, reset_i⟩
14        od
15 Other: do forever
16              forall P_j ∈ N(i) do lr_{ji} :=  read (r_{ji})
17              if color_i ≠ lr_{parent,i}.color then
18                    color_i := lr_{parent,i}.color
19                    if lr_{parent,i}.reset =true then
20                        reset_i := true
21                        invoke_i := false
22                        InitializeState(DA)
23                    else reset_i := false
24              else
25                    if (∀ P_j ∈ children(i)  (lr_{ji}.color = color_i)) then
26                        if reset_i =false then invoke_i :=  FaultDetect()
27                        if (∀ P_j ∈ children(i)  (lr_{ji}.ResetRequest = false))
28                                and invoke_i = false then
29                            ResetRequest_i :=  false
30                        else
31                            ResetRequest_i :=  true
32                    write r_{i,parent}.⟨color, ResetRequest⟩ :=
33                            ⟨color_i, ResetRequest_i⟩
34              forall P_j ∈ children(i) do
35                    write r_{ij}.⟨color, reset⟩ := ⟨color_i, reset_i⟩
36        od
```

Figure 5.1
Self-stabilizing reset

The code for the algorithm, which appears in figure 5.1, is written for the case when neighboring processors communicate by writing and reading in shared communication registers. Note that the same techniques can be used for the case of message passing by employing a self-stabilizing data-link algorithm on each link, as suggested in section 4.2.

Figure 5.1 includes code for the root processor and for non-root processors. The root processor repeatedly reads the value in the communication registers of each of its children (line 2 of the code). The root chooses a new color whenever all of its children report that their subtrees are colored according to the current color of the root (lines 3 and 4). Whenever the root chooses a new color, it checks whether a processor is requesting a reset (lines 5 and 6). If some processor is requesting a reset, then the root assigns *true* to *reset$_i$*, indicating that the distributed reset algorithm is active. In addition, the root assigns *false* to *invoke$_i$* and, by doing so, P_i "turns off" the signal request of the failure detector (line 10). Note that it is assumed that the failure detector at P_i is not activated as long as the the value of *reset$_i$* is *true*. Moreover, in line 11 of the code, the procedure *InitializeState($\mathcal{DA}$)* is invoked, changing the state of both the failure detector $\mathcal{D}$ and the algorithm $\mathcal{AL}$ to a predefined initial state. Then the state components of both $\mathcal{D}$ and $\mathcal{AL}$ are not changed as long as the value of *reset$_i$* is *true*. Note that the predefined states of $\mathcal{AL}$ and $\mathcal{D}$ include a definition for the internal state as well as a definition for the content of communication register fields. Thus the procedure *InitializeState($\mathcal{DA}$)* involves write operations to the communication registers. In line 13 of the code, the computed values of *color$_i$* and *reset$_i$* are actually written to the communication registers that are written by P_i and read by P_i's children.

The code for a non-root processor starts with read operations from the parent and the children of P_i (line 16). If P_i discovers that its parent is colored with a new color, it checks whether the wave of the new color carries a reset command from the root (line 17 through 19). If a reset command has arrived at P_i, P_i assigns *true* to *reset$_i$*, *false* to *invoke$_i$*, and executes the procedure *InitializeState($\mathcal{DA}$)*. Otherwise, when the color of the parent of P_i is not new, P_i checks whether it can report (in line 32) to its parent that its subtree is colored with the current color of P_i's parent. P_i also checks (in lines 26 to 28) and reports (in line 32) whether a reset is requested. First the result of the transient failure detector is used (line 26). Note that the failure detector result is *not* considered (in line 26) when a *reset* is in progress. Otherwise, during the period in which the reset is not yet completed, the transient failure detector might not stop triggering resets and no reset will be successfully completed. In lines 27 and 28 of the code, P_i gathers the reset requests of its children (if it is a non-leaf processor) together with its own reset request (stored in *invoke*$_i$) and assigns *true* to *ResetRequest*$_i$ if at least one such request exists (line 31). P_i then reports to its parent that its subtree is colored with the color of the parent and, at the same time, reports whether a processor in its subtree has requested a reset (lines 32 and 33). P_i repeatedly writes its current color and reset values to the communication registers that are shared with its children (lines 34 and 35).

Correctness Proof Outline The correctness proof for the reset algorithm is based on the correctness of the self-stabilizing leader-election and spanning-tree construction algorithm, the correctness proof of the self-stabilizing β synchronizer algorithm, and the fair composition technique. Observe that the algorithm in figure 5.1 is an extension of the β synchronizer in the sense that the operation on the color variables is identical in both algorithms. Therefore, every fair execution has a suffix in which the root repeatedly colors the tree according to the specifications of the β synchronizer.

To complete the proof outline, it is necessary to show that the reset algorithm, composed with a failure detector $\mathcal{D}$, ensures that, starting in any configuration, every fair system execution reaches a safe configuration of the algorithm $\mathcal{AL}$. Consider an execution that starts with the root choosing a new color. If the value of the reset variable of the root is true, then every processor P_i initializes its state and sets invoke$_i$ to false (lines 19 through 22); therefore, a successful reset takes place. Otherwise, let a be the step of the root P_i in which P_i chooses the next color.

The reset variable of every processor is set to false during the propagation of the new color to the leaves. Thus, every processor uses the failure detector to check the consistency of the system when the processor reports the new color to its parent. In addition, during this color report phase, the root receives a report (the value of the *Reset Request* variables of its children) that at least one invoke variable exists with the value *true*.

Exercises

5.1. Design a self-stabilizing randomized algorithm for every fixed-output task in an anonymous system.

5.2. As a function of n, what is the minimal radius of the views required to implement a transient failure detector for the rooted tree-construction abstract task? (see definition 5.1.) *Hint:* The radius is less than $n/2$.

5.3. Design a failure detector for the synchronous consensus algorithm presented in section 2.8 such that the radius of the view of each processor is as small as possible. Detail the actions of the *InitializeState* procedure for the combination of the failure detector and the non-stabilizing algorithm in figure 2.6.

5.4. Design a self-stabilizing reset algorithm using an α synchronizer as a building block.

5.5. The self-stabilizing reset algorithm presented in figure 5.1 assumes the existence of a spanning tree. Two algorithms that can be composed with the reset algorithm are mentioned in this chapter, the leader election algorithm of section 2.9 and the update algorithm presented in section 4.4. Does the choice influence the time and space complexities of the reset algorithm?

Notes

The first stabilizer, presented in [KP93], repeatedly collects snapshots of the system and checks their consistency. The process of collecting distributed snapshots does not interfere with the activity of the algorithm. A collected snapshot describes not a certain configuration of the system reached during the execution, but a configuration c from which there exists an execution E starting in c and reaching the current configuration. An important observation made in [KP93] was that, if the snapshot represents a safe configuration, then the current system configuration is safe. The snapshot distributed algorithm was introduced in [CL85].

The method for converting a fixed output algorithm to a self-stabilizing algorithm using logs of states or a synchronizer was suggested in [AV91].

The terms *local detection* and *local checking* were suggested in [AKY90; APSV91], where each processor P_i checks a predicate on the state of P_i and a neighbor P_j; a fault is detected if the result of the predicate evaluation is false. Unreliable failure detectors for systems in which processors may stop operating were introduced in [CT96]. Transient fault detectors that uses different sizes of views are introduced in [BDDT98]. Monitoring consistency by using pyramids is suggested in [AD97].

Self-stabilizing reset is considered in several papers; see [AG94; AO94; IL94], to mention only a few.

6 Convergence in the Presence of Faults

The focus of this chapter is the integration of self-stabilization with other fault models, such as crash failures and Byzantine failures, both of which have been studied extensively. Crash failures are failures that cause a processor to stop operating. Algorithms that tolerate crash failures in some of the processors and achieve their goal in spite of the failures are of practical interest, since processors do crash from time to time due to power supply problems, user activity, or software problems.

In addition, software (and sometimes hardware) may contain flaws; therefore, the behavior of a faulty processor is not limited to ceasing to operate, as assumed in the crash-faults model. Obviously, the effect of software bugs cannot be determined in advance. How does one model the behavior of a faulty processor?

The Byzantine fault model assumes that the processor is controlled by an adversary that "fights" against the rest of the processors in order to prevent them from reaching their goal. A Byzantine processor can send any message at any time to each of its neighbors. Initially, algorithms that tolerate Byzantine faults were designed for flight devices that must be extremely robust. Several processors that are executing programs for the task communicate the result and decide which result is correct. Unfortunately, it is well known that, if one-third (or more) of the processors are Byzantine, it is impossible to achieve basic tasks such as consensus in distributed systems.

For example, consider a system of three processor P_1, P_2, and P_3 that are connected to one another. Each processor has a single input bit. The task of the non-faulty processors is to choose the same value. Moreover, when the non-faulty processors have the same input, that input must be chosen. Assume there is a distributed algorithm $\mathcal{AL}$ that achieves consensus in the presence of a single Byzantine processor in the above system. Note that if we prove that no non-stabilizing algorithm can ensure that consensus is eventually achieved (assuming the executions start in a particular initial configuration), then it is clear that no self-stabilizing algorithm for this task exists.

Consider a six-processor ring P_1, P_2, P_3, P_1', P_2', P_3', where P_1 is connected to P_3' and each P_x, $x \in \{1, 2, 3\}$, is identical to P_x'. P_x and P_x' run the same program as defined by $\mathcal{AL}$ for P_x in the three-processor system. P_x and P_x' may have different input values. In particular, let the input values of the processors in the ring be $0, 0, 0, 1, 1, 1$ for P_1, P_2, P_3, P_1', P_2', P_3', respectively. Analyze the executions of $\mathcal{AL}$ on the ring. Note that $\mathcal{AL}$ is designed to be executed on a system with only three processors P_1, P_2 and P_3; we examine it only to prove the impossibility result using a ring of six processors. Furthermore, no processor is faulty in the executions examined. Thus, P_2 and P_3 must choose 0 since they both have input 0 and the information received from P_1 and P_1' in the ring can be produced by a single Byzantine processor, namely P_1 in the three-processor system. On the other hand, P_1' and P_2' both have input 1 and the communication with P_3 and P_3' during the execution can be produced by a Byzantine processor. Thus P_1' and P_2' must choose 1. The final observation is the output of P_3 and P_1'. Recall that no processor is faulty in the ring execution. Thus, both P_3 and P_1' are non-faulty and the communication pattern between P_2 and P_3 and between P_1' and P_2' may be produced by a single Byzantine processor in the three-processor system that is connected to P_3 and P_1'. Thus, P_3 and P_1' must decide on one input. The proof is complete, since we have previously proved that P_3 must choose 0 and P_1' must choose 1.

Is this a special case? Is it perhapes possible to reach consensus when the number of processors is $3f$, where $f > 1$ is the number of Byzantine processors? The rough idea for proving the impossibility result is logically to partition the system into three clusters of processors, one of which contains all the Byzantine processors. Each cluster can be replaced by a single superprocessor that simulates the execution of the cluster (including the communication within and outside the cluster). Thus the existence of an algorithm for the case $3f$, $f > 1$, implies existence for the case $f = 1$, which in turn we proved impossible.

Now that we have proved the limitations of algorithms designed to cope with Byzantine faults, we may ask: Is it reasonable to assume that during *any* period of the execution less than one-third of the processors are faulty? What happens if, for a short period, more than one-third of the processors are faulty, or perhaps temporarily crashed? What happens if messages sent by non-faulty processors are lost in one instant of time? The answer to these questions is similar in flavor to the answer concerning the influence of program flaws. Such temporary violations of the assumptions can be viewed as leaving the system in an arbitrary initial state that could have been chosen by a malicious adversary and from which the algorithm resumes.

An algorithm designed to cope with both Byzantine faults and transient faults may be able to cope with severe faults that are not tolerated by an algorithm that copes with only one type of faults. Self-stabilizing algorithms that cope with ongoing faults and stabilize in spite of these faults are presented in this chapter. The existence of such algorithms demonstrates once again the generality of the self-stabilization concept. One can require stabilization whenever certain conditions hold, for example convergence to a safe configuration when less than one-third of the processors are Byzantine. To demonstrate the integration of self-stabilization with other fault concepts, we start by presenting self-stabilizing algorithms for the elegant and simple digital clock-synchronization problem. The digital clock-synchronization problem assumes a synchronous system in which the processors are activated by a global clock pulse. We follow this with the case of asynchronous systems.

6.1   Digital Clock Synchronization

The digital clock-synchronization problem is defined for a system of n identical processors connected to a global common clock pulse. Each processor maintains a digital clock value. In every pulse each processor executes a step in which it reads the value of its neighbors' clocks and uses these values to calculate its new clock value. In other words, a pulse triggers read operations by all the processors, and once the read operations by all the processors are finished, the processors choose new clock values and change state accordingly. The term *lock-step* is sometimes used for such synchronous processor activation.

Starting in a configuration in which every processor has an arbitrary clock value, the processors should reach a safe configuration c in which: (1) all the clock values are identical, and (2) in every execution that starts in c, the clocks are incremented by one in every pulse. Note that the fact that the processors are identical does not contradict the existence of a deterministic algorithm for the task, since we are interested in reaching a symmetric configuration in which all the clock values are identical (unlike, e.g., the leader-election task).

```
1   upon a pulse
2       forall Pⱼ ∈ N(i) do send (j, clockᵢ)
3       max := clockᵢ
4       forall Pⱼ ∈ N(i) do
5           receive(clockⱼ)
6           if clockⱼ > max then max := clockⱼ
7       od
8       clockᵢ := max + 1
```

Figure 6.1
Self-stabilizing digital clock synchronization (unbounded)

The first self-stabilizing algorithm for synchronizing digital clocks that we describe uses an unbounded number of clock values. The code for the algorithm appears in figure 6.1. Let *max* be the maximal clock value that a processor P_i reads from a neighbor during a certain pulse. P_i assigns the value $max + 1$ to its own clock. This simple algorithm is self-stabilizing, since from any initial configuration that follows at least d pulses (where d is the diameter of the system), the clocks are synchronized and incremented by one in any later pulse.

Let P_m be a processor with the maximal clock value in the first configuration. The correctness of the algorithm can be easily proven by an induction on the distance from P_m; we assume that, following i pulses, every processor of distance i from P_m holds the (current) maximal clock value. The algorithm uses unbounded clocks, which is a serious drawback in self-stabilizing systems. Every implementation of the algorithm must use bounded memory for the clock (e.g., a sixty-four-bit register). As already remarked, the assumption that a sixty-four-bit digital clock is "unbounded" for every implementation because it will take 2^{64} time units to reach the upper bound (which is large enough for every possible application) does not hold in the design of self-stabilizing systems, where a single transient fault may cause the clock immediately to reach the maximal clock value.

We discuss two self-stabilizing algorithms that use bounded clock values. The first bounded algorithm is almost identical to the unbounded algorithm, the only difference being that the clocks are incremented modulo M where $M > (n + 1)d$ (note that for ease of description the values we choose for M are not the minimal possible value). The code of the algorithm appears in figure 6.2.

```
1  upon a pulse
2      forall P_j ∈ N(i) do send (j, clock_i)
3      max := clock_i
4      forall P_j ∈ N(i) do
5          receive(clock_j)
6          if clock_j > max then max := clock_j
7      od
8      clock_i := (max + 1) mod ((n + 1)d + 1)
```

Figure 6.2
Self-stabilizing digital clock synchronization (bounded) I

```
1   upon a pulse
2       forall P_j ∈ N(i) do send (j, clock_i)
3       min := clock_i
4       forall P_j ∈ N(i) do
5           receive(clock_j)
6           if clock_j < min then min := clock_j
7       od
8       clock_i := (min + 1) mod (2d + 1)
```

Figure 6.3
Self-stabilizing digital clock synchronization (bounded) II

Note that, if the system is initialized in a configuration in which the values of the clocks are less than $M - d$, then the clocks are synchronized before the modulo operation is applied. Once the clocks are synchronized, the value zero is assigned to the clocks simultaneously in the pulse immediately after a configuration in which the clock values are all $M - 1$. The correctness proof for the first algorithm uses the pigeonhole principle, showing that, in any configuration, there must be two clock values x and y such that $y - x \geq d + 1$ and there is no other clock value between. Furthermore, since each processor chooses an existing clock value and increments it by one, it holds at the first pulse of the execution that no clock can be assigned a value greater than the value of $x + 1$ and less than the value of $y + 1$. Similarly, until y is incremented to M, it holds that, following the ith pulse, no clock value is greater than $x + i$ and smaller than $y + i$. Thus, after $M - y + 1$ pulses, the system reaches a configuration in which there is no clock value that is greater than $M - d$. In the next d rounds, the maximal clock value propagates, and the system reaches a configuration in which all the clocks are synchronized.

The other bounded algorithm, in figure 6.3, uses the minimal, instead of the maximal, clock value read by a processor. For this version, it is sufficient to use $M > 2d$. As in previous algorithms, the number of distinct clock values can only be reduced during the execution. Actually, it is shown that the number of clock values is reduced to a single clock value. Two cases are considered. In the first, no processor assigns zero to its clock during the first d pulses. A simple induction on the distance from a processor that holds the minimal clock value in the first configuration proves that, following $i \leq d$ pulses, all neighbors at distance i from this processor have the minimal clock value in the system. In the other case, a processor assigns zero to its clock during the first d pulses. Here it is easy to see that, in d pulses after this assignment, a configuration c is reached such that there is no clock value in c, that is greater than d. In the first d pulses that follow c, no processor assigns zero to its clock. Thus, the arguments for the first case hold.

Digital Clocks with a Constant Number of States

One may wonder whether the number of clock values be further reduced. Can this number be a fixed constant that is related to neither the diameter of the system nor the number of processors in the system? The following elegant lower bound on the number of states per processor proves that there is no uniform digital clock-synchronization algorithm that uses only a constant number of states per processor. To prove the lower bound, we restrict our attention to systems with ring communication graphs. This is a special case of general communication graph systems; therefore, a lower bound for this special case implies a lower bound for the general communication graph case.

To present the main ideas of the lower bound, we start in a restricted case in which a processor can read only the clock of a subset of its neighbors, and we prove a lower bound for a unidirected ring. In a unidirected ring every processor has a left and a right neighbor. The left and right neighbor relation is global in the following sense: if P_i is the left neighbor of P_j then P_j is the right neighbor of P_i. In a unidirected ring a processor can read the state of its left neighbor.

Given any self-stabilizing digital clock-synchronization algorithm for a unidirected ring, denote the transition function of every processor by f. Each transition is denoted by $s_i^{t+1} = f(s_{i-1}^t, s_i^t)$, where s_i^t and s_{i-1}^t are the states of P_i and its left neighbor, respectively, at time t, and s_i^{t+1} is the state of P_i at time $t + 1$. Assume that the number of states of every processor is a constant; in other words, the number of possible states is not a function of the number of the processors in the ring. Let $|S|$ be the constant number of states of a processor. The idea is to choose a sufficiently large ring for which the given algorithm will never stabilize. The proof shows that a configuration exists for a sufficiently large ring such that the states of the processors rotate: in every step, the state of every processor is changed to the state of its right processor.

Figure 6.4 depicts our next argument. Let s_1 and s_2 be two states in S; e.g., the first two states according to some arbitrary ordering of the states. Use s_1 and s_2 to construct an infinite sequence of states such that $s_{l+2} = f(s_l, s_{l+1})$ (the upper two lines of figure 6.4 are such a sequence). There must be a sequence of states $s_j, s_{j+1}, \cdots, s_{k-1}, s_k$ — that is, a subset of the above infinite sequence

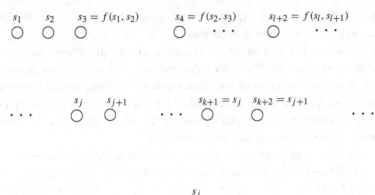

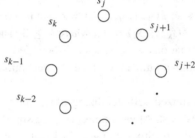

Figure 6.4
Digital clocks with a constant number of states are impossible

— such that $f(s_{k-1}, s_k) = s_j$ and $f(s_k, s_j) = s_{j+1}$ and $k \geq j + 3$; or, equivalently, $s_{k+1} = s_j$ and $s_{k+2} = s_{j+1}$. Consider the sequence of pairs (s_1, s_2), (s_5, s_6), (s_9, s_{10}), $\cdots$, $(s_{4(i-1)+1}, s_{4(i-1)+2})$ $\cdots$. Any sequence of $|S|^2 + 1$ such pairs has at least one pair (s_j, s_{j+1}) that appears more than once. Thus, any segment of $2(|S|^2 + 1)$ states in the infinite sequence can be used in our proof.

Now, we are convinced that there is a sequence $s_j, s_{j+1}, \cdots, s_{k-1}, s_k$ in which the combination s_{k+1}, s_{k+2} and the combination s_j, s_{j+1} are identical. Therefore, it holds that $f(s_{k-1}, s_k) = s_j$ and $f(s_k, s_j) = s_{j+1}$. Now construct a unidirected ring of processors using the sequence $s_j, s_{j+1}, \cdots, s_{k-1}, s_k$, where the processor in state s_k is the left neighbor of the processor in state s_j (see the lower portion of figure 6.4). Each processor uses its own state and the state of its left neighbor to compute the next state; in accordance with our construction, the state s_{j+i} is changed to s_{j+i+1} for every $0 \leq i < k - j$, and the state s_k is changed to s_j. We conclude that, in each pulse, the states are rotated one place to the left. Note that the above is true in an infinite execution starting in the configuration defined above.

Is it possible that such an infinite execution will stabilize? Since the states of the processors encodes the clock value and the set of states is not changed during an infinite execution (it just rotates around the ring), we must assume that all the states encode the same clock value. On the other hand, the clock value must be incremented in every pulse. This is impossible, since the set of states is not changed during the infinite execution.

In the more complicated case of bidirectional rings, the lower-bound proof uses a similar approach. We denote a transition by $s_i^{t+1} = f(s_{i-1}^t, s_i^t, s_{i+1}^t)$. In this case, there must exist a sequence of states $s_1, s_2, \cdots, s_k$ of length $O(|S|^3)$ such that, for every $i > 2$, $f(s_{i-1}, s_i, s_{i+1}) = s_{i+2}$ and $f(s_{k-2}, s_{k-1}, s_k) = s_1$, $f(s_{k-1}, s_k, s_1) = s_2$, $f(s_k, s_1, s_2) = s_3$, where $k \geq 3$. The reason is that the number of state combinations, s_{i-1}, s_i, s_{i+1}, is bounded by $|S|^3$. The proof is completed by the rotation argument, where every activation results in a double rotation.

Note that a randomized self-stabilizing algorithm that uses a constant number of clocks does exist. At each pulse, a processor P_i randomly chooses a clock value $clock$ that is either its own clock value or the clock value of a neighbor. P_i assigns $(clock + 1) \mod M$ to $clock_i$. Again, this choice ensures that the number of distinct clock values can only be reduced during the execution. A simple sl-game winning strategy can be used. Choose a particular node P_l; if each processor repeatedly chooses a clock value of a neighbor in a shortest path to P_l, then the system reaches a safe configuration within d pulses. Thus, in every infinite execution, the algorithm stabilizes with probability 1.

Until this point, we have studied self-stabilizing algorithms for digital clock synchronization. In the following sections, we present algorithms that cope with other types of faults in addition to transient faults.

6.2 Stabilization in Spite of Napping

We are interested in clock synchronization algorithms that can tolerate hybrid faults: these should work starting from an arbitrary initial configuration and should tolerate processors that exhibit faults during and after convergence.

Several self-stabilizing algorithms that synchronize digital clocks in the presence of (permanent) faults are known. An algorithm that tolerates both transient and permanent faults is, of course, more resilient to faults than an algorithm that tolerates only one of these types of faults.

The first set of results concerns a complete communication graph in which each processor can communicate with all other processors. A self-stabilizing clock synchronization algorithm copes with permanent *napping* faults if processors can repeatedly stop and (possibly) resume operation during and after the convergence of the algorithm to a safe configuration. Note that napping faults are more severe than crash failures, since a crashed processor can be seen as a napping processor that does not resume operation. A clock synchronization algorithm that copes with transient and napping faults is called a *wait-free self-stabilizing* clock-synchronization algorithm. A non-faulty processor P_i synchronizes its clock even when all $n - 1$ other processors are faulty; in other words, P_i does not wait for other processors to participate in the algorithm. What is the meaning of synchronization when $n - 1$ processors are faulty? How can the single operational processor be synchronized with itself? The answer to these questions is simple: the synchronization algorithm should ensure that each non-faulty operating processor ignores the faulty processors and increments its clock value by one in every pulse.

A processor P_i *adjusts* its clock in a certain step if the value of its clock is not incremented by one in this step. The requirements of an algorithm that is both self-stabilizing and copes with napping faults are called *adjustment* and *agreement*. We require that a fixed integer k exists such that, starting in an arbitrary configuration, once a processor P_i has been working correctly for at least k time units and as long as P_i continues to work, the following *adjustment* and *agreement* properties hold:

- *adjustment:* P_i does not adjust its clock, and

- *agreement:* P_i's clock agrees with the clock of every other processor that has also been working correctly for at least k time units

Because a working processor must synchronize its clock in a fixed amount of time regardless of the actions of the other processors and because the system can be started in an arbitrary configuration, such algorithms are called *wait-free self-stabilizing* algorithms.

Note that trivial algorithms that fulfill only one of the above requirements exist. An algorithm in which a processor increments its clock by one in every pulse without communicating with its neighbors fulfills the adjustment requirement, and an algorithm in which the clock value of every processor is always 0 fulfills the agreement requirement.

Does an algorithm that fulfills both requirements exist? We first present a simple *wait-free self-stabilizing* algorithm with $k = 1$ that uses unbounded clocks: a (non-crashed) processor reads the clocks of all the other processors in every step, chooses the maximal clock value in the system, denoted by x, and assigns $x + 1$ to its clock.

Starting in an arbitrary configuration, immediately after an execution of a step by a processor P_i, the clock of P_i holds the maximal clock value. Hence as long as P_i does not crash, it does not adjust its clock; in other words, P_i increments its clock by one in every pulse. Moreover, the clock of P_i and every other processor that is not crashed hold the maximal clock value in the system. Thus, the clocks of all non-crashed processors that executed $k = 1$ steps agree. Does the algorithm tolerate transient faults as well as napping faults? Transient faults may cause the system to reach an arbitrary configuration c with arbitrary clock values. Still, after this arbitrary configuration c, the clock of every processor P_i holds the maximal clock value immediately after each of P_i's steps.

At this point, we already know that self-stabilizing algorithms that use bounded memory are more attractive than self-stabilizing algorithms that use unbounded memory. One might suggest a similar technique for bounded clocks. Instead of incrementing the clock values by one, an identical algorithm that increments the clock values by one modulo some integer M might be used. Unfortunately, this suggestion will not work, since the clock of a napping processor that holds $M - 1$ may cause all the active processors repeatedly to assign zero to their clocks and to violate the adjustment requirement for every possible integer k.

We now present a technique for a wait-free self-stabilizing clock synchronization algorithm that uses a bounded clock value M and a bounded number of states for a processor. The idea is to use a mechanism for identifying crashed processors and ignoring their clock value. Every two processors P_i and P_j have an "arrow" indicating which of them was recently active. In every step it executes, P_i makes sure that it is not *behind* P_j. Using the analogy of the arrow, P_i makes sure that it is not the tail of the arrow by trying to direct the arrow toward itself, while P_j does the same from the other side. Immediately after both processors execute a step, the arrow has no direction; i.e., P_i is not behind P_j and P_j is not behind P_i.

Interestingly, there is a simple self-stabilizing implementation of this arrow. The implementation is based on the concept of the famous *scissors, paper, stone* children's game in which two children randomly choose an element in the set scissors, paper and stone. Every time they chose different elements a winner is declared according to the following rules: it is possible to wrap a stone with paper, to break scissors with a stone, and to cut paper with scissors.

Each processor P_i has an $order_{ij}$ variable for each neighbor P_j that holds a value from $\{0, 1, 2\}$. P_i writes in $order_{ij}$ and *every* processor can read $order_{ij}$. The arrow has no direction when the value of $order_{ij}$ is equal to the value of $order_{ji}$. When $order_{ij}$ is not equal to $order_{ji}$, the arrow is directed. In this case, we define the *behind* relation by the missing value x, which is the value from $\{0, 1, 2\}$ such that $x \neq order_{ij}$ and $x \neq order_{ji}$. The convention we use is that the value that follows x in the clockwise direction is behind the other value. In other words, P_i is *behind* P_j if and only if $(order_{ij} + 1)$ mod $3 = order_{ji}$.

P_i identifies all napping processors P_j by incrementing $(order_{ij} + 1)$ mod 3 as long as P_j is not behind P_i. To get a clearer understanding of this mechanism, we observe the steps of two processors P_i and P_j in a specific execution. This execution starts in a configuration in which the arrow has no direction and continues with a step of P_i and P_j. In each step, both processors try to signal each other that they are executing a step by directing the arrow toward themselves. Thus, P_i increments $order_{ij}$ by 1 modulo 3 and P_j does the same. This results in a configuration in which the arrow is not directed. The same holds as long as both processors continue to execute steps. Immediately after the first time in which only one of the two processors, say P_i, executes a step, P_j is behind P_i. When P_j resumes operation, it finds that it is behind P_i and increments $order_{ji}$ by 1 modulo 3. Note that, if P_i executes a step, too, P_i does not increment $order_{ij}$ since P_j is behind P_i.

This order mechanism is used for selecting (bounded) clock values. The clock values of the napping processors are ignored. At each pulse, P_i reads the order variables between every two processors P_j and P_l, $1 \leq j, l \leq n$ in the system. Let $\mathcal{NB}$ be the set of processors that are not behind any other processor according to the order variables P_i read. If $\mathcal{NB}$ is not empty, then P_i chooses the maximal clock value x among the clock values of the processors in $\mathcal{NB}$ and assigns $(x + 1)$ mod M to its clock. Otherwise, P_i does not change its clock value.

THEOREM 6.1:   The above algorithm is a wait-free self-stabilizing clock-synchronization algorithm with $k = 2$.

Proof The proof shows that, starting with any values in the *order* variables and the *clock* variables, the algorithm meets the adjustment and agreement requirements.

First note that all processors that take a step at the same pulse, see the same view, and compute the same $\mathcal{NB}$. We must show that, if any processor P_i executes more than $k = 2$ successive steps, then the agreement and adjustment requirements hold following its second step.

Assume P_i executes more than k successive steps. Our first observation is that $\mathcal{NB}$ is not empty following the first step of P_i. Moreover, while P_i continues to execute steps without stopping, it remains in $\mathcal{NB}$. The reason is that P_i executes a step in which it increments every order variable $order_{ij}$ such that P_j is not behind P_i.

Since $\mathcal{NB}$ is not empty following the first step of P_i, and since all processors that execute a step see the same set $\mathcal{NB}$, all the processors that execute a step following the first step of P_i choose the same clock value. Thus, following the second step of P_i and while P_i does not stop to execute steps, the clock values of the processors that belong to $\mathcal{NB}$ are the same.

Every processor that executes a single step belongs to $\mathcal{NB}$, and the value of the clocks of all processors in $\mathcal{NB}$ is the same; thus the agreement requirement holds. Every processor chooses the maximal clock value M of a processor in $\mathcal{NB}$ and increments M by 1 modulo M; thus, the adjustment requirement holds as well.

The proof of the theorem assumes an arbitrary starting configuration for the execution with any combination of *order* and *clock* values. Thus our algorithm is both wait-free and self-stabilizing. ∎

6.3   Stabilization in Spite of Byzantine Faults

In this section we suggest enhancing the fault tolerance property of a system that copes only with Byzantine faults by designing a self-stabilizing algorithm that stabilizes in the presence of f Byzantine faults. Self-stabilizing algorithms work correctly when started in any initial system state. Thus, even if the system loses its consistency due to an unexpected temporary violation of the assumptions on it (e.g., more than one-third of the processors are faulty, unexpected message loss), the system synchronizes the clocks when subsequently the assumptions hold (e.g., fewer than one-third of the processors experience Byzantine faults).

Byzantine processors may exhibit arbitrary two-faced behavior, inform-
ing each of their neighbors of a different clock value at the same pulse. Such
behavior is impossible when each processor writes its clock value in a communication register that can be read by every other processor. To capture the
power of the Byzantine processor, we assume that every two processors have
an independent means of communication, either by using two communication
registers r_{ij} and r_{ji} between every two processors P_i and P_j or by message
passing. In the first case, the Byzantine processor P_i may write different clock
values in its registers, so the clock value in r_{ij} may be different from the clock
value in r_{ik}. In the synchronous message passing case, it is assumed that a pulse
triggers a send operation of each processor P_i and that the messages sent arrive
to their destination before the next pulse. Non-Byzantine processors send messages only at the beginning of a pulse. Thus, no message of a non-Byzantine
processor is in transit when a new pulse starts.

Since the system can be started in an arbitrary configuration — e.g., a
configuration that is a result of all processors being Byzantine — we assume
that messages may be present in every link when the first pulse starts. The
system starts to stabilize and to synchronize the clocks in every execution period in which fewer than one-third of the processors are non-faulty. In such a
period of execution, there is no message in every link that connects two non-
faulty processors at every pulse after the second pulse: the messages sent at the
first pulse arrive before the second pulse (note that the links obey the first-in
first-out message-delivery order). Clearly, a Byzantine processor may simultaneously send conflicting messages to its neighbors in such a synchronous
message passing system.

We now consider a randomized self-stabilizing clock-synchronization algorithm that uses bounded clock values and copes with Byzantine faults. First,
let us state the requirements for a randomized self-stabilizing algorithm for digital clock synchronization in the presence of Byzantine processors. The clocks
are assumed to be bounded by an integer M. The algorithm should fulfill the
requirements in every "long enough" execution period in which fewer than
one-third of the processors exhibit Byzantine behavior. We require that, starting in an arbitrary configuration and in the presence of at least $2n/3 + 1$ non-
faulty processors, the system reach a configuration within k expected number
of rounds, for some constant k, such that the following properties hold:

• *agreement*: the clocks of all the non-faulty processors hold the same value,
and

- *adjustment*: in any (possible) subsequent step, each processor increments its clock by 1 modulo M.

The algorithm is designed for systems with a fully connected communication graph. At each pulse, each processor P_i reads the clock values of the other processors in the system. P_i uses the value of its clock and that of the clocks of the other processors in order to choose a new clock value. There are two basic rules for choosing a clock value, *increment* and *reset*. The *increment* rule is used when P_i finds $n - f - 1$ clock values that are identical to its own clock value. In this case, P_i increments its clock value by one modulo M. Note that, when the clocks of the non-faulty processors are synchronized, P_i finds at each pulse that there are $n - f - 1$ clocks in the system with an identical value to its own clock value. In some sense, P_i cannot hope to receive more such identical values, since f processors may send arbitrary clock values. The *reset* rule is used when P_i finds fewer than $n - f - 1$ clocks with clock values equal to its own clock value. In this case, P_i assigns 0 to its clock.

The above simple rules for choosing the next clock value ensure that, at any pulse after the first pulse of the execution, any two processors that increment their clocks have identical clock values. This is because there is a limited amount of evidence. Assume for a moment that two non-faulty processors P_i and P_j simultaneously apply the above increment rule while having different clock values, e.g. x and y, respectively. Let $f' \leq f$ be the number of faulty processors in the system and $n - f'$ the number of non-faulty processors. P_i must receive $n - f - 1$ x values, of which at least $n - f - f' - 1$ values are from non-faulty processors, while P_j must receive at least $n - f - f' - 1$ y values from non-faulty processors. Thus, the total number of non-faulty processors must be at least $2n - 2f - 2f'$ (including P_i and P_j in the summation). But we know that the number of non-faulty processors is $n - f'$, which is less than $2n - 2f - 2f' = n - f' + (n - 2f - f')$, because f and f' are smaller than one-third of n.

We can conclude that, after the second pulse, the set of clock values of the non-faulty processors includes no more than two clock values and that, if two such distinct values exist, then one of them is zero.

This seems almost to achieve the clock synchronization task; one may be tempted to say, "Just wait for the set of non-faulty processors to increment their clock values to reach $M - 1$ and then, in the very next pulse, all the non-faulty processors hold a clock value of zero. Once all the non-faulty processors have

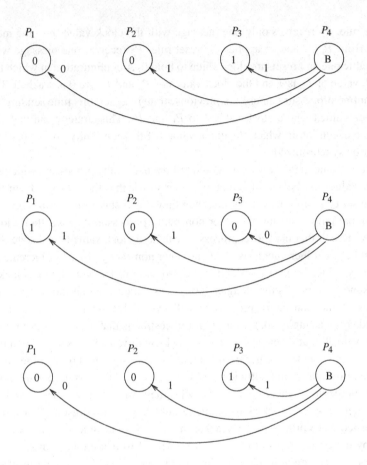

Figure 6.5
The Byzantine processor avoids synchronization

identical clock values, they receive $n - f - 1$ clock values that are identical to their clock values, increment their clock values, and stay synchronized."

Unfortunately, the Byzantine processors can prevent the non-faulty processors from reaching zero simultaneously. For example, figure 6.5 shows four processors P_1, P_2, P_3 and P_4, of which P_4 is the only faulty processor. Start in a configuration in which the clock values of P_1 and P_2 are zero while the clock value of P_3 is one. At the first pulse, P_4 sends a message with clock value 0 to P_1 and messages with clock value 1 to P_2 and P_3. P_1 receives $n - f - 1 = 2$ messages with clock value 0 (namely, from P_2 and P_4) and applies the increment rule. P_2 receives only one message with the clock value 0 — the message from P_1 — and so applies the reset rule. P_3 receives one message with the value one and resets its clock value to hold 0. A configuration in which the clock value of P_1 is 1 and the clock values of P_2 and P_3 are 0 is reached. The Byzantine processor can use the previous strategy again, this time sending P_3 a clock value 0 and a clock value 1 to P_1 and P_2. This strategy can yield an infinite execution in which the clock values of the non-faulty processors will never be synchronized.

If, in some magical way, we could tell the non-faulty processors with zero clock value just before incrementing their clock that they do not form the entire set of non-faulty processors, then they could stay in their state for one additional pulse, causing the other non-faulty processors to reset their clock values. Recall that because a processor with zero clock value is in a state that is just before it increments its clock, no other non-faulty processor increments its clock value, so every non-faulty processor assigns the value 0 in its clock.

Randomization is the "magic" tool we use to ensure that the set of clock values of the non-faulty processors will eventually, with high probability, include only a single clock value. One suggestion is that every processor with clock value 0 that receives $n - f - 1$ clocks with value 0 toss a coin and use the result to decide whether to increment its clock to 1 or stay with the value 0. This proposal is not sufficient for stabilization, since, even after the non-faulty processors synchronize their clocks, they still can lose synchronization after they assign their clock to 0, due to unlucky coin toss results. Thus, it is suggested that a processor that reaches the 0 clock value in a "normal" way — i.e., by incrementing its clock value from $M - 1$ to 0 at the last pulse — and is about to increment its clock at the current pulse should increment its clock without tossing a coin. The code for a processor P_i executing this algorithm appears in figure 6.6. Whenever a pulse occurs, P_i sends its clock value to its neighbors (line 2 of the code). P_i then tries to receive the clock values of its neighbors; since a Byzantine neighbor may not send a message, P_i limits the time it waits to receive such a message (as noted in line 4 of the code).

To implementat of the above mechanism, a processor must use a local variable *LastIncrement* that indicates whether the last rule applied was a reset or an increment. In the context of self-stabilizing algorithms, this variable may be corrupted as well, causing a processor to make wrong decisions about whether to toss a coin or not. However, it is clear that this variable holds the right value after the first pulse.

```
01 upon a pulse
02      forall P_j ∈ N(i) do send (j,clock_i)
03      forall P_j ∈ N(i) do
04          receive(clock_j) (* unless a timeout*)
05      if |{j | j ≠ i, clock_i = clock_j}| < n − f − 1 then
06          clock_i := 0
07          LastIncrement_i := false
08      else
09          if clock_i ≠ 0 then
10              clock_i := (clock_i + 1) mod M
11              LastIncrement_i := true
12          else
13              if LastIncrement_i = true then clock_i := 1
14              else clock_i := random({0, 1})
15              if clock_i = 1 then LastIncrement_i := true
16              else LastIncrement_i := false
```

Figure 6.6
Digital clocks in the presence of Byzantine processors

During any execution that contains at least M pulses, there must exist a configuration such that a non-faulty processor receives $n - f - 1$ clock values that are 0, because either all or a majority the non-faulty processors hold the clock value 0. Assume for a moment that there exists a sequence of M successive pulses during which no processor receives $n - f - 1$ clock values that are 0. Thus, non-faulty processors do not assign the value 1 to the clock at any of these pulses. In such a case, none of the non-faulty processors changes their clock value after the first time the clock is assigned to 0. But every non-faulty processor must assign its clock value to the value 0 at least once every M successive pulses (either because it increments its clock in every pulse or because it resets its clock value). So during this sequence of M successive pulses, we reach a configuration in which the clock of all the non-faulty processors is 0. However, in this configuration, every processor receives $n - f - 1$ clock values that are 0. We can conclude that at least one non-faulty processor assigns 1 to its clock in every M successive pulses.

An additional observation is that if, during a pulse that follows the first pulse, a non-faulty processor P_i increments its clock value to be 1 without tossing a coin, then, just before this pulse, all the non-faulty processors' clock values were 0. The variable *LastIncrement* is assigned during every pulse. Thus, since we are considering a pulse that follows the first pulse, P_i indeed increments its clock at the previous pulse. Since no more than one clock value may be incremented in a pulse by the non-faulty processors (while the other values are assigned to 0), it holds that all the non-faulty processors have clock values of 0 just before P_i increments its clock to 1 without tossing a coin.

The next theorem uses the scheduler-luck game to analyze the randomized algorithm. Recall that the scheduler-luck game has two competitors: *scheduler* (adversary) and *luck*. The goal of the scheduler is to prevent the algorithm from reaching a safe configuration, while the goal of luck is to help the algorithm reach a safe configuration. For our algorithm, a configuration is *safe* if, for all non-faulty processors, the logical clocks are equal and *LastIncrement* is true.

THEOREM 6.2:   In expected $M \cdot 2^{2(n-f)}$ pulses, the system reaches a configuration in which the value of every non-faulty processor's clock is 1.

Proof We present a strategy for luck to win the scheduler-luck game with $2(n-f)$ interventions and within $M+2$ pulses. The strategy of luck is (1) wait for the first pulse to elapse, and then, (2) wait until a pulse in which a non-faulty processor with clock value 0 receives $n-f$ clock values that are 0. This occurs within the next M pulses. In case (2.1), at this pulse all the non-faulty processors are either tossing a coin or assigning 1 without tossing. Then luck intervenes no more than $n-f$ times and fixes the coin toss results of all the non-faulty processors to be 1. Otherwise (2.2), if there is a non-faulty processor P_i that is neither about to toss a coin nor to assign 1 without tossing, then luck intervenes and fixes all the coin toss results (less than $n-f$) to be 0. Note that, because of the existence of P_i, there must be a non-faulty processor P_j with a non-zero clock value just before the current pulse. Thus, according to the above observation concerning processors that assign 1 without tossing a coin, it holds in this case that no processor assigns 1 without tossing a coin. Because some non-faulty processors received $n-f$ clock values that are 0, it holds that, following the current pulse, the clock values of all the non-faulty processors are 0. Therefore, in the next pulse, case (2.1) is reached and luck can intervene and fix at most $n-f$ coin toss results to ensure that the desired global state is reached.   ∎

According to theorem 6.2, the system reaches a configuration in which the value of every non-faulty processor's clock is 1 in expected time $M \cdot 2^{2(n-f)}$. It is easy to see that, in each successive pulse, all the non-faulty processors have the same clock value. Thus, the agreement requirement holds. Since the clocks of the non-faulty processors are incremented by 1 at every pulse, the adjustment requirement holds as well.

Note that the probability that all the processors assign the number 1 simultaneously is exponentially small as a function of the number of processors. In some cases, a large number of processors is used to ensure reliability, and such systems may tolerate processor failures. If we measure the *reliability* of a system by the ratio f/n — the ratio of the number of faulty (Byzantine) processors that the system can tolerate to the total number of processors — then, asymptotically, we need an infinite blowup to reach a reliability of one-third. The above is implied by the impossibility of tolerating more than one-third of the processors being Byzantine. On the other hand, to reach reliability 0.25, the number of processors needed is four. Hence, optimal reliability is almost achieved by the use of four processors. It is thus reasonable to have a small number of processors when a single processor can compute a task efficiently and further processors are added only to ensure reliability. In such a case, the algorithm described above can synchronize the clocks efficiently, as long as M is small.

In a system of four processors (one of which is Byzantine) and a maximal clock value $M = 2$, the system reaches a safe configuration within expected $2 \cdot 2^6 = 128$ pulses. On the other hand, if M is 2^{64}, then the time for convergence is too long for any practical application. In the next section, we present the *parallel composition* technique, which can be used to achieve an exponentially better convergence rate while keeping the maximal clock value no smaller than 2^{64}.

Parallel Composition for Fast Convergence

In the fair composition of self-stabilizing algorithms presented in section 2.7, an output of one self-stabilizing algorithm, called the *server* algorithm, is used by another self-stabilizing algorithm, called the *client* algorithm. The composition is not cyclic in the sense that the *server* algorithm does not use a value of any variable of the *client* algorithm. Otherwise, the stabilization of the *server* algorithm cannot be proven without considering the actions of the *client* algorithm. We note, however, that it is sometimes useful to consider several algorithms $\mathcal{AL}_1$, $\mathcal{AL}_2$, $\cdots$, $\mathcal{AL}_i$ that interact among themselves and argue about the stabilization of each algorithm $\mathcal{AL}_j$ when considering its possible interaction with the other algorithms. Algorithms that use such a composition are presented in sections 4.6 and 5.2.

Here we present *parallel composition*, a composition technique that can be used in a synchronous system (or in asynchronous systems that use self-stabilizing synchronizers, like those presented in section 4.5). The idea is that, in every step of a processor P_i, P_i will execute a step of several independent versions of a self-stabilizing algorithm. The output of all these versions is then used to compute the output of P_i.

In this section, we use the parallel composition technique to reduce the convergence time of the algorithm in figure 6.6. A *Chinese remainder counter* based on the Chinese remainder theorem (see [Knu81]) is used.

THEOREM 6.3:   Let m_1, m_2, m_3, $\cdots$, m_r be positive integers that are relatively prime in pairs, i.e., $gcd(m_j, m_k) = 1$ when $j \neq k$. Let $m = m_1 m_2 \cdots m_r$, and let $a, u_1, u_2, \cdots, u_r$ be integers. Then there is exactly one integer u that satisfies the conditions $a \leq u < a+m$ and $u \equiv u_j$ (modulo m_j) for $1 \leq j \leq r$.

Choose $a = 0$ and the smallest r primes 2, 3, 5, $\cdots$, m_r, where r is chosen such that $2 \cdot 3 \cdot 5, \cdots, m_{r-1} < M \leq 2 \cdot 3 \cdot 5 \cdots m_r$. Each processor executes, in parallel, r versions of the algorithm in figure 6.6. The lth version uses the lth prime m_l in the above series for the value of M_l, where M_l is the bound on the clock value used by the lth version (line 10 of figure 6.6). A message sent by P_i carries the value of r clocks $clock_i^1, clock_i^2, \cdots, clock_i^r$, where only the value $clock_i^l$ is used by the lth algorithm version. The computation of the new clock value of some version l uses only the values received for this particular version, and therefore is independent of the computation of all other versions. Thus, the lth version converges within expected $M_l \cdot 2^{2(n-f)}$ pulses. The expected time for all the versions to be synchronized is therefore no greater than $(m_1 + m_2 + \cdots + m_r) \cdot 2^{2(n-f)}$.

For instance, assume $M = 2 \cdot 3 \cdot 5$; thus three parallel versions are sufficient. Following the stabilization period, the values of $(clock_i^1, clock_i^2, clock_i^3)$ maintained by the processor P_i can be $(1, 0, 4)$. One pulse later, the value of $(clock_i^1, clock_i^2, clock_i^3)$ should be $(0, 1, 0)$. In detail, the value of $clock_i^1$ is incremented by 1 modulo 2, the value of $clock_i^2$ is incremented by 1 modulo 3, and the value of $clock_i^3$ is incremented by 1 modulo 5. In the following pulses, the values of $(clock_i^1, clock_i^2, clock_i^3)$ are $(1, 2, 1)$, then $(0, 0, 2)$, $(1, 1, 3)$, and so on. From the Chinese remainder theorem, it is clear that the clock value combination $(1, 0, 4)$ will appear again only after all the other possible clock combinations have appeared.

According to the Chinese remainder theorem, every combination of the clock values of these r versions can be mapped to a distinct value in the range 0 to $2 \cdot 3 \cdot 5 \cdots m_r$. A well-known technique such as Garner's method (see

[Knu81]) can be used to convert the clock values of the r versions into a single clock value that is incremented by one at every pulse. The above example demonstrates the way the parallel composition can be used to achieve fast convergence.

6.4 Stabilization in the Presence of Faults in Asynchronous Systems

In this section we examine the self-stabilizing property of an asynchronous algorithm when crashes are possible. We show that, for some tasks, a single faulty processor may cause the system not to stabilize.

The impossibility result concerns counting the number of processors in the presence of exactly one single crashed processor. A special case is considered, namely that of a ring communication graph. Processors have distinct identifiers. In a ring of n processors, the state of each processor should eventually encode the number $n - 1$.

First, let us describe a simple non-terminating, non-stabilizing algorithm that starts in a predefined initial state and counts the number of processors in the ring in the presence of exactly one crash. In fact, we design the non-stabilizing algorithm to count the number of non-crashed processors in the presence of *at most* one crashed processor. Let P_i, P_j, P_k be three consecutive processors in the ring. P_j reads r_{ij} and r_{kj} and writes in r_{ji} and r_{jk}.

Each communication register r_{xy} contains a list of processors. P_j writes a list of processors $(P_l, P_m, \cdots)$ that are to its left (right) in r_{jk} (r_{ji}, respectively). At the beginning of execution, all the lists are empty. P_j repeatedly reads the list $(P_l, P_m, \cdots, P_x, P_j, \cdots)$ from the register r_{kj} and assigns it to the local variable lr_{kj}. Then P_j removes the suffix of the list in lr_{kj} that starts with P_j, if such a suffix exists. P_j concatenates P_k to the front of the list and writes the result $(P_k, P_l, P_m, \cdots, P_x)$ in r_{ji}. Similarly, P_j repeatedly reads the list $(P_l, P_m, \cdots, P_y, P_j, \cdots)$ in r_{ij}, removes the suffix of the list that starts with P_j, concatenates P_i to the front of the list, and writes the result $(P_i, P_l, P_m, \cdots P_y)$ in r_{jk}. This simple algorithm ensures that the lists of every processor P_j accumulate more and more knowledge concerning the ring and eventually contain all the non-crashed processors that are to the left and to the right of P_j. Thus, each processor can compute the number of processors in the system.

Is it possible to design a self-stabilizing algorithm for the counting task? As we now show, the answer is negative. Note that the impossibility of counting the number of non-crashed processors in a ring implies the impossibility of an algorithm that counts the number of non-crashed processors in a distributed system with a general communication graph.

Assume there exists a self-stabilizing algorithm that counts the number of processors in a ring in the presence of exactly one crashed processor. Let P_j be a crashed processor, starting in an arbitrary configuration. Once the system reaches a safe configuration, the state of each processor P_i, $i \neq j$, must encode the number $n - 1$. Since the initial state of the system may be arbitrary, convergence must occur regardless of the contents of the registers of P_j (the registers in which P_j writes).

Consider a system consisting of three processors P_1, P_2, and P_3 that are connected in a ring so P_{i+1} is the neighbor to the right of P_i for $1 \leq i \leq 2$ and P_1 is the neighbor to the right of P_3. Assume that P_1 is crashed; every fair execution of the self-stabilizing counting algorithm $\mathcal{AL}$ must reach a safe configuration. Once a safe configuration is reached, the state of every processor except P_1 encodes the number 2. Note that there must exist a safe configuration for every possible value x and y of $r_{1,2}$ and $r_{1,3}$, respectively. In every (asynchronous) execution that starts in a safe configuration, no processor should change its estimate of the number of processors.

Consider a system consisting of four processors P_1, P_2, P_3, and P_4. Assume that P_1 is crashed and the value of $r_{1,2}$ is x. The system must reach a safe configuration c', and once a safe configuration is reached, the state of each processor except P_1 should encode the number 3. Let z be the value of $r_{4,3}$ in c'. There must exist an execution E of our first system (the system with three processors) such that the value of $r_{1,2}$ is x and the value of $r_{1,3}$ is z. During E, P_2 and P_3 must reach a state that encodes the number 2. Since the system is asynchronous, one can stop P_4 following c' until P_2 and P_3 change state to encode the number 2, as is done in E. Thus, c' is not a safe configuration and hence the system never reaches a safe configuration.

Exercises

6.1. Can a smaller number than $((n + 1)d + 1)$ be used in line 8 of figure 6.2 without changing any other statement in the code? Prove stabilization or present a contradicting example.

6.2. Consider digital clock-synchronization algorithms for a line of processors $P_1, P_2, \cdots, P_n$, where P_i, $2 \leq i \leq n - 1$, communicates with the processors

P_{i-1} and P_{i+1}; similarly, P_1 communicates with P_2 and P_n with P_{n-1}. Assume that processors have no sense of direction: the fact that P_i considers P_{i-1} its left neighbor does not imply that P_{i-1} considers P_i its right neighbor. Will the algorithm presented in figure 6.2 stabilize when the increment operations are modulo 3? Prove your answer or present a contradicting example.

6.3. Will the unbounded algorithm presented in figure 6.1 stabilize if the minimal clock value plus one is assigned to $clock_i$? Will it stabilize if the average clock value (counting only the integer part of the average result) is used?

6.4. Does there exist a self-stabilizing algorithm that estimates the number of processors in an asynchronous ring of n processors in the presence of at most one crashed processor, such that the output of every non-crashed processor is not smaller than $n - 2$ and not greater than $n + 2$?

6.5. In this chapter it is proved that consensus is not possible when the number of processors is less than $3f + 1$ if f of these processors are Byzantine. Prove that there is no self-stabilizing phase synchronization algorithm when there are only $3f$ processors. (*Hint:* Consider two safe configurations c_1 and c_2 for a three processor system, each with a different clock value.)

Notes

The Byzantine fault model was introduced in [LSP82]. Motivation for designing systems that tolerate severe faults was given in [WLG+78]. The limitations of a distributed system that tolerates Byzantine faults were discussed in [LMS85; DHS86; FLM86]. The lower bound of the number of processors, namely $3f + 1$ processors, that is necessary to tolerate f Byzantine processors is based on the proof in [FLM86].

The self-stabilizing digital clock-synchronization problem was introduced in [GH90], where a solution that uses unbounded clock values was presented.

The first bounded self-stabilizing algorithms for the problem were presented in [ADG91]; there it was assumed that a processor reads one neighbor at a pulse, which requires the enlargement of M by a factor of the maximal degree of a node.

The elegant lower bounds for the number of clock values per processor were presented in [LS95]. A randomized algorithm for the problem that uses a constant number of clock values per processor was presented in [HG95].

Self-stabilizing algorithms for the digital clock-synchronization problem that cope with faults during convergence were presented in [DW93; PT94; DW95; Dol97]. The combination of transient faults and Byzantine faults was suggested in [BYZ89; ZB92]. Parallel composition for fast convergence was used for synchronizing digital clocks in [DW95] and for fast leader election in [AKM+93].

The impossibility result for asynchronous systems is based on [AH93]. Extensions were proposed in [Mas95; BKM97]. More about combining other fault models with self-stabilization can be found in [GP93; Dol97].

7 Local Stabilization

Locality is a desired property of self-stabilizing algorithms. The motivation is to avoid situations in which a small number of transient faults cause an entire system to start a global convergence activity in which the system behaves in an unspecified and undesired way. The terms *superstabilizing*, *fault containment*, *time-adaptive*, and *local stabilization* are used to describe an algorithm that converges to a safe configuration in a graceful way following the occurrence of a limited number of faults.

7.1 Superstabilization

Let us first study the combination of self-stabilization and dynamic systems. In a *dynamic* system, communication links and processors may fail and recover during normal operation. Algorithms for dynamic systems are designed to cope with such failures and to recover without global reinitialization. These algorithms consider only global states that are reachable from a predefined initial state under a *restrictive sequence of failures*; under such restrictions, the algorithms attempt to cope with failures with as few adjustments as possible. In contrast to self-stabilizing algorithms that were not designed to guarantee a particular behavior between the time of a transient fault and restoration to a legitimate state, dynamic algorithms make guarantees about behavior at all times (e.g., during the period between a failure event and the completion of necessary adjustments).

Superstabilizing algorithms combine benefits of both self-stabilizing and dynamic algorithms. Roughly speaking, an algorithm is superstabilizing if it is self-stabilizing and if, when started in a safe configuration and a topology change occurs, it converges to a new safe configuration in a graceful manner. In particular, it should preserve a *passage* predicate during the convergence to a new safe configuration and should exhibit a fast convergence rate.

The passage predicate is defined with respect to a class of topology changes. A topology change typically falsifies legitimacy. The passage predicate must therefore be weaker than legitimacy but strong enough to be useful; ideally, it should be the strongest predicate that holds when a legitimate state undergoes a topology change event. One example of a passage predicate is the existence of at most one token in the token-passing task; in a legitimate state, exactly one token exists, but a processor crash could lose the token but not falsify the passage predicate. Similarly, for the leader-election task, the passage predicate could specify that no more than one leader exists.

In addition to the complexity measures used to evaluate self-stabilizing algorithms, superstabilizing algorithms are also evaluated by their *superstabilizing time* and *adjustment measure*. The *superstabilizing time* is the maximum number of rounds it takes for an algorithm starting from a legitimate state, to undergo a single topology change and then reach a legitimate state. The *adjustment measure* is the maximum number of processors that must change their local states, upon a topology change from a legitimate state, so that the algorithm reaches a legitimate state.

Many distributed algorithms have been designed to cope with continuous dynamic changes. These algorithms make certain assumptions about the behavior of processors and links during failure and recovery; for instance, most of them do not consider all possible combinations of crashes, assume that every corrupted message is identified and discarded, and assume bounded link capacity. Recall, that according to our proof in section 3.2, when crashes are possible and the link capacity is not known, an arbitrary configuration can be reached.

The primary goal of self-stabilizing algorithms is to recover from transient faults, and this goal has influenced their design and analysis. For instance, for a correct self-stabilizing algorithm, there are no restrictions on the behavior of the system *during* the convergence period: the only guarantee is convergence to a legitimate state.

Self-stabilization's treatment of a dynamic system differs from that of dynamic algorithms in how topology changes are modeled. Dynamic algorithms assume that topology changes are *events* signaling changes in incident processors. In particular, an initial state is defined for the processors executing a dynamic algorithm. When the system starts operating, each processor that joins the execution of the algorithm initializes its state.

Self-stabilizing algorithms take a necessarily more conservative approach that is entirely state-based: a topology change results in a new state from which convergence to a legitimacy is guaranteed, with no use of signals of events. Yet, when the system is in a legitimate state and a fault happens to be detected, can the behavior during the convergence be constrained to satisfy some desired safety property? For instance, is it possible in these situations for the algorithm to maintain a "nearly legitimate" state during convergence? A self-stabilizing algorithm that does not ignore the occurrence of events will perform better: it will be initialized in a predefined way and react better to dynamic changes during the execution.

The issue can be motivated by considering the problem of maintaining a spanning tree in a network. Suppose the spanning tree is used for virtual circuits between processors in the network. When a tree link fails, the spanning tree becomes disconnected, but, virtual circuits entirely within a connected component can continue to operate. In the superstabilizing approach, the system restores a spanning tree so that existing virtual circuits in the connected components remain operating; thus, a least-impact legitimate state can be realized by simply choosing a link to connect the components.

The time complexity of a self-stabilizing algorithm is the worst-case measure of the time spent to reach a legitimate state from an arbitrary initial state. But is this measure appropriate for self-stabilization for dynamic systems? Perhaps a better measure would be the worst case: starting from an arbitrary legitimate state, considering a topology change, and then measuring the time needed to reach a legitimate state again. This approach can be motivated by considering the probability of certain types of faults: while a transient fault is rare (but harmful), a dynamic change in the topology may be frequent. Note that the issue of time complexity is orthogonal to the issue of whether an algorithm converges while preserving a passage predicate.

We present a self-stabilizing and superstabilizing algorithm for the graph coloring task. The graph coloring task is to assign a *color* value to each processor, such that no two neighboring processors are designated by the same color. The distributed coloring algorithms that are presented below do not cope with the theoretical difficulty of minimizing the number of colors. The algorithms use $\Delta + 1$ colors, where Δ is an upper bound on a processor's number of neighbors. The goal is to demonstrate the superstabilizing property and the complexity measures that are related to superstabilization. Each processor P_i has a register field $color_i$.

A self-stabilizing coloring algorithm should ensure that, for every two neighboring processors P_i and P_j, it eventually holds that $color_i \neq color_j$ and that no color variable changes value.

Let us first explain the code of the algorithm presented in figure 7.1. A processor P_i has an internal variable $GColors$ that is used to store the set of colors of P_i's neighbors. $GColors$ accumulates the colors of P_i's neighbors that have an identifier greater than i (this is done in lines 2 through 5 of the code).

Then P_i checks whether its color is that of one of the processors with a greater identifier and, if so, chooses a new color different from the colors of these processors (this is done in lines 7 and 8 of the code). Finally, P_i writes the value of $color_i$ to $r_i.color$.

```
01 do forever
02     GColors := ∅
03     for m := 1 to δ do
04         lr_m := read (r_m)
05             if ID(m) > i then GColors := GColors ∪ lr_m.color
06     od
07     if color_i ∈ GColors then
08             color_i := choose(\\ GColors)
09     write r_i.color := color
10 od
```

Figure 7.1
Self-stabilizing coloring algorithm for P_i

Assume that a link between two processors is added or that a new processor is added to the system. Note that we assume that the above addition does not violate the restriction that each processor have no more than Δ neighbors. The new system state that is reached due to the dynamic change may not be a safe configuration for this system. For instance, it is possible that two processors that became neighbors due to the link addition have the same color. Clearly, a safe configuration is reached when each processor follows the algorithm presented in figure 7.1. However, it is possible that, during the convergence, almost every processor will change its color.

For example, consider a system in the form of a chain $P_1, P_2, \cdots, P_n$ where, for every $1 \leq i \leq n - 1$, P_i is connected to P_{i+1}, and where the link between P_{n-1} and P_n is inoperative. If the link between P_{n-1} and P_n recovers while $color_n = color_{n-1}$, it is then possible that, during the execution of the algorithm in figure 7.1, every processor will change its color. Such a scenario can be avoided by using the topology change as a signal for P_n and P_{n-1} to change colors in a careful way. Figure 7.2 presents a superstabilizing algorithm for the coloring task. Each processor repeatedly reads the color of its neighbors and uses the variables $AColors$ and $GColors$ to store the set of colors it finds. In particular, $AColors$ stores the set of colors of all the neighbors and $GColors$ stores the set of colors of the neighbors that have a greater identifier (lines 2 through 8 of the code).

A special symbol $\perp$ is used by the superstabilizing algorithm to flag a non-existent color. When a link connecting the processors P_i and P_j recovers, both P_i and P_j receive an interrupt signal, $recover_{ij}$ and $recover_{ji}$, respectively. Assume, without loss of generality, that $j > i$; in such a case, the interrupt $recover_{ij}$ triggers an assignment $color_i := \perp$ (lines 14 and 15 of the

```
01 do forever
02     AColors := ∅
03     GColors := ∅
04     for m := 1 to δ do
05         lr_m := read (r_m)
06         AColors := AColors ∪ lr_m.color
07         if ID(m) > i then GColors := GColors ∪ lr_m.color
08     od
09     if color_i =⊥ or color_i ∈ GColors then
10         color_i := choose(\\ AColors)
11     write r_i.color := color
12 od
13 interrupt section
14     if recover_ij and j > i then
15         color_i := ⊥
16         write r_i.color := ⊥
```

Figure 7.2
Superstabilizing coloring algorithm for P_i

code). In our example P_{n-1} assigns ⊥ to $color_{n-1}$ and $r_{n-1}.color$. Then P_{n-1} chooses a color different from the color of P_n and P_{n-2}. Thus, a safe configuration is reached. To prove superstabilization of an algorithm, one needs first to prove that the algorithm is self-stabilizing. Consider an execution of the superstabilizing algorithm in figure 7.2 in which no topology change occurs. In every configuration that follows the first asynchronous cycle of the algorithm, the values of $color_i$ and $r_i.color$ of every processor P_i are not equal to ⊥. Moreover, processors execute only lines 1 to 12 of the code during the execution. Thus, following the first asynchronous cycle, the processor P_n with the largest identifier has a fixed color. The proof continues by induction, proving that the processor P_{n-1} with the second largest identifier chooses a color that is fixed through the entire execution during the next cycle. The proof uses the fact that the color of P_n is already fixed, so that when P_{n-1} is a neighbor of P_n, P_{n-1} does not choose the color of P_n. The same argument is used repeatedly to prove that P_i chooses a color that is different from the color of every neighbor P_j with $j > i$ in the jth cycle, and that this color remains fixed.

The terms *passage predicate, superstabilizing time complexity*, and *adjustment measure* can be demonstrated using the superstabilizing coloring algorithm in figure 7.2. The passage predicate ensures that the color of neighboring processors is always different in any execution that starts in a safe configuration and in which only a single edge may fail or recover before the next safe configuration is reached. Superstabilizing time complexity is measured by the number of cycles required to reach a safe configuration following a topology change. Clearly, the superstabilizing time complexity of the algorithm in figure 7.2 is one cycle (while the stabilizing complexity is $O(n)$ cycles). The adjustment measure for our algorithm is the number of processors that change color upon a topology change; this is only one processor, when the topology changes considered are link addition or removal.

7.2   Self-Stabilizing Fault-Containing Algorithms

The goal of superstabilizing algorithms is to cope with dynamic systems. A change in the topology of the system may require a state change of processors that are far from the portion of the system in which the topology change (such as the crash of a processor) occurred. Moreover, it is possible for a single dynamic change to require a state change of every processor in the system. For example, consider the rooted spanning-tree task in which every processor except one chooses one of its neighbors as its parent. Consider a safe configuration of a ring of processors P_1, P_2, $\cdots$, P_n, where P_1 communicates with both P_2 and P_n. By the definition of the rooted spanning-tree task, there is a single edge that is not marked as a tree edge. Clearly, the failure of an edge that is neighboring to the root disconnects the original ring communication graph and may force approximately half of the processors to change their parent.

A less severe fault model is one that considers only transient faults. Unlike the case of dynamic changes, it is possible to repair the system configuration after the occurrence of f transient faults by changing the state of the f processors that experienced a fault back to their original state in the safe configuration. The goal of self-stabilizing fault-containing algorithms is to ensure that: (1) from any arbitrary configuration, a safe configuration is reached, and (2) starting from a safe configuration that is followed by transient faults that corrupt the state of f processors, a safe configuration is reached within $O(f)$ cycles.

In this section we present a self-stabilizing fault-containing algorithm for fixed output tasks. The algorithm is designed for synchronous systems. A fixed input for this algorithm is assumed; for example, the input for each processor is its fixed local topology and the output is a description of a single spanning tree of the entire system.

```
01 upon a pulse
02      ReadSet_i := ∅
03      forall P_j ∈ N(i) do
04          ReadSet_i := ReadSet_i ∪ read(Processors_j)
05      ReadSet_i := ReadSet_i \\ ⟨i, *, *⟩
06      ReadSet_i := ReadSet_i ++⟨*, 1, *⟩
07      ReadSet_i := ReadSet_i ∪ {⟨i, 0, I_i⟩}
08      forall P_j ∈ processors(ReadSet_i) do
09          ReadSet_i := ReadSet_i \\ NotMinDist(P_j, ReadSet_i)
10      write Processors_i := ConPrefix (ReadSet_i)
11      write O_i := ComputeOutput_i (Inputs(Processors_i))
```

Figure 7.3
Fixed-output synchronous algorithm for processor P_i

Before we start, let us first design a self-stabilizing algorithm for all such fixed-input fixed-output tasks. To do this, we assume that the variable I_i contains the fixed-input of the processor P_i and that the variable O_i is the output variable of P_i, to which the result of the algorithm should be assigned. Interestingly, a version of the self-stabilizing update algorithm presented in section 4.4 is a self-stabilizing (synchronous and asynchronous) algorithm for any fixed-input fixed-output task. In this version, the tuples $⟨id, dis⟩$ in $Processors_i$, $ReadSet_i$ used by the update algorithm are replaced by $⟨id, dis, I_{id}⟩$, where I_{id} is the fixed input of the processor P_{id}. Every processor P_i includes a tuple $⟨id, 0, I_i⟩$ in $Processors_i$. The code of the algorithm appears in figure 7.3. Each processor P_i reads all the tuples from the $Processors$ variables of its neighbors (in lines 3 and 4 of the code), then removes all the tuples with identifier i from the set of tuples that were read. The distance field in each of the remaining tuples is incremented by 1 (in line 6 of the code) and a tuple $⟨id, 0, I_i⟩$ is added to the read set. Next, for each tuple in the read set a tuple with the smallest distance is chosen and all the rest are eliminated from $ReadSet_i$. The $ConPrefix$ function eliminates all tuples with distance field x such that there exists a distance $y < x$ that is present in any tuple of $ReadSet_i$. The semantics of the operators $\\$ and $++$ are implied in a straightforward manner from the above description. The function $ComputeOutput_i$ uses the inputs of the processors appearing in $Processors_i$ to determine the global output. Clearly, when every processor has the correct input value of all the processors, the computed output is correct. Thus, we need only show that eventually each processor has the correct value of the input values; this is implied by the assignment in line 7 of figure 7.3 and the fact that every processor P_j copies the tuple with $id = i$ from a processor P_k that is at a smaller distance from P_i than the distance from P_j to P_i.

Does the algorithm presented in figure 7.3 have the fault-containment property? Starting in a safe configuration c of the algorithm presented in figure 7.3, is it possible to change the state of a few of the processors and cause an output change in a large portion of the system? Note that no input is changed, and therefore the outputs in c and the safe configuration that follows the faults, occurrence must be identical. The answer to the above question is positive. Consider a system with a chain communication graph, $P_1, P_2, \cdots, P_n$. In a safe configuration, P_n has a tuple $\langle 1, n - 1, I_1 \rangle$ in $Processors_n$. Assume that a transient fault has changed this tuple to $\langle 1, 1, I_1' \rangle$. In such a case, at the first pulse after the occurrence of the faults, the processor P_{n-1} will assign a tuple $\langle 1, 2, I_1' \rangle$ in $Processors_{n-1}$. Thus, since $I_1 \neq I_1'$, P_{n-1} assigns a wrong output to O_{n-1}. Moreover, the propagation of the wrong input I_1' will continue during approximately the next $n/2$ pulses, causing approximately half of the processors to write a wrong output to their output variables.

On the other hand, a processor P_i that is about to change the value of O_i may take the following conservative approach: P_i waits d pulses before the $ComputeOutput_i$ function is invoked and the result is written in O_i. The above technique ensures stabilization from every arbitrary state and also ensures that, starting in a safe configuration followed by several simultaneous transient faults, only the output of the processors that experienced a fault can be changed, and each such change is a change to the correct output value. However, in this case, the time it takes for the output correction is $O(d)$, which may be much greater than the number f of processors that experienced a transient fault.

As a first step toward the solution, let us assume that, when a processor P_i writes a new value in O_i using the value of the I fields in $Processors_i$, it also writes the $evidence$ for computing O_i in a variable A_i. The evidence for computing O_i is the values of the I fields in $Processors_i$. Each tuple of the update algorithm also includes a field A; hence, each tuple in $Processors_i$ and $ReadSet_i$ is $\langle id, dis, I, A \rangle$. The code of the algorithm appears in figure 7.4. The first part of the code (lines 2 through 10) is a version of the update algorithm in which two additional fields, I and A, are included in every tuple.

The additional A variable enables the processors that experienced a fault to learn quickly about the inputs of remote processors. Most of the A variables of the processors within distance $2f + 1$ or less from a processor are the set of correct inputs. Thus, the value of the A variables should not be changed for a

```
01 upon a pulse
02     ReadSet_i := ∅
03     forall P_j ∈ N(i) do
04         ReadSet_i := ReadSet_i ∪ read(Processors_j)
05         if RepairCounter_i ≠ d + 1 then
06             RepairCounter_i := min(RepairCounter_i, read(RepairCounter_j))
07     od
08     ReadSet_i := ReadSet_i \\ ⟨i, *, *, *⟩
09     ReadSet_i := ReadSet_i + +⟨*, 1, *, *⟩
10     ReadSet_i := ReadSet_i ∪ {⟨i, 0, I_i, A_i⟩}
11     forall P_j ∈ processors(ReadSet_i) do
12         ReadSet_i := ReadSet_i \\ NotMinDist(P_j, ReadSet)
13     write Processors_i := ConPrefix (ReadSet_i)
14     if RepairCounter_i = d + 1 then
15         if (O_i ≠ ComputeOutput_i (Inputs(Processors_i))) or
16             (∃⟨*, *, *, A⟩ ∈ Processors_i | A ≠ Inputs(Processors_i)) then
17                 RepairCounter_i := 0
18     else
19         RepairCounter_i := min(RepairCounter_i + 1, d + 1)
20         write O_i := ComputeOutput_i (RepairCounter_i,
21             MajorityInputs(Processors_i))
22         if RepairCounter_i = d + 1 then
23             A_i := Inputs(Processors_i)
```

Figure 7.4
Self-stabilizining fault-containing algorithm for processor P_i

time sufficient to let faulty processors collect the value of the A variables from their neighborhood. Faulty processors maintain a repair counter to indicate the distance from which the A variables have been collected since the fault was detected. The repair counter is incremented by 1 in every pulse, measuring the distance for which the tuples of the update algorithm are correct. The faulty processor has no idea of the diameter of the faulty region, but eventually the repair counter will reach $2f + 1$ (and continue to be incremented). From this point, the values of at least $2f + 1$ A variables are known and the computed output, which is based on the majority of the processors within the distance indicated by the repair counter, is correct.

Before we continue describing the algorithm, let us discuss the main idea behind the fast repair. A safe configuration is a configuration in which, for every tuple $\langle x, dis, I, A \rangle$ in $Processors_i$, the value of dis is the distance of P_x from P_i, the value of I is the input of P_x, and the value of A is a set of all the inputs of the processors. Moreover, the values in the $ReadSet$ variables are such that no change in the value of the tuples is possible. Starting in a safe configuration that is followed by transient faults affecting a set of processors, no processor changes the value of A_i for $d + 1$ pulses. These A variables are the basis of the fast recovery.

The repair process starts by assigning $RepairCounter_i := 0$ (in line 17 of the code). The trigger for starting a repair process is an indication that a fault occurred. First the current output of the processor is checked by applying the function $ComputeOutput_i$ to the inputs of the system appearing in the I fields of the $Processors$ set (line 15). Then the A field of every tuple in $Processors_i$ is checked to see that it is identical to the collection of the input fields I of all the tuples. The repair counter is then incremented in every pulse (line 19). The computed output considers the majority of A values among the tuples with distance-field value less than or equal to the value of $RepairCounter_i$ (lines 20 and 21). Finally, the evidence A_i is recorded only when $RepairCounter_i$ is $d + 1$ (lines 22 and 23).

7.3 Error-Detection Codes and Repair

In the previous section we considered only fixed-output tasks. In this section we present a scheme that can be used to correct the state of algorithms for ongoing long-lived tasks. This scheme is designed to convert non-stabilizing algorithms for such tasks to self-stabilizing algorithms for the same tasks.

Up to this point we have assumed that a transient fault can change the state of a processor arbitrarily, and have evaluated a self-stabilizing algorithm by the maximal number of cycles it takes to converge to a safe configuration. Here we propose a different metric for evaluating a self-stabilizing algorithm. Starting from a safe configuration c after which k processors experience a transient fault, a new configuration c' is reached. The states of the processors that experienced a fault can be chosen as the states that result in the longest convergence time. We call this model of faults that assumes the worst-case state changes the *malicious transient faults* model.

Self-stabilizing algorithms designed with the worst case measure in mind minimize the convergence time in the worst case scenario of transient faults. However, roughly speaking these algorithms may have larger *average convergence time* than other algorithms. To define the average convergence time in the context of local stabilization, we first define the *probability of a configuration*. In the *nonmalicious transient fault model* a transient fault assigns to the processor P_i that experiences a fault a state that is chosen with equal probability from the state space of P_i. The probability $pr(c, k, c')$ of reaching a particular configuration c' from a safe configuration c due to the occurrence of k faults is the combined probability that every processor experiencing a fault changes its state to the state in c'. Let *WorstCase(c)* be the maximal number of cycles before the system reaches a safe configuration when it starts in c. The *average convergence time* following the occurrence of k non-malicious transient faults is the sum of the products $\Sigma pr(c, k, c') \cdot WorstCase(c)$ over all possible configurations c'.

Error-detection codes can be used to reduce the average convergence time. Each processor maintains a variable *ErrorDetect* with the error-detection code *ed* of its current state s. The error-detection scheme is a function that computes a pair s, ed given s. Given an algorithm that does not use an error-detection code to identify non-malicious transient faults, we replace every step a by a step a' that first examines whether the value of *ErrorDetect* variable fits the state component, then executes either a if the above assertion holds or a special step a'' otherwise. Finally, the resulting state s' is augmented by ed' using the function of the error-detection code.

A transient fault can corrupt all the memory bits of a processor. Thus, the probability that, following such a corruption, the value of the *ErrorDetect* variable will fit the state of a processor decreases as the number of bits added to each processor to implement the *ErrorDetect* variable increases.

The repair scheme described below uses error-detection codes and the pyramid data structure described in section 5.2. The repair scheme is designed for synchronous systems and can be used to correct the state of algorithms for ongoing long-lived tasks. First, assume that every transient fault is identified by the error-detection code. Recall that the pyramid data structure consists of d snapshots and the base of the pyramid is a snapshot of the entire system. Roughly speaking, the processors that identify a corruption of their memories initialize their states and start collecting state information from the neighboring processors that did not experience faults. Then the faulty processors reconstruct their pyramids and the execution continues.

First let us assume that every transient fault is identified by the error-detection code. Then we consider the (rare) case in which the error-detection code does not identify the occurrence of transient faults. Let c' be the configuration reached following the occurrence of transient faults from a safe configuration. The processors in c' are categorized as *faulty, border non-faulty*, or *operating*, where every processor that identifies the occurrence of a fault (due to the error-detection code) assigns *faulty* to a *status* variable and resets its pyramid (to have only nil values). One would like to stop the entire system at this stage and use the data in the non-corrupted pyramid to reconstruct the corrupted pyramid. For example, the pyramid of a non-faulty processor P_i that is next to a faulty processor P_j has almost all the information stored in the pyramid for P_j prior to the occurrence of the fault. In particular, P_i has the full snapshot of the base of P_j's pyramid. In our distributed system it is impossible immediately to stop the operation of the processors in the system. Instead, a processor that identifies that it is next to a faulty processor changes its *status* variable to *border non-faulty*.

A border non-faulty processor does not change its pyramid until it receives an indication that all the faulty processors are finished reconstructing their pyramids. A topology-collection procedure is the tool for such an indication. When a processor experiences a transient fault that is identified by the error-detection code, it assigns its local topology (the links connected to itself) to a topology variable. In every time unit, a faulty processor and a border non-faulty processor send the topology known to them so far to their neighbors and receive the topology the neighbors send. Thus, faulty and border non-faulty processors collect the topology of the corrupted region within a number of rounds that is equal to the diameter of the corrupted region. Moreover, in one additional round the information collected at each such processor indicates that the information in the pyramid of every processor next to a faulty processor has arrived (together with its local topology). The following test is used to identify that the information required to reconstruct the pyramid is still missing: each processor checks whether the topology collected so far includes an edge attached to a faulty processor such that the status of the other node connected to this edge is still unknown. The pyramid is reconstructed when the above test returns false. However, part of the information needed to reconstruct the pyramids is missing; specificelly, the latest states of the faulty processors that were recorded in the pyramids of faulty processors are missing. The reconstruction procedure at each processor uses the information collected from the other pyramids and the transition functions of the processors to reconstruct the missing data.

Faulty and border non-faulty processors can use the topology information and a local round counter that counts the number of rounds since the occurrence of the fault (detection of the transient fault) to conclude when the rest of the processors will reconstrut their pyramids. Thus, these processors can simultaneously change their status to operating.

Now that we have described how faults are handled when every transient fault is identified by the error-detection code, let us consider an arbitrary state.

Note that an arbitrary state can be reached because of transient faults that are not detected by the error-detection code. Transient fault detectors and *watchdog counters* are used to cope with such states. Whenever an error is detected by the transient fault detectors, the processors that detect the fault start counting, letting the repair procedure try to fix the system. Once a watchdog counter reaches its upper bound, the system is examined again by the transient fault detector and a reset is triggered if a fault is still detected. The upper bound for the watchdog counter is computed as the upper bound for repairing transient faults, which is $O(d)$.

Exercises

7.1. Design a superstabilizing leader election algorithm in a system with a complete communication graph. Assume that the events $recover_{ij}$, $crash_{ij}$, and $recover_i$ trigger an interrupt at processor P_i. Note that a topology change is a node addition or node removal. A node removal or addition is associated with edge recoveries or crashes such that a complete communication graph is obtained. The passage predicate ensures that, starting in a safe configuration that is followed by a processor crash, no more than one leader exists in each configuration. Compute the superstabilizing time complexity of your algorithm.

7.2. Does there exist a superstabilizing algorithm for leader election in a system with a complete communication graph such that exactly one leader exists in each configuration that is reached by a single topology change that follows a safe configuration?

7.3. Design a self-stabilizing fault-containing α synchronizer that uses error-detection codes and recovers in one cycle following the occurrence of a single transient fault.

7.4. Design a repair scheme that uses error-detection codes for a fixed output algorithm. Your scheme should use less memory than the scheme presented in this chapter for an ongoing long-lived algorithm (an algorithm with no fixed output).

7.5. Design a repair scheme that uses error-detection codes (and less memory than the scheme presented in this chapter) for the following resource allocation problem: no two neighboring processors are simultaneously in the critical section and every processor is in the critical section infinitely often.

Notes

Distributed algorithms for dynamic networks have been studied extensively. We mention here [AAG87; AGR92; DW97], which are only a few of the results in the area. Some of the research works that have proposed using self-stabilization for dynamic networks are [DIM93; KP93; APSV91; AG94]. Superstabilizing algorithms were presented in [DH95; DH97], where several examples of superstabilizing algorithms and a general scheme for converting a self-stabilizing algorithm to a superstabilizing algorithm were presented. A superstabilizing algorithm for high-speed networks was presented in [AACD$^+$96]. Superstabilizing algorithms are further studied in [UKMF97].

Two related terms are *masking* and *nonmasking fault tolerance*. *Masking fault-tolerant algorithms* are algorithms that cope with a predefined set of faults in a predefined way, while *nonmasking fault-tolerant algorithms* are self-stabilizing algorithms that can be started in an arbitrary configuration but exhibit arbitrary behavior during convergence [AK95].

The fault-containment approach was introduced in [GGHP96; GG96; GGP96]. In [KPS97], the term *time-adaptive* is used for a general scheme based on voting to achieve fault containment. The use of encryption schemes to ensure that processors identify transient failures was suggested in [YB95; Yen96] to achieve mutual exclusion that is safer, with high probability, than previous algorithms. In [AD97], a local stabilizer that uses error-detection codes was introduced. The local stabilizer of [AD97] converts any algorithm (fixed-output, non-fixed-output, or even interactive) to cope with f faults within $O(f)$ cycles.

8 Self-Stabilizing Computing

In this chapter we present several theoretical results concerning computations of Turing machines.

8.1 The Computation Power of Self-Stabilizing Systems

Extensive research has been performed on self-stabilization using a constant amount of memory per processor. If such a system exists, then there is no need to know in advance how many processors will be connected to form the system. In some of the self-stabilizing algorithms presented so far, the memory usage of a processor depends on the number of processors. Alternatively, it is assumed that a bound on the number of processors, or on the diameter of the system, is known to every processor. In contrast, in a system with a constant amount of memory per processor, the memory usage of each processor is fixed — k bits — no matter how many processors are connected to the system. A self-stabilizing algorithm that uses a constant amount of memory per processor can be implemented by, e.g., microprocessors that are fabricated uniformly. Moreover, the number of processors connected to the system can be changed dynamically without changing the amount of memory used by each processor.

In this section we ask the following question: is the computation power of a self-stabilizing distributed system composed of processors with a constant amount of memory identical to the computation power of a single processor with that total amount of memory? In other words, does the fact that the memory is distributed among several processors reduce the computation power of the system? The single processor with the total amount of memory is modeled by a Turing machine. Note that the program itself is stored in the memory of the processors — the program of a Turing machine is the transition table of the Turing machine. To eliminate the transition table size factor, let us consider only a specific universal Turing machine [HU79]. We show that the constant-memory processors in the distributed system can simulate the universal Turing machine in a self-stabilizing fashion.

To do this, we first present a token-passing algorithm for a chain of processors $P_1, P_2, \cdots, P_n$. The token-passing algorithm we chose is a version of Dijkstra's second mutual exclusion algorithm that is designed to work with steps that are either read or write (without assuming the existence of a powerful central daemon that activates one processor at a time). The processors have a sense of direction: P_1 knows that it is the leftmost processor and P_n knows that it is the rightmost processor. Every other processor P_i, $1 < i < n$, knows that P_{i-1} is its left neighbor and P_{i+1} is its right neighbor.

Token-Passing with a Constant Number of States

Two neighboring processors P_i and P_j communicate by two shared registers r_{ij} and r_{ji}. P_i writes in r_{ij} and reads from r_{ji}. Each register r_{ij} has a *color* field $r_{ij}.color$ that can store three values, 0, 1, 2. The processor P_1 repeatedly performs the following actions in the following order:

1. P_1 reads the value of $r_{2,1}.color$ into a local variable $lr_{2,1}.color$. We say that a *token* arrives at P_1 when the value of $lr_{2,1}.color$ is changed to the value of $r_{1,2}.color$.

2. If the value of $lr_{2,1}.color$ is equal to the value of $r_{1,2}.color$, P_1 increments the value of $r_{1,2}.color$ by 1 modulo 3.

A processor P_i, $1 < i < n$, repeatedly performs the following actions in the following order:

1. P_i reads the value of $r_{i-1,i}.color$ into $lr_{i-1,i}.color$. We say that a *left token* arrives at P_i when the value in $lr_{i-1,i}.color$ is changed by the above assignment.

2. P_i writes the value of $lr_{i-1,i}.color$ into $r_{i,i+1}.color$.

3. P_i then reads the value of $r_{i+1,i}.color$ into $lr_{i+1,i}.color$. If $lr_{i+1,i}.color = lr_{i-1,i}.color$, P_i writes $r_{i,i-1}.color := lr_{i+1,i}.color$. We say that a *right token* arrives at P_i when the value of $lr_{i+1,i}.color$ is changed to the value of $lr_{i,i-1}.color$.

P_n, the last processor in the chain, repeatedly performs the following actions:

1. P_n reads $r_{n-1,n}.color$ into $lr_{n-1,n}.color$. We say that a *token* arrives at P_n when the value of $lr_{n-1,n}.color$ is changed.

2. P_n writes the value of $lr_{n-1,n}.color$ into $r_{n,n-1}.color$.

Now we are ready to describe an execution of the algorithm following its stabilization phase. A safe configuration for the token-passing task for our algorithm is a configuration in which the value of all the color fields of the registers and the color fields of the internal variables have an identical value, e.g., the color 1. The algorithm starts when P_1 changes the value in

$r_{1,2}.color$ to 2. P_2 then reads this value into $lr_{1,2}.color$ and changes the value of $r_{2,3}.color$ to 2. In general, the new value 2 propagates from $r_{i,i+1}.color$ to $lr_{i,i+1}.color$ and then to $r_{i+1,i+2}.color$, until it is copied to $lr_{n-1,n}$. The value 2 is then copied from $lr_{n-1,n}$ to $r_{n,n-1}$. Roughly speaking, at this stage the propagation of the new value is over and the acknowledgment is now propagating toward P_1. A processor P_i, $1 < i < n - 1$, copies the value of $r_{i+1,i}.color$ into $r_{i,i-1}.color$. Once P_1 finds that the value 2 has returned, it uses the value 0 as a new value that propagates in the system.

The stabilization of the above algorithm is proven by the following lemmas.

LEMMA 8.1:   In every fair execution, P_1 changes the value of $r_{1,2}.color$ infinitely often.

Proof Assume that there is a configuration c_0 after which the value of $r_{1,2}.color$ is fixed. By the fairness of the execution, P_2 is activated infinitely often after c_0, and therefore copies the value of $r_{1,2}.color$ into $lr_{1,2}.color$ and into $r_{2,3}.color$ infinitely often. Thus a configuration c_1 is reached after which the values of $r_{1,2}.color$, $lr_{1,2}.color$ and $r_{2,3}.color$ are identical. Similarly, following c_1, P_3 is activated infinitely often and a configuration c_2 is reached after which the values of $lr_{2,3}.color$ and $r_{3,4}.color$ are equal to the value of $r_{1,2}.color$. The above argument can be repeated until a configuration c_{n-2} is reached, after which the value of every $r_{i,i+1}.color$ and $lr_{i,i+1}.color$, $1 \leq i \leq n - 1$, is identical to the value of $r_{1,2}.color$.

The proof continues by arguing that the values of $r_{i+1,i}.color$ and $lr_{i+1,i}.color$ for $1 \leq i \leq n - 1$ are equal, from some point of the execution, to the value of $r_{1,2}.color$, first considering $r_{n,n-1}.color$ and $lr_{n,n-1}.color$ and then continuing with decreasing values of i. Hence we can conclude that, from some configuration, the values of all the color fields are identical to the value of $r_{1,2}.color$. The proof is complete, since P_1 is activated infinitely often following the above configuration and thus must change the value of $r_{1,2}.color$, and so on. ∎

The next lemma proves that the system reaches a safe configuration.

LEMMA 8.2:   In every fair execution, a configuration is reached in which all the color fields of the communication registers and internal variables have identical values.

Outline of proof: Lemma 8.1 proves that the value of $r_{1,2}.color$ is changed infinitely often. Thus the value of $lr_{2,1}.color$ is changed infinitely often as well. Consider an execution E that contains four successive changes of $r_{1,2}.color$. Let $color^i$ be the color assigned to $r_{1,2}.color$ in the ith color change of $r_{1,2}.color$. E contains the following steps, in the specified order:

1. P_1 writes $color^1$ to $r_{1,2}.color$
2. P_1 reads $color^1$ in $r_{2,1}.color$
3. P_1 writes $color^2$ to $r_{1,2}.color$
4. P_1 reads $color^2$ in $r_{2,1}.color$
5. P_1 writes $color^3$ to $r_{1,2}.color$
6. P_1 reads $color^3$ in $r_{2,1}.color$

Therefore P_2 must write $color^2$ to $r_{1,2}.color$ between steps 2 and 4. In addition, P_2 must write $color^3$ to $r_{1,2}.color$ between steps 4 and 6. Hence, between steps 2 and 6, P_2 must read $color^3$ in $r_{1,2}.color$. Since $color^1$, $color^2$ and $color^3$ are distinct, the read operation of P_2 must occur after step 5 and before step 6. Thus, between steps 5 and 6, P_2 reads $color^3$ in $r_{1,2}.color$ and writes $color^3$ in $r_{2,1}.color$. Immediately after this write operation, it holds that $r_{1,2}.color = lr_{1,2}.color = r_{2,1}.color$. From this stage, P_2 changes the color of ($r_{2,3}.color$ and) $r_{2,1}.color$ only to the current color of $r_{1,2}.color$.

The proof continues by considering the color changes of P_2 (which are in accord with the color changes of P_1), proving that P_3 always changes eventually color to the color of P_1. ∎

Note that three colors are necessary to guarantee that such a safe configuration is reached. To demonstrate the problems of using only two colors, consider a system with two processors P_1 and P_2. P_1 writes to $r_{1,2}.color$ and reads from $r_{2,1}.color$. Similarly, P_2 writes to $r_{2,1}.color$ and reads from $r_{1,2}.color$. P_1 stores the value it reads from $r_{2,1}.color$ in $lr_{2,1}.color$. Analogously, P_2 stores the values read from $r_{1,2}.color$ in $lr_{1,2}.color$.

The programs for P_1 and P_2 appear in figure 8.1. The state of P_1 is defined by the values of its program counter and the color fields $r_{1,2}.color$ and $lr_{2,1}.color$. Analogously, the state of P_2 is defined by the values of its program counter and the color fields $r_{2,1}.color$ and $lr_{1,2}.color$. Note that, following the first write operation, the value of the internal variables $color_1$ and $color_2$ are identical to the value in $r_{1,2}.color$ and $r_{2,1}.color$, respectively. The first write operation by P_1 and P_2 is executed during the first cycle of the execution.

```
01 P₁: do forever
02          lr₂,₁.color := read(r₂,₁.color)
03          if color₁ = lr₂,₁.color then (* token arrives *)
04                color₁ := 1 − lr₂,₁.color
05          write r₁,₂.color := color₁
06      od
07 P₂: do forever
08          lr₁,₂.color := read(r₁,₂.color)
09          if color₂ ≠ lr₁,₂.color then (* token arrives *)
10                color₂ := lr₁,₂.color
11          write r₂,₁.color := color₂
12      od
```

Figure 8.1
Balance-unbalance algorithm

The value of the program counter in any configuration is a line number in the code that starts an atomic step. The processor's program has two atomic steps: a read atomic step and a write atomic step. The read atomic step of P_1 starts in line 2 and its write atomic step starts in line 3. Lines 8 and 9 are the first lines of the read and write atomic steps of P_2, respectively. Let us describe a state of a processor by a tuple that includes the next step to be executed and the values of its internal variable and communication register. For example, the tuple $\langle read, 0, 1 \rangle$ describing the state of P_1 includes the following information: the next atomic step of P_1 is one in which P_1 reads, the value of $r_{1,2}.color$ is 0, and the value of $lr_{2,1}.color$ is 1. A configuration is a pair of states (s_1, s_2) where s_1 is the state of P_1 and s_2 is the state of P_2.

Our goal is to prove that at least three color values are required. We present a fair execution in which there is no safe configuration. A processor *holds a token* if its next step is a step in which it writes. The *token-passing* task is identified by executions in which every processor holds a token infinitely often and there is no configuration in which more than one processor holds a token. Let us repeat that a configuration is safe if all the values of the color fields are identical. The execution starts in a configuration $(\langle write, 0, 0 \rangle, \langle write, 1, 0 \rangle)$ and activates P_2 twice and then P_1 twice, and so on. The description of the execution is:

$$(\langle write, 0, 0 \rangle, \langle write, 1, 0 \rangle) \xrightarrow{P_2, w}$$
$$(\langle write, 0, 0 \rangle, \langle read, 1, 1 \rangle) \xrightarrow{P_2, r}$$
$$(\langle write, 0, 0 \rangle, \langle write, 0, 1 \rangle) \xrightarrow{P_1, w}$$

$$(\langle read, 0, 1 \rangle, \langle write, 0, 1 \rangle) \xrightarrow{P_1, r}$$
$$(\langle write, 1, 1 \rangle, \langle write, 0, 1 \rangle)$$

During this execution, every color value is changed to the opposite value. Thus, if P_2 is activated twice more and then P_1 is activated twice, a configuration identical to the first configuration is reached. Hence it is possible to continue to activate P_2 and P_1 forever to repeat the same pattern of configurations, none of which is a safe configuration. Note that, in the infinite execution obtained by repeating the above pattern, there is a configuration in which both P_1 and P_2 can change color simultaneously, for example the configuration $(\langle write, 0, 0 \rangle, \langle write, 1, 0 \rangle)$. Thus, both P_1 and P_2 hold a token simultaneously infinitely often.

Computing with Bounded Memory

To show that every input-output task can be computed in a self-stabilizing fashion by processors with a constant amount of memory, we define the following input-output mechanism. In addition to accessing its neighbors' communication registers, each processor P_i repeatedly reads one symbol of input from its external *input register* I_i and writes one symbol of output to its *output register* O_i. The content of I_i and O_i are either 0,1 or $\perp$. We view the concatenation of the input symbols as a fixed word in $\{0, 1\}^l \perp^{n-l}$, where $n \geq l$.

We require that, for any finite n, when the algorithm is executed by a system of n processors and is started in any possible configuration c with input $w \perp^{n-l}$ ($n \geq l$), then: any fair execution that starts with c has a suffix in which the output of every processor P_i is constant. Moreover, this constant output is 1 (0, respectively) if the Turing machine accepts (rejects) w using no more than n working tape cells; otherwise, the output is $\perp$.

To simulate the execution of the Turing machine, we use the self-stabilizing token-passing algorithm presented above. In our description, we use the terms *send* and *receive* token, which are implemented by the token-passing algorithm in an obvious way. By the self-stabilizing property of the token-passing algorithm, it eventually holds that a single token exists and that this single token is sent repeatedly from the rightmost processor in the chain to the leftmost processor and back again. The token can carry information: a value is written in a token field just before it is transferred to a neighbor (the token is transferred by changing the value of $r_{i,i+1}.color$ or the value of $r_{i-1,i}.color$). To do this, every processor P_i, $1 < i < n$, has *token* fields in its registers — namely, $r_{i,i-1}.token$ and $r_{i,i+1}.token$ — while P_1 has $r_{1,2}.token$ and P_n has $r_{n,n-1}.token$. A processor writes to $r_{ij}.token$ just before changing the value of $r_{ij}.color$. In what follows, we consider the token as an entity with data fields that moves in the system. For example, we later use the value of the field $token.carry$ to implement a distributed counter.

Each processor maintains the information of a single working tape cell. In a well-initialized simulation, a single processor is marked to hold the head of the Turing machine. Whenever the token reaches the processor that holds the head of the Turing machine, the value of the working tape cell and the current state of the Turing machine are used to calculate the transition of the Turing machine. The transition itself includes modification of the contents of the working tape cell, state change of the Turing machine, and movement of the head mark to a neighboring processor.

The system can be started in any possible configuration, and in particular in a configuration in which no head mark exists. Obviously, in an execution that starts in such a configuration, the Turing machine will not make any move. Thus we need to control the activity of the Turing machine. To overcome this difficulty, we propose using an implementation of a distributed binary counter in which each processor maintains two bits of the counter. An increment operation of the distributed counter starts when the token reaches the leftmost processor and continues until the rightmost processor is reached. If the increment operation at a processor P_n produces a carry, the carry is sent to P_{n-1}, and P_{n-1} in turn increments its portion of the counter by 1. In general, a carry is sent to P_{i-1} whenever the increment operation at P_i results in a carry. Otherwise, the portion of the counter at P_{i-1} remains unchanged: it is not affected by the increment operation of the distributed counter that is performed during the traversal of the token from P_n to P_1.

The system is initialized when counter overflow occurs — when the increment of the distributed counter results in a carry at P_1. Thus, from every possible initial state and no matter what the arbitrary counter value is in this configuration, the system eventually reaches a configuration in which a counter overflow occurs. A counter overflow triggers a reset that initializes the working cells to hold the inputs.

In more detail, each processor P_i maintains two bits of the distributed counter in $CounterBits_i$. When a token arrives at P_n, P_n computes the new value for $CounterBits_n$ after incrementing it by 1 and, at the same time, computes the carry. For example, if $CounterBits_n = 11$ then the value of $CounterBits_n$ is changed to 00 and the carry that is sent in $token.carry$

is 1. (Recall that we use an abstraction in which the token is an entity that can be sent from a processor to its neighbor.) Similarly, when a token with $token.carry = 1$ arrives at a processor P_i with $CounterBits_i = 11$, the value of $CounterBits_n$ is changed to 00 and the carry sent in $token.carry$ is 1.

A reset procedure is invoked when an overflow occurs in $CounterBits_1$. The following activities occur during the reset: (1) every processor P_i writes its input to $WorkSymbol_i$, which is the ith cell of the virtual Turing machine working tape; (2) every processor P_i, except P_1, sets a flag $HeadMark_i$ to be false, while P_1 sets $HeadMark_1$ to be true; (3) the binary bits of each processor are set to 00; and (4) $\perp$ is assigned to the output O_i. The computation of the Turing machine is simulated during the traversal of the token from P_1 to P_n. Whenever a processor P_i with $HeadMark_i = true$ receives a token that traverses in this direction, the Turing machine transition table is used to determine the value for $WorkSymbol_i$, the movement of the head, and the new Turing machine state. The movement of the Turing machine head is done together with the token movement: a right movement is done when the token moves toward P_n and a left movement when the token returns toward P_1. For example, when $HeadMark_i = true$ and the token arrives at P_i from the left, P_i uses the Turing machine transition table to determine the value of $WorkSymbol_i$, the direction in which the head should move and the new state of the Turing machine. In our example, assume that the direction in which the Turing machine head should move is left. P_i sends the token to the right; the token eventually reaches P_n and then returns toward P_1. During the token return, when P_i receives the token it sets $HeadMark_i = false$ and send the token to P_{i-1} with a signal to set $HeadMark_{i-1} := true$.

To prove that the system eventually produces the right output, we use the floating output technique presented in section 2.8. Once the Turing machine enters a state in which it accepts or rejects, the token carries the information about acceptance or rejection to every processor. Each processor P_i copies the result to its output O_i and then P_1 resets the system. The reset procedure invoked is identical to that triggered by a counter overflow; the only difference is that the (floating) output O_i is not changed. Hence, once the system completes the first computation following the first reset, the same output is recomputed repeatedly and no change is made in the value of O_i.

A key observation is that the number of Turing machine configurations with a tape of size n and alphabet $\{0, 1\}$ is at most $Cn^2 2^n$. The reason is that there are n possibilities for the location of the first $\perp$ and no more than 2^n possible working tape contents until the location of the first $\perp$. There are n

possibilities for the location of the Turing machine head and C possibilities for the current Turing machine state, where for certain universal Turing machines $C \leq 56$ [HU79].

The counter ensures that from every initial configuration a reset is invoked within $Cn^2 2^n$ Turing machine configurations. The reset is invoked either when the simulated Turing machine enters the accept or reject state or because of a distributed counter overflow. The distributed counter may have an arbitrary initial value. Therefore the first counter overflow occurs within $2^{2n} > Cn^2 2^n$ (for $n > 14$) Turing machine transitions. The second overflow occurs only if the Turing machine does not accept or reject the input word during $2^{2n} > Cn^2 2^n$ transitions. In this last case, the Turing machine must have been in a certain configuration more than once since the last reset — therefore the computation of the Turing machine enters an "infinite loop" and a reset execution is in place.

Note that the above result is an "existence result" and is not designed as an efficient algorithm for performing the simulation of the Turing machine.

8.2 Queue Machine

A *queue machine* Q is a finite-state machine equipped with a queue. The queue initially contains a non-empty word from Σ^+ for some (finite) alphabet Σ. In each step of its computation, Q performs the following: (1) reads and deletes a letter from the head of the queue; (2) adds zero or more letters from Σ to the tail of the queue; and (3) changes a state. The computation terminates when the queue becomes empty, which prevents Q from performing any further steps. It is interesting to note that an oblivious Turing machine (which is as powerful as a Turing machine) is a variant of the queue machine. However, the fact that the input and work alphabets of a queue machine are identical causes the queue machine to be unable to perform simple tasks, such as deciding the length of the input word or even deciding whether the input word contains a specific letter.

Define a *token controller* as a special type of queue machine. Assume that the alphabet Σ contains a subset $\mathcal{T}$ of *token letters*. A queue machine is a *token controller* if, starting with a non-empty queue of arbitrary content and in an arbitrary state of the finite-state machine, the queue eventually contains exactly one occurrence of a letter from $\mathcal{T}$.

The token controller is an abstraction of the token-passing task presented in section 4.2, where the sender is the finite-state machine that receives (finite-

```
01 do forever
02     dequeue(color,CounterBit,Token)
03     if color = TokenColor then (* token arrives *)
04         begin
05             if carry = 1 then enqueue (color, 1, false)
06             TokenColor := (color + CounterXor + 1) (mod 3)
07             CounterXor := 0
08             carry := 1
09             Token := true
10         end
11     CounterXor := CounterXor ⊕ CounterBit
12     NewCounterBit := carry ⊕ CounterBit
13     carry := carry ∧ CounterBit
14     enqueue (TokenColor, NewCounterBit, Token)
15     Token := false
16 od
```

Figure 8.2
Token controller

length) messages and sends messages in response. The messages in transit on the link from the sender to the receiver and from the receiver to the sender form the content of the queue. In the queue controller, it is assumed that messages are not lost for a period long enough to ensure stabilization.

One implication of the lower-bound result of section 4.2 is that, if a token controller does exist, the asymptotic number of letters in the queue must be $\Omega(\log t)$, where t is the number of steps of Q. The queue can contain any number of arbitrary letters. Therefore, the finite state machine that is designed to control the queue (and uses the same set of letters that can appear in the queue) cannot perform even such a simple task as counting the letters in the queue. The queue may contain any combination of letters that convinces the finite-state machine that it scanned all the letters in the queue and a few additional letters. The above observation is true even if the finite-state machine is initialized to a special initial state. Hence the existence of a finite-state machine that can control any number of letters in its queue is surprising.

The program for the queue controller appears in figure 8.2. To control the queue the sender uses three colors to color the messages it sends. The sender has a variable *TokenColor* in which it stores the current color it uses to color the messages. Whenever a message with *color* = *TokenColor* arrives, the sender concludes that all the messages in the queue are of the same color and assigns a new color to *TokenColor*. Clearly, the sender's conclusion about the common color of the messages in the queue may be wrong at the beginning of the execution. However, we show that eventually the sender's conclusion is correct.

Definitions and ideas similar to those presented in sections 2.10 and 4.2 are used. Let us repeat and modify the definitions we use. Let $\mathcal{L}(c) = l_1, l_2, l_3, \cdots, l_k$ be the sequence of the labels of the messages in the queue in configuration c. The label l_1 is the label of the last message sent by the sender and the label l_k is the label of the message that is the first to arrive at the sender.

A segment of labels $\mathcal{S}(c) = l_j, l_{j+1}, \cdots, l_{j+n}$ in $\mathcal{L}(c)$, is a maximal sequence of labels in $\mathcal{L}(c)$ such that all the labels in $\mathcal{S}(c)$ are identical. The contents of the queue in a configuration c can be described by the segments of the queue $\mathcal{L}(c) = \mathcal{S}_1(c), \mathcal{S}_2(c), \cdots, \mathcal{S}_j(c)$, where $j = SegmentsNumber(\mathcal{L}(c))$, the number of segments in $\mathcal{L}(c)$.

We use the term *pseudo-stabilized configuration* for every configuration c in which the *MsgLabel* of the next (pending) message m_k to arrive at the sender has a value equal to the value of *TokenColor* in c. Note that a pseudo-stabilized configuration c is a safe configuration when $SegmentsNumber(\mathcal{L}(c))=1$. Let c_1 and c_2 be two successive pseudo-stabilized configurations in an arbitrary execution. According to our discussion in section 4.2, $SegmentsNumber(\mathcal{L}(c_1)) \geq SegmentsNumber(\mathcal{L}(c_2))$. Moreover, if the number of segments in c_1 and c_2 is the same, then the sender must choose in c_1 the label of $\mathcal{S}_{j-1}$ to be the new *TokenColor* value. Thus, if the number of segments is never reduced, then the sender must always choose the color of the next segment to arrive. Thus, the colors of the segments in c_1 uniquely define the sequence of colors that the sender must choose in an execution in which the number of segments in the pseudo-stabilized configurations is fixed.

Consider the pseudo-stabilized configuration c_1 in which: $\mathcal{L}(c_1)=\mathcal{S}_1(c_1)$, $\mathcal{S}_2(c_1),\mathcal{S}_3(c_1),\mathcal{S}_4(c_1)$ and the colors of $\mathcal{S}_1(c_1)$, $\mathcal{S}_2(c_1)$, $\mathcal{S}_3(c_1)$, and $\mathcal{S}_4(c_1)$ are 1, 2, 3, and 1, respectively. c_1 is a pseudo-stabilized configuration and hence a new color is chosen. The sender can choose a new color that is either 2 or 3. A choice of 2 leads to a pseudo-stabilized configuration c_2' in which $\mathcal{L}(c_2') = \mathcal{S}_1(c_2'), \mathcal{S}_2(c_2'), \mathcal{S}_3(c_2')$, where the colors of $\mathcal{S}_1(c_2'), \mathcal{S}_2(c_2')$, and $\mathcal{S}_3(c_2')$, are 2, 1, and 2, respectively. (Here $\mathcal{S}_1(c_2')$ consists of messages sent in response to receiving $\mathcal{S}_4(c_1)$ and $\mathcal{S}_3(c_1)$.) Therefore, a choice of 2 reduces the number of segments in the next pseudo-stabilized configuration. On the other hand, a choice of 3, which is the color of $\mathcal{S}_{j-1}(c_1)$, preserves the number of segments in the next pseudo-stabilized configuration c_2, resulting in segments with colors 3, 1, 2 and 3. The same arguments holds for c_2 and the next pseudo-stabilized configuration c_3, so that the next label that must be chosen in c_2 is the color of $\mathcal{S}_{j-1}(c_2)$, namely 2. Thus, the sequence of colors that the sender must choose in order to preserve the number of segments starting in c_1 is $[3, 2, 1]^\infty$.

In general, the colors of the segments in the first pseudo-configuration define the period of the infinite sequence that must be used in order to preserve that number of segments. Moreover, if the sender chooses a color not according to this infinite periodic sequence and the number of segments in the pseudo-stabilized configuration is greater than one, then the number of segments is reduced.

Let us present an aperiodic sequence to be used later in reducing the number of segments. Define $xor(x)$ as the parity of the binary representation of x. For example, the binary representation of 5 is 101 and therefore $xor(5) = 0$. Our first observation is that the sequence $XorSeq = xor(0), xor(1), xor(2), xor(3), \cdots = 0, 1, 1, 0, \cdots$ is *aperiodic*. An infinite sequence is *periodic* if it has a suffix that is an infinite repetition of a finite sequence; an *aperiodic* sequence is a sequence that is not periodic.

LEMMA 8.3:   The infinite sequence $XorSeq$ is aperiodic.

Proof   Assume that there exist numbers l and p such that the suffix of $XorSeq$ that follows the first l elements of $XorSeq$ is periodic with period of length p. First consider the case in which $xor(p) = 1$. Let $l_1 = 2^k$ such that $2^{k-1} > l$ and $l_1 > 2p$, $xor(l_1 + p) = 0$ and $xor(l_1) = 1$, which implies that the suffix that follows l has no period p. We still must consider the case in which $xor(p) = 0$. Let $l_2 = 2^j$ such that $2^j \leq p < 2^{j+1}$. In other words, the value that the most significant bit of p represents is 2^j. By our choice of l_2 it holds that $xor(p + l_2) = xor(p) = 0$. Thus, $xor(l_1 + p + l_2) = 1$ while $xor(l_1 + l_2) = 0$. ∎

One idea is to use $XorSeq$ as a source of an aperiodic sequence. However, the use of a counter by the finite-state machine queue controller (i.e., the sender) is not possible. The alphabet of the letters in the queue is fixed as well; only the number of letters in the queue may grow. Can one implement a distributed binary number using a finite number of letters in the queue? Each letter in the queue can represent a color and a binary bit. The value of the bits in a segment of a pseudo-stabilized configuration defines a counter value in which the least significant bit is in the letter of the segment that will be read first. The queue controller increments the value of a segment counter while reading its letters. This can be done by using a variable to store the carry. In addition, the queue controller computes the value of $xor(counter)$ and uses this value to determine the next color to choose.

Note that an overflow of a counter increases the number of letters (messages) in the queue (line 5 of the code). The rate of memory growth implied by this overflow is equal to the rate of growth of the number of bits of a counter as a function of the number of increments — namely logarithmic growth. This logarithmic memory-growth rate matches the lower bound proved in section 4.2.

To complete the correctness proof, we need to convince ourselves that the sequence of colors obtained by the algorithm in figure 8.2 is aperiodic.

THEOREM 8.1: In any execution in which the number of segments in the pseudo-stabilized configuration is fixed, the sequence of colors produced by the token controller of figure 8.2 is aperiodic.

Proof First we show that the sequence of the *CounterXor* used in line 6 of the code is aperiodic. Since the number of segments x is assumed to be fixed we can refer to a certain segment and its counter during the execution. According to lemma 8.3, the *CounterXor* value computed by the token controller due to a particular segment is aperiodic. The *CounterXor* sequence produced by the token controller is a combination of the *CounterXor* sequences produced due to each sequence. Let $b_1^1, b_2^1, b_3^1, \cdots$ be the *CounterXor* sequence due to the first segment (where segments are ordered according to their appearance in the first configuration). In general, $b_1^i, b_2^i, b_3^i, \cdots$ is the *CounterXor* sequence due to the ith segment, $1 \le i \le x$. The combined sequence of *CounterXor* values produced by the token controller is $X = b_1^1, b_1^2, \cdots b_1^x, b_2^1, b_2^2, \cdots, b_2^x, b_3^1, \cdots$. We now show that if X is eventually periodic with period length y, then each sequence $b_1^i, b_2^i, b_3^i, \cdots$ is eventually periodic with period length y. If X has period of length y then it also eventually has period of length yx. Thus, $b_1^i, b_2^i, b_3^i, \cdots$ has a period of length y.

To complete the proof we need to argue that the sequence of colors obtained in line 6 of figure 8.2 using the *CounterXor* sequence is aperiodic. To do so, observe that when the sequence of colors is periodic then the combined *CounterXor* sequence is periodic. ■

Exercises

8.1. Compute the time complexity for the stabilization of the token-passing algorithm presented in section 8.1.

8.2. The token-passing algorithm presented in section 8.1 requires storing three values 0, 1, and 2 in each register. This, requires registers with at least two bits that have one additional value, i.e., 3 (this value may be mapped to be equivalent to the value 2). Design a self-stabilizing token-passing algorithm for a system of two processors P_1 and P_2 such that $r_{1,2}$ is a two-bit register while $r_{2,1}$ is only a single-bit register.

8.3. Design a self-stabilizing β synchronizer assuming a rooted tree-structured system and using the token-passing algorithm of section 8.1.

8.4. Use the idea of a token controller to implement a self-stabilizing token-passing algorithm in a ring of a fixed memory processors. All the processors are identical except for a single processor. Assume that communication is done by sending messages in a clockwise direction and the number of message in transit is greater than zero but not bounded.

8.5. The lower bound presented in section 4.2 proves that the memory of the system must grow in a logarithmic rate. The memory of the sender and the number of bits of each message grow at a logarithmic rate for the algorithm presented in figure 4.1. The queue controller uses finite memory but increases the number of messages in the queue. Design a self-stabilizing token controller in which the number of messages in the queue does not change and each message has a fixed number of bits. The only logarithmic increase that your algorithm may have is an increase in the number of bits it uses.

Notes

Using a constant amount of memory per processor for different distributed tasks has been considered in several works, e.g., [MOOY92; AD94; AO94; IL94]. The study of different computation models such as computations performed by self-stabilizing Turing machine was addressed in [GHR90]. The queue machine was introduced in [DIM97a].

References

[AACD+96]H Abu-Amara, B Coan, S Dolev, A Kanevsky, and JL Welch. Self-stabilizing topology maintenance protocols for high-speed networks. *IEEE/ACM Transactions on Networking*, 4:902–912, 1996. Conference version in *High-Speed Networking and Multimedia Computing*, SPIE 2188, pp. 380-390, 1994.

[AAG87]Y Afek, B Awerbuch, and E Gafni. Applying static network protocols to dynamic networks. In *FOCS87: Proceedings of the 28th Annual IEEE Symposium on Foundations of Computer Science*, pages 358–370, 1987.

[AB93]Y Afek and GM Brown. Self-stabilization over unreliable communication media. *Distributed Computing*, 7:27–34, 1993.

[AB97]Y Afek and A Bremler. Self-stabilizing unidirectional network algorithms by power supply. *Chicago Journal of Theoretical Computer Science* 3, 1998.

[AD94]J Abello and S Dolev. On the computational power of self-stabilizing systems. *Theoretical Computer Science*, Vol. 182, pp. 159-170, 1997. Conference version in *Journal of Computing and Information*, 1:585–603, 1994.

[AD97]Y Afek and S Dolev. Local stabilizer. In *ISTCS97: Proceedings of the 5th Israeli Symposium on Theory of Computing and Systems*, pages 74–84, 1997.

[ADG91]A Arora, S Dolev, and MG Gouda. Maintaining digital clocks in step. *Parallel Processing Letters*, 1:11–18, 1991.

[ADHK97]U Abraham, S Dolev, T Herman, and I Koll. Self-stabilizing l-exclusion. In *Proceedings of the Third Workshop on Self-Stabilizing Systems*, pages 48–63. Carleton University Press, 1997.

[ADW95]H Attiya, S Dolev, and JL Welch. Connection management without retaining information. *Information and Computation*, 123:155–171, 1995.

[AEY91]E Anagnostou and R El-Yaniv. More on the power of random walks: uniform, bounded self-stabilizing protocols. In *WDAG91: Distributed Algorithms 5th International Workshop Proceedings*, LNCS 579, pages 31–51. Springer-Verlag, 1991.

[AEYH92]E Anagnostou, R El-Yaniv, and V Hadzilacos. Memory adaptive self-stabilizing protocols. In *WDAG92: Distributed Algorithms 6th International Workshop Proceedings*, LNCS 647, pages 203–220. Springer-Verlag, 1992.

[AG93]A Arora and MG Gouda. Closure and convergence: a foundation of fault-tolerant computing. *IEEE Transactions on Software Engineering*, 19:1015–1027, 1993.

[AG94]A Arora and MG Gouda. Distributed reset. *IEEE Transactions on Computers*, 43:1026–1038, 1994.

[GH91]MG Gouda and T Herman. Adaptive programming. *IEEE Transactions on Software Engineering*, 17:911-921, 1991.

[AGR92]Y Afek, E Gafni, and A Rosen. The slide mechanism with applications in dynamic networks. In *PODC92: Proceedings of the Eleventh Annual ACM Symposium on Principles of Distributed Computing*, pages 35–46, 1992.

[AH93]E Anagnostou and V Hadzilacos. Tolerating transient and permanent failures. In *WDAG93: Distributed Algorithms 7th International Workshop Proceedings*, LNCS 725, pages 174–188. Springer-Verlag, 1993.

[AK93]S Aggarwal and S Kutten. Time-optimal self-stabilizing spanning tree algorithm. In *FSTTCS93: Proceedings of the 13th Conference on Foundations of Software Technology and Theoretical Computer Science*, LNCS 761, pages 400–410. Springer-Verlag, 1993.

[AK95]A Arora and SS Kulkarni. Designing masking fault-tolerance from nonmasking fault-tolerance. In *SRDS95: Proceedings of the 14th Symposium on Reliable Distributed Systems*, pages 174–185, 1995.

[AKM+93]B Awerbuch, S Kutten, Y Mansour, B Patt-Shamir, and G Varghese. Time optimal self-stabilizing synchronization. In *STOC93: Proceedings of the 25th Annual ACM Symposium on Theory of Computing*, pages 652–661, 1993.

[AKY90]Y Afek, S Kutten, and M Yung. Memory-efficient self-stabilization on general networks. In *WDAG90: Distributed Algorithms 4th International Workshop Proceedings*, LNCS 486, pages 15–28. Springer-Verlag, 1990.

[AO94]B Awerbuch and R Ostrovsky. Memory-efficient and self-stabilizing network reset. In *PODC94: Proceedings of the Thirteenth Annual ACM Symposium on Principles of Distributed Computing*, pages 254–263, 1994.

[APSV91]B Awerbuch, B Patt-Shamir, and G Varghese. Self-stabilization by local checking and correction. In *FOCS91: Proceedings of the 31st Annual IEEE Symposium on Foundations of Computer Science*, pages 268–277, 1991.

[AS95]G Antonoiu and PK Srimani. A self-stabilizing distributed algorithm to construct an arbitrary spanning tree of a connected graph. *Computers and Mathematics with Applications*, 30:1–7, 1995.

[AS97]G Antonoiu and PK Srimani. Distributed self-stabilizing algorithm for minimum spanning tree construction. In *Euro-par'97 Parallel Processing Proceedings*, LNCS 1300, pages 480–487, Springer-Verlag 1997.

[AV91]B Awerbuch and G Varghese. Distributed program checking: a paradigm for building self-stabilizing distributed protocols. In *FOCS91: Proceedings of the 31st Annual IEEE Symposium on Foundations of Computer Science*, pages 258–267, 1991.

[Awe85]B Awerbuch. Complexity of network synchronization. *Journal of the Association for Computing Machinery*, 32:804–823, 1985.

[Bar96]VC Barbosa. *An Introduction to Distributed Algorithms*. MIT Press, 1996.

[BDDT98]J Beauquier, S Delaet, S Dolev, and S Tixeuil. Transient fault detectors. In *DISC98: International Symposium on DIStributed Computing*, LNCS 1499, pages 62-74. Springer-Verlag, 1998.

[BGM93]JE Burns, MG Gouda, and RE Miller. Stabilization and pseudo-stabilization. *Distributed Computing*, 7:35–42, 1993.

[BGW89]GM Brown, MG Gouda, and CL Wu. Token systems that self-stabilize. *IEEE Transactions on Computers*, 38:845–852, 1989.

[BJ95]J Beauquier and C Johnen. Space-efficient distributed self-stabilizing depth-first token circulation. In *Proceedings of the Second Workshop on Self-Stabilizing Systems*, pages 4.1–4.15, 1995.

[BKM97]J Beauquier and S Kekkonen-Moneta. On ftss-solvable distributed problems. In *Proceedings of the Third Workshop on Self-Stabilizing Systems*, pages 64–79, 1997.

[BP89]JE Burns and J Pachl. Uniform self-stabilizing rings. *ACM Transactions on Programming Languages and Systems*, 11:330–344, 1989.

[BS88]A Baratz and A Segall. Reliable link initialization procedures. *IEEE Transactions on Communications*, 36:144–152, 1988.

[BSW69]K Bartlett, R Scantlebury, and P Wilkinson. Full-duplex transmission over half-duplex links. *Communications of the Association for Computing Machinery*, 12:260–261, 1969.

[BYZ89]F Bastani, I Yen, and Y Zhao. On self-stabilization, non-determinism and inherent fault tolerance. In *Proceedings of the MCC Workshop on Self-Stabilizing Systems*, MCC Technical Report No. STP-379-89, 1989.

[CD94]Z Collin and S Dolev. Self-stabilizing depth-first search. *Information Processing Letters*, 49:297–301, 1994.

[CFG92]JM Couvreur, N Francez, and MG Gouda. Asynchronous unison. In *ICDCS92: Proceedings of the 12th International Conference on Distributed Computing Systems*, pages 486–493. IEEE Computer Society Press, 1992.

[CGK95]I Cidon, I Gopal, and S Kutten. New models and algorithms for future networks. *IEEE Transactions on Information Theory*, 41:769–780, 1995.

[CL85]KM Chandy and L Lamport. Distributed snapshot: determining global states of distributed systems. *ACM Transactions on Computer Systems*, 3:63–75, 1985.

[CT96]TD Chandra and S Toueg. Unreliable failure detectors for asynchronous systems. *Journal of the ACM*, 43(2):225-267, 1996.

[CV96]A Costello and G Varghese. Self-stabilization by window washing. In *PODC96: Proceedings of the Fifteenth Annual ACM Symposium on Principles of Distributed Computing*, pages 35–44, 1996.

[CW97]JA Cobb and M Waris. Propagated timestamps: a scheme for the stabilization of maximum-flow routing protocols. In *Proceedings of the Third Workshop on Self-Stabilizing Systems*, pages 185–200. Carleton University Press, 1997.

[CYH91]NS Chen, HP Yu, and ST Huang. A self-stabilizing algorithm for constructing spanning trees. *Information Processing Letters*, 39:147–151, 1991.

[Deb95]XA Debest. Remark about self-stabilizing systems. *Communications of the Association for Computing Machinery*, 38:115–117, February 1995.

[DGS96]S Dolev, M Gouda, and M Schneider. Memory requirements for silent stabilization. In *PODC96: Proceedings of the Fifteenth Annual ACM Symposium on Principles of Distributed Computing*, pages 27–34, 1996.

[DH95]S Dolev and T Herman. Superstabilizing protocols for dynamic distributed systems. In *Proceedings of the Second Workshop on Self-Stabilizing Systems*, pages 3.1–3.15, 1995.

[DH97]S Dolev and T Herman. Superstabilizing protocols for dynamic distributed systems. *Chicago Journal of Theoretical Computer Science*, 1997.

[DHS86]D Dolev, JY Halpern, and HR Strong. On the possibility and impossibility of achieving clock synchronization. *ACM Transactions on Programming Languages and Systems*, 32:230–250, 1986.

[Dij73]EW Dijkstra. *EWD391: Self-stabilization in spite of distributed control*, pages 41–46. Springer-Verlag, 1973 (Original date is 1973, printed in 1982).

[Dij74]EW Dijkstra. Self stabilizing systems in spite of distributed control. *Communications of the Association for Computing Machinery*, 17:643–644, 1974.

[Dij86]EW Dijkstra. A belated proof of self-stabilization. *Distributed Computing*, 1:5–6, 1986.

[DIM89]S Dolev, A Israeli, and S Moran. Self-stabilization of dynamic systems. In *Proceedings of the MCC Workshop on Self-Stabilizing Systems*, MCC Technical Report No. STP-379-89, 1989.

[DIM91]S Dolev, A Israeli, and S Moran. Uniform dynamic self-stabilizing leader election. In *WDAG91: Distributed Algorithms 5th International Workshop Proceedings*, LNCS 579, pages 167–180. Springer-Verlag, 1991.

[DIM93]S Dolev, A Israeli, and S Moran. Self-stabilization of dynamic systems assuming only read/write atomicity. *Distributed Computing*, 7:3–16, 1993. Conference version in *PODC90: Proceedings of the 9th Annual ACM Symp. on Principles of Distributed Computing*, pp. 103–117, 1990.

[DIM95]S Dolev, A Israeli, and S Moran. Analyzing expected time by scheduler-luck games. *IEEE Transactions on Software Engineering*, 21:429–439, 1995.

[DIM97a]S Dolev, A Israeli, and S Moran. Resource bounds for self-stabilizing message-driven protocols. *SIAM Journal on Computing*, 26:273–290, 1997. Conference version in *PODC91: Proceedings of the 10th Annual ACM Symp. on Principles of Distributed Computing*, pp. 281–293, 1991.

[DIM97b]S Dolev, A Israeli, and S Moran. Uniform dynamic self-stabilizing leader election. *IEEE Transactions on Parallel and Distributed Systems*, 8:424–440, 1997.

[Dol93]S Dolev. Optimal time self-stabilization in dynamic systems. In *WDAG93: Distributed Algorithms 7th International Workshop Proceedings*, LNCS 725, pages 160–173. Springer-Verlag, 1993. Journal version in *Journal of Parallel and Distributed Computing*, Vol. 42, pp. 122-127, 1997.

[Dol94]S Dolev. Optimal time self-stabilization in uniform dynamic systems. In *6th IASTED: International Conference on Parallel and Distributed Computing and Systems*, pages 25–28, 1994.

[Dol97]S Dolev. Possible and impossible self-stabilizing digital clock synchronization in general graphs. *Journal of Real-Time Systems*, 12:95–107, 1997.

[Dol98]S Dolev. Optimal time self-stabilization in uniform dynamic systems. *Parallel Processing Letters*, 8:7–18, 1998.

[DPW95]S Dolev, DK Pradhan, and JL Welch. Modified tree structure for location management in mobile environments. In *INFOCOM95: 14th Annual Joint Conference of IEEE Computer and Communications Societies (Volume 2)*, pages 530–537, 1995. Journal version in *Computer Communications*, special issue on mobile computing, Vol. 19, No. 4, pp. 335-345, April 1996.

[DTOF94]AK Datta, V Thiagarajan, E Outley, and M Flatebo. Stabilization of the X.25 connection management protocol. In *ICCI94: Sixth International Conference on Computing and Information*, pages 1637–1654, 1994.

[DW93]S Dolev and JL Welch. Wait-free clock synchronization. In *PODC93: Proceedings of the Twelfth Annual ACM Symposium on Principles of Distributed Computing*, pages 97–107. ACM, 1993.

[DW95]S Dolev and JL Welch. Self-stabilizing clock synchronization in the presence of Byzantine faults. In *Proceedings of the Second Workshop on Self-Stabilizing Systems*, pages 9.1–9.12, 1995.

[DW97]S Dolev and JL Welch. Crash-resilient communication in dynamic networks. *IEEE Transactions on Computers*, pages 14–26, 1997.

[FD94]M Flatebo and AK Datta. Two-state self-stabilizing algorithms for token rings. *IEEE Transactions on Software Engineering*, 20:500–504, 1994.

[FDG94]M Flatebo, AK Datta, and S Ghosh. Self-stabilization in distributed systems. In *Readings in Distributed Computing Systems*, chapter 2, pages 100–114. IEEE Computer Society Press, 1994.

[FDS94]M Flatebo, AK Datta, and AA Schoone. Self-stabilizing multi-token rings. *Distributed Computing*, 8:133–142, 1994.

[FLM86]MJ Fischer, N Lynch, and M Merritt. Easy impossibility proofs for distributed consensus problems. *Distributed Computing*, 1:26–39, 1986.

[FLMS93]A Fekete, N Lynch, Y Mansour, and J Spinelli. The impossibility of implementing reliable communication in the face of crashes. *Journal of the Association for Computing Machinery*, 40:1087–1107, 1993.

[GG96]S Ghosh and A Gupta. An exercise in fault-containment: self-stabilizing leader election. *Information Processing Letters*, 59:281–288, 1996.

[GGHP96]S Ghosh, A Gupta, T Herman, and SV Pemmaraju. Fault-containing self-stabilizing algorithms. In *PODC96: Proceedings of the Fifteenth Annual ACM Symposium on Principles of Distributed Computing*, pages 45–54, 1996.

[GGP96]S Ghosh, A Gupta, and SV Pemmaraju. A fault-containing self-stabilizing algorithm for spanning trees. *Journal of Computing and Information*, 2:322–338, 1996.

[GH90]MG Gouda and T Herman. Stabilizing unison. *Information Processing Letters*, 35:171–175, 1990.

[GHR90]MG Gouda, RR Howell, and LE Rosier. The instability of self-stabilization. *Acta Informatica*, 27:697–724, 1990.

[GM91]MG Gouda and N Multari. Stabilizing communication protocols. *IEEE Transactions on Computers*, 40:448–458, 1991.

[Gou95]MG Gouda. The triumph and tribulation of system stabilization. In *WDAG95: Distributed Algorithms 9th International Workshop Proceedings*, LNCS 972, pages 1–18. Springer-Verlag, 1995.

[GP93]AS Gopal and KJ Perry. Unifying self-stabilization and fault-tolerance. In *PODC93: Proceedings of the Twelfth Annual ACM Symposium on Principles of Distributed Computing*, pages 195–206, 1993.

[HC92]ST Huang and NS Chen. A self-stabilizing algorithm for constructing breadth-first trees. *Information Processing Letters*, 41:109–117, 1992.

[Her90]T Herman. Probabilistic self-stabilization. *Information Processing Letters*, 35:63–67, 1990.

[HG95]T Herman and S Ghosh. Stabilizing phase-clocks. *Information Processing Letters*, 54:259–265, 1995.

[HH92]SC Hsu and ST Huang. A self-stabilizing algorithm for maximal matching. *Information Processing Letters*, 43:77–81, 1992.

[HU79]JE Hopcroft and JD Ullman. *Introduction to Automata Theory, Languages and Computation*. Addison-Wesley, 1979.

[IL94]G Itkis and L Levin. Fast and lean self-stabilizing asynchronous protocols. In *FOCS94: Proceedings of the 35th Annual IEEE Symposium on Foundations of Computer Science*, pages 226–239, 1994.

[Joh97]C Johnen. Memory-efficient self-stabilizing algorithm to construct BFS spanning trees. In *Proceedings of the Third Workshop on Self-Stabilizing Systems*, pages 125–140. Carleton University Press, 1997.

[JPT95]JH Joepman, M Papatriantafilou, and P Tsigas. On self-stabilization in wait-free shared memory objects. In *WDAG95: Distributed Algorithms 9th International Workshop Proceedings*, LNCS 972, pages 273–287. Springer-Verlag, 1995.

[JV96]M Jayaram and G Varghese. Crash failures can drive protocols to arbitrary states. In *PODC96: Proceedings of the Fifteenth Annual ACM Symposium on Principles of Distributed Computing*, pages 247–256, 1996.

[Kes88]JLW Kessels. An exercise in proving self-stabilization with a variant function. *Information Processing Letters*, 29:39–42, 1988.

[Knu81]DE Knuth. *The Art of Computer Programming*, Vol. 2. Addison-Wesley, 1981.

[KP93]S Katz and KJ Perry. Self-stabilizing extensions for message-passing systems. *Distributed Computing*, 7:17–26, 1993.

[KPS97]S Kutten and B Patt-Shamir. Time-adaptive self-stabilization. In *PODC97: Proceedings of the 16th Annual ACM Symposium on Principles of Distributed Computing*, pages 149–158, 1997.

[Kru79]HSM Kruijer. Self-stabilization (in spite of distributed control) in tree-structured systems. *Information Processing Letters*, 8:91–95, 1979.

[Lam83]L Lamport. Solved problems, unsolved problems and non-problems in concurrency, Invited address. In *PODC84: Proceedings of the Third Annual ACM Symposium on Principles of Distributed Computing*, pages 63–67, 1983.

[Lam86]L Lamport. The mutual exclusion problem: part ii—statement and solutions. *Journal of the Association for Computing Machinery*, 33:327–348, 1986.

[LMS85]L Lamport and PM Melliar-Smith. Synchronizing clocks in the presence of faults. *Journal of the Association for Computing Machinery*, 32:1–36, 1985.

[LS95]C Lin and J Simon. Possibility and impossibility results for self-stabilizing phase clocks on synchronous rings. In *Proceedings of the Second Workshop on Self-Stabilizing Systems*, pages 10.1–10.15, 1995.

[LSP82]L Lamport, R Shostak, and M Pease. The Byzantine generals problem. *ACM Transactions on Programming Languages and Systems*, 4:382–401, 1982.

[LV92]M Li and PMB Vitanyi. Optimality of wait-free atomic multiwriter variables. *Information Processing Letters*, 43:107–112, 1992.

[Mas95]T Masuzawa. A fault-tolerant and self-stabilizing protocol for the topology problem. In *Proceedings of the Second Workshop on Self-Stabilizing Systems*, pages 1.1–1.15, 1995.

[MOOY92]A Mayer, Y Ofek, R Ostrovsky, and M Yung. Self-stabilizing symmetry breaking in constant space. In *STOC92: Proceedings of the 24th Annual ACM Symposium on Theory of Computing*, pages 667–678, 1992.

[PT94]M Papatriantafilou and P Tsigas. Self-stabilizing wait-free clock synchronization. In *Proceedings of the 4th Scandinavian Workshop on Algorithm Theory*, LNCS 824, pages 267–277. Springer-Verlag, 1994. Journal version in *Parallel Processing Letters*, 7(3), pages 321-328, 1997.

[PY94]G Parlati and M Yung. Non-exploratory self-stabilization for constant-space symmetry-breaking. In *Algorithms ESA 94*, LNCS 855, pages 183–201. Springer-Verlag, 1994.

[Sch93]M Schneider. Self-stabilization. *ACM Computing Surveys*, 25:45–67, 1993.

[Seg83]A Segall. Distributed network protocols. *IEEE Transactions on Communications*, 29:23–35, 1983.

[SG89]JM Spinelli and RG Gallager. Event-driven topology broadcast without sequence numbers. *IEEE Transactions on Communications*, 37:468–474, 1989.

[SRR95]SK Shukla, DJ Rosenkrantz and SS Ravi. Observations on self-stabilizing graph algorithms for anonymous networks, In *Proceedings of the Second Workshop on Self-Stabilizing Systems*, pages 7.1–7.15, 1995.

[Sto93]FA Stomp. Structured design of self-stabilizing programs. In *Proceedings of the 2nd Israel Symposium on Theory of Computing and Systems*, pp. 167–176, 1993.

[Tan96]A Tanenbaum. *Computer Networks*. Prentice-Hall, 1996.

[Tch81]M Tchuente. Sur l'auto-stabilisation dans un reseau d'ordinateurs. *RAIRO Informatique Theoretique*, 15:47–66, 1981.

[Tel94]G Tel. *Introduction to Distributed Algorithms*. Cambridge University Press, 1994.

[UKMF97]E Ueda, Y Katayama, T Masuzawa, and H Fujiwara. A latency-optimal superstabilizing mutual exclusion protocol. In *Proceedings of the Third Workshop on Self-Stabilizing Systems*, pages 110–124. Carleton University Press, 1997.

[Var94]G Varghese. Self-stabilization by counter flushing In *PODC94: Proceedings of the 13th Annual ACM Symposium on Principles of Distributed Computing*, pages 244–253, 1994.

[Var97]G Varghese. Compositional proofs of self-stabilizing protocols. In *Proceedings of the Third Workshop on Self-Stabilizing Systems*, pages 80–94. Carleton University Press, 1997.

[WLG$^+$78]JH Wensley, L Lamport, J Goldberg, MW Green, KN Levitt, PM Melliar-Smith, RE Shostak, and CB Weinstock. Sift: Design and analysis of fault-tolerant computer for aircraft control. *Proceedings of the IEEE*, 66:1240–1255, 1978.

[YB95]IL Yen and FB Bastani. A highly safe self-stabilizing mutual exclusion algorithm. In *Proceedings of the Second Workshop on Self-Stabilizing Systems*, pages 18.1–18.13, 1995.

[Yen96]IL Yen. A highly safe self-stabilizing mutual exclusion algorithm. *Information Processing Letters*, 57:301–305, 1996.

[ZB92]Y Zhao and FB Bastani. A self-adjusting algorithm for Byzantine agreement. *Distributed Computing*, 5:219–226, 1992.

Index

Printed in the United States
By Bookmasters